2/27/75

For My Family

THE FICTION OF PHILIP ROTH

813.
54
ROTH

John N. McDaniel

HADDONFIELD HOUSE
HADDONFIELD, NEW JERSEY

Library of Congress Cataloging in Publication Data

McDaniel, John N   1941-
    The fiction of Philip Roth.

    "Philip Roth: a bibliography": p.
    Includes bibliographical references.
    1. Roth, Philip--Criticism and interpretation.
I. Title.
PS3568.0855Z8   813'.5'4   74-8804
ISBN 0-88366-002-4

ERRATA

Page v, line 9: *For* advise *read* advice

Page 4, line 8: *For* "The Land of Opportunity and the Age of Self-Fulfillment" *read* "The Land of Opportunity in the Age of Self-Fulfillment"

Page 21, following last line: *Add* unwilling "defender of the faith" by saying *no* to much

Page 23, line 7: *For* or, at, least *read* or, at the least,

Page 95, line 24: *For* soverign *read* sovereign

Page 170, line 10: *For* I magined *read* I imagined

Page 200, line 36: *For* point *read* pointing

Page 217, footnote 9: *For* Britian *read* Britain

Page 218, footnote 11: *For* "Realism and Contemporary Novel" *read* "Realism and the Contemporary Novel"

Page 225, footnote 12: *For* "The Act of Fiction" *read* "The Art of Fiction"

Page 230, footnote 31, line 8: *For* pin *read* pain

Page 231, footnote 34: *For* "The Act of Fiction" *read* "The Art of Fiction"

advise about the book were offered by Webb Salmon, Griffith Pugh, Larry Burk, Larry Mapp, Thomas McDaniel, and Grover Grubbs. I am particularly grateful to Fred Standley, of Florida State University, not only for his sensitive and helpful comments on the manuscript but also for his unwavering confidence in the value of this present study. Mrs. Cynthia Walker and Mrs. Barbara Humphrys uncomplainingly typed and retyped portions of this book, a chore that was above the call of duty. I extend my deep appreciation to Philip Roth for his generous response to my many questions, for his allowing me to review the galleys for his *My Life As A Man*, and for his permitting me such freedom to quote from the many stories on which he holds exclusive copyright. And for the patience and understanding of my wife Jean, my appreciation is, quite simply, inexpressible.

Permission to quote from Roth's works has been generously granted as follows: From *Goodbye, Columbus*,

Bibliography from the April-June 1974 issue. From "Writing American Fiction" copyright © 1961 by *Commentary*. Reprinted from the March 1961 issue. From "Jewishness and the Younger Intellectuals" copyright © 1961 by *Commentary*. Reprinted from the April 1961 issue. From "Writing About Jews" copyright © 1963 by *Commentary*. Reprinted from the December 1963 issue. From "The Proceedings of the Second American Israel Dialogue" copyright © 1963 by *Congress Bi-Weekly*. Reprinted from Volume 30, Number 12, dated September 16, 1963. From *The New Novel in America* by Helen Weinberg copyright © 1970 Cornell University Press. Reprinted by permission of *Daedalus,* Journal of the American Academy of Arts and Sciences, Boston, Massachusetts, Spring 1963, *Perspectives on the Novel.* From "Recollections from Beyond the Last Rope" copyright © 1959 by *Harper's Magazine.* Reprinted from the July 1959 issue by special permission. From "On Satirizing Presidents: An Interview with Philip Roth" copyright © 1971 by *Atlantic.* Reprinted from the December 1971 issue. From "On the Breast: An Interview" by Alan Lelchuk. Reprinted with permission from *The New York Review of Books.* Copyright © 1972 Nyrev, Inc. From "Philip Roth's Exact Intent" interview with George Plimpton. Copyright © 1969 in *The New York Times Book Review* . Reprinted from the February 23 issue. From "Reading Myself" by Philip Roth. Reprinted with permission from *The Partisan Review.*

Preface

When I first became involved in writing a critical text on Philip Roth's fiction, some of my friends and colleagues displayed reactions ranging from amusement to surprise. One such friend summarized a not uncommon reaction when he asked quizzically, "What's a nice Protestant boy like you doing in a neighborhood like *that*?" I am not at all sure that I could answer the question now any better than I could when it was asked; I have come to feel, however, that Roth's "neighborhood" is not confined within clearly marked ethnic or religious borders, and that in Roth's fiction the ever-changing voices — alternately caustic, whining, exasperated, truculent, naive, sardonic, *hopeful* — are speaking in accents that even a nice Protestant boy has heard before: the voices of real men and women, Jewish and otherwise; these men and women attempt to grapple with the mysteries of themselves and their world — a world that is by no means exclusively "Jewish."

When Roth began publishing fiction in the late 1950's, his most vocal supporters and critics came from the Jewish community. In the last decade and a half, Roth's increasing popularity and stature as a major American writer have been accompanied by an increasing amount of critical attention, although, interestingly enough, such attention is still largely concerned with Roth's Jewishness. There can be no doubt that the so-called "Jewish question" is both a legitimate and illuminating area of inquiry, but it seems to me that to leave matters there is to leave unexplored the larger question of Roth's fictional world: its characters, its themes, its values. What I have attempted to do in the following pages is to make some inroads into that fictional world, and into the critical controversies surrounding it, for the purpose of clarifying Roth's place within the community of writers, Jewish and non-Jewish, now practicing their craft in America.

Chapter I examines Roth's artistic stance as revealed by his fiction and by his own comments. I use one of Roth's first published stories, "The Contest for Aaron Gold," and one of his most recent stories, " 'I Always Wanted You to Admire My Fasting'; Or, Looking at Kafka," as points of departure for a preliminary discussion. The basic esthetic and religious values informing Roth's artistic vision are discussed; additionally, the chapter outlines some of the prevailing critical opinions in regard to Roth's achievement and assesses the appropriateness of regarding Roth as a "Jewish" writer.

Chapters II and III are predicated on the critical assumption that Roth's fictional heroes provide the clearest way of seeing into Roth's fiction and that Roth's distinctiveness as a writer is best illustrated by comparing his fictional heroes to those of such Jewish-American writers as Saul Bellow and Bernard Malamud. Chapter II utilizes the prototypal character designated as the activist hero (a term that was coined by David L. Stevenson and further defined by Albert Guerard and Helen Weinberg) as a convenient index of Roth's early fictional hero types; Chapter III utilizes the prototypal character designated as the victim-hero as a convenient index of Roth's later fictional hero types. Proceeding chronologically, I analyze Roth's fiction, with particular attention to the possibilities for heroic response, for the purpose of suggesting Roth's most crucial artistic concerns and of emphasizing the most salient features of his artistic development.

Chapter IV is an exploration of Roth's recent fiction, fiction, that is, produced after the high-water mark of *Portnoy's Complaint.* I suggest that Roth's most recent work dramatizes the two different modes in which his best fiction has been rendered. After this analysis, there follows, in Chapter V, an exploration of the implications of Roth's fiction and artistic creed. The tentative conclusion reached is that Roth may best be assessed, in broad terms, as a writer whose artistic intentions are "moral," whose artistic method is "realistic," and whose central artistic concern is with man *in* society; furthermore, I discuss the importance of Roth's significant shift away from the activist hero and toward the victim-hero in his artistic development. These assessments are offered as ways of specifying Roth's uniqueness in the contemporary literary tradition, particularly among writers of contemporary Jewish-American fiction.

Throughout this study I have focused primarily on the fiction itself, in that such a focus has been noticeably absent in critical treatment of Roth's artistry. Whenever possible I have also brought to bear Roth's own comments — not only because he speaks intelligently and forcefully about himself and his fiction, but also because his observations provide an often ignored or misunderstood context for assessing the scope of his fiction and the direction it has taken. My hope is that instincts of tidiness on my part have not obscured the most obvious fact about Roth the writer: despite the consistency of his artistic vision, he demonstrates an evident willingness for experimentation, exploration, and change.

A Note on the Text

I have used three abbreviations which have been incorporated into the text and footnotes. Full information for these articles is given in the Bibliography at the end of the book:

WAF — "Writing American Fiction" (an essay by Roth)
WAJ — "Writing About Jews" (an essay by Roth)
SDI — "Second Dialogue in Israel" (symposium)

Whenever possible — that is, in all cases except for *The Breast, The Great American Novel,* and *My Life As A Man* — the pagination cited for Roth's novels is in reference to the paperback editions (see Bibliography).

Contents

I   The Fiction of Philip Roth: An Introduction   1

II   The Activist Hero in Roth's Fiction   37

III   The Victim-Hero in Roth's Fiction   90

IV   Post-*Portnoy*: Roth's Most Recent Fiction   149

V   Distinctive Features of Roth's Artistic Vision   199

     Notes   217

     Philip Roth: A Bibliography   235

I

The Fiction of Philip Roth:
An Introduction

American society has always been at war with its writers, and most frequently it has won its battles. James Fenimore Cooper spent his last years in England; Henry James, Ezra Pound, and T.S. Eliot early set sail for Europe; Herman Melville, Hart Crane, Sylvia Plath, and John Berryman, to name an obvious few, were driven to suicidal despair, while other writers, like J.D. Salinger, have simply become silent. The deeply ingrained romantic tradition, characterized, as Richard Chase says, by "a willingness to abandon moral questions or to ignore the spectacle of man in society,"[1] is symptomatic of the general and widespread restraint our authors have showed in examining social life, a restraint more imposed than chosen, we are likely to feel. Certainly an H.L. Mencken, a Sinclair Lewis, a John Dos Passos has occasionally appeared to raise an attack, but such social observers represent a minor, aggressive flank in the overall strategy of retreat.

Today American writers are more acutely overmatched than ever before. "Truth" about collective life in America has passed from the hands of the intellectuals and artists to the microphones and printing presses of mass media. Most novelists no longer address themselves directly to social problems, but rather approach them on the sly, through techniques of symbol, fantasy, myth, and fable. "When we try to visualize American society at the present time, to perceive it imaginatively, I believe that most of us find it extremely difficult to visualize it in terms of specific human situations,"[2] complains John Aldridge, in accents that are painfully familiar to the contemporary writer. The "deeply lodged suspicion of the times," says Benjamin DeMott, is that *"events and individuals are unreal, and that power to alter the course of the age, of my life and your life, is actually vested nowhere."*[3] "The facts of contemporary experience are constantly beyond belief," Raymond Olderman asserts, and "calling those facts absurd does not seem to subdue them."[4] Novels as different as Burrough's *Naked Lunch*, Hawkes's *Second Skin*, and Pyncheon's *Gravity's Rainbow* share in common a dreamlike world, one that is cosmic rather than societal, surrealistic rather than realistic, more imaginary than real. One is tempted to think that many modern writers have come to agree with Sergius O'Shaughnessy, the narrator of Norman Mailer's *The Deer Park*, when he suggests that the real world is psychically painful and therefore best avoided:

> I had the idea that there were two worlds. There was a real world as I called it, a world of wars and boxing clubs and children's homes on back streets, and this real world was a world where orphans burned orphans. It was better not even to think of this. I liked the other world in which almost everybody lived. The imaginary world.

In search of what Ihab Hassan has called radical innocence, many of our writers turn from unimaginable realities of American experience, to mourn and celebrate the possibilities of everyman, the archetypal self who lives at anytime except *now*, anyplace except *here:* Bellow's Henderson, cavorting through a mythic Africa to terminate, joyfully, in barren Newfoundland; Malamud's S. Levin, suffering and enduring in the imaginary state of Cascadia, somewhere in the American Northwest; Barth's heroes, lost in the funhouse, at the end of some road, traveling backward in time, into colonial Maryland, into Araby, into the labyrinths of history and tradition, away, in any event, from the recognizable present. "The individual's sense of his own potency, his power to effect change and mold events, seems in steady decline," says Hassan in his perceptive analysis of the non-realistic aspects of much contemporary American literature; "it is no great wonder that men choose to withdraw from the public realm of action."[5]

Philip Roth is a singular figure in recent American fiction: he is a social realist who adamantly refuses to withdraw from the field, even though he sees around him no smiling aspects of American life. Taking as his domain the recognizable present, Roth has been the most prolific — and the most controversial — writer in America in the last decade and a half. His immense popularity in the universities and the marketplace has raised appreciative eyebrows and elicited cries of outrage, in some cases both at the same time. Irving Howe reveals the ambivalence that Roth's fiction typically generates when he says, "His reputation has steadily grown these past few years, he now stands close to the center of our culture (if that is anything for him to be pleased about)," and "we are in the presence not only of an interesting writer but also of a cultural 'case.'"[6]

Roth's wonderfully rich and varied works — the sharp-edged and well-crafted stories in the *Goodbye, Columbus* collection (1959), the gloomily realistic *Letting Go* (1962) and *When She Was Good* (1967), the serio-comic *Portnoy's Complaint* (1969), the fabulistic *The Breast* (1972), the satiric *Our Gang* (1971) and *The Great American Novel*

(1973), the candidly autobiographical *My Life As A Man* (1974) — illustrate important insights into America's cultural predicament as Roth sees it from his own vantage point: up close and personal, as the television commentators say. No other living writer has so rigorously and actively attempted to describe the destructive element of experience in American life — the absurdities and banalities that impinge upon self-realization in this "The Land of Opportunity and the Age of Self-Fulfillment" (as David Kepesh in *The Breast* says). And no other writer so clearly bridges the buoyant optimism of Jewish-American writers of the fifties and the dark, despairing world view of such recent writers as John Hawkes, Thomas Pyncheon, Joseph Heller, Ken Kesey, Anthony Burgess and Jerzy Kosinski. Yet Roth is more often than not dismissed as a cultural "case," as if that explained away the variety and vision of his fiction or mitigated the acute embarrassment that accompanies the spectacle of brash young soldiers obstinately continuing in losing battles.

But of course Howe is right: Roth *is* a cultural "case" in that he has been both attracted to and repelled by the shaping forces of society — and who of us has not? Here, perhaps, is a key to the popularity that Roth enjoys as a spokesman for a growing sense of disgust, outrage and impotence felt by so many Americans who view the Vietnam War, the Watergate affair, the sensationalism of the press, the fatuousness of popular novels, television sit-coms, broadway shows, indeed the entire phenomenon of American society, with fascination and repulsion. As Norman Podhoretz says in taking issue with Howe, "Roth is now central not because he has sold out . . . but because in the course of his literary career more and more people have come along who are exactly in tune with the sense of things he has always expressed in his work and who have accordingly and in increasing numbers come to recognize him as their own."[7] If we are compelled, as Lionel Trilling believes, by the writer

whose inner struggle "provides us with the largest repre-
sentation of the culture in which we, with him, are
involved,"[8] then quite possibly Roth's popularity is explained in part by a growing public awareness that his
struggle is in some ways our own.

2

Roth's struggle with American culture has developed along
two fronts, one religious and the other artistic. By far the
more important of the two has been the artistic battle, one
that calls upon the artist to confront American society, "the
real thing," head-on. This, Roth feels, is a confrontation that
is essential to the writing of fiction and to the writer of
fiction. It is, then, with some regret that Roth discovers how
uncommon his artistic stance is — and how alone he seems to
be in his fight. In a seminal essay entitled "Writing American
Fiction" Roth charges that there has been "a voluntary
withdrawal of interest by the writer of fiction from some of
the grander social and political phenomena of our times."
(*WAF*, p.227) Some of our best writers, says Roth, have
"given up on making an imaginative assault upon the
American experience." (*WAF*, p.226) Roth argues that the
private, energetic, "bouncy" language in the fiction of
Herbert Gold, Norman Mailer, Saul Bellow, Grace Paley, and
others, is symptomatic of the "writer's loss of the community as subject":

> In fact, it is paradoxical really, that the very prose style
> which, I take it, is supposed to jolt and surprise us, and
> thereby produce a new and sharper vision, turns back
> upon itself, and the real world is in fact veiled from us
> by this elaborate and self-conscious language-making. I
> suppose that in a way one can think of it as a

sympathetic, or kinetic, response to the clamor and din of our own mass culture, an attempt to beat the vulgar world at its own game.   (*WAF*, p. 231)

For Roth the world *is* vulgar, but — and here his affinities with social realism are evident — he believes it is the writer's task to make an imaginative assault on "the corruptions and vulgarities and treacheries of American public life." (*WAF*, p. 225) Roth's complaint, like Portnoy's is a sweeping observation about the cultural predicament facing the sensitive, creative individual: American reality, Roth concludes, "stupefies, it sickens, it infuriates, and finally it is even a kind of embarassment to one's own meager imagination" (*WAF*, p. 224), and hence it is understandable, perhaps, that many modern writers continue in the romantic strategy of evasion, which involves, as Walter Allen notes, the "opting out of society."[9] Roth understands what is meant when John Barth says that a basic motivation for writing stories is the "impulse to imagine alternatives to the world" and that the writer often feels compelled "to re-invent philosophy and the rest — make up your own whole history of the world."[10] Nonetheless, Roth clearly (even, as Stanley Edgar Hyman suggests, arrogantly) refuses to admire the note of affirmation or approve the evasion of the "real world" that he perceives in the writings of Salinger, Styron, Malamud, Bellow, Mailer, Gold: "When the self can only be celebrated as it is excluded from society, and as it is exercised or admired in a fantastic one, we then, I think, do not have much reason to be cheery." (*WAF*, p. 233)

It is difficult to overestimate the importance of the hard core of social realism at the center of Roth's artistic creed: it qualifies the most romantic of Roth's early stories and explains his most recent ventures into social and political satire (*Our Gang, The Great American Novel*) and fantasy (*The Breast*); it gives credence to Roth's exploration of stereotypes and stereotypic attitudes promulgated by mass media and accepted by some segments of the American public; and, perhaps most importantly, it generates the central conflicts and basic themes found in Roth's fiction. It is a social realism that offers us, as Raymond Williams says,

> a valuing of a whole way of life, a society that is larger than any of the individuals composing it, and at the same time valuing creations of human beings who, while belonging to and affected by and helping to define this way of life, are also, in their own terms, absolute ends in themselves. . . . Every aspect of personal life is radically affected by the quality of the general life, yet the general life is seen at its most important in completely personal terms. We attend with our whole senses to every aspect of the general life, yet the center of value is always in the individual human person — not any one isolated person but the many persons who are the reality of the general life.[11]

In emphasizing the predicament that the modern writer faces, Roth suggests a broader predicament, one that is faced, he feels, by many people. Although he has the writer specifically in mind, there is no doubt that the problem he describes is *cultural.* Making note of Benjamin DeMott's observation that there seems to be today a kind of "universal descent into unreality," Roth goes on to observe that he too is often overwhelmed by the "unreality" of the world that he wants to describe in his fiction:

> . . . For a writer of fiction to feel that he does not really live in the country in which he lives — as represented by *Life* or by what he experiences when he steps out his front door — must certainly seem a serious occupational impediment. For what will be his subject? His

landscape? It is the tug of reality, its mystery and magnetism, that leads one into the writing of fiction — what then when one is not mystified but stupefied? not drawn but repelled?

(*WAF*, p.225)

Roth's observation is by no means new. As long ago as 1956, Lionel Trilling remarked, "It is now life and not art that requires the willing suspension of disbelief."[12] But what if the writer whose art is fed by the life around him cannot suspend his disbelief? The danger facing the writer, Roth believes, is that "when the predicament produces in the writer not only feelings of disgust, rage, and melancholy, but impotence, too, he is apt to lose heart and finally, like his neighbor, turn to other matters, or to other worlds." (*WAF*, p. 233) "What the hell," exclaimed John Barth recently, as if confirming Roth's observation, "reality is a nice place to visit but you wouldn't want to live there, and literature never did, very long. . . . Reality is a drag."[13] Yet it is precisely this predicament that fascinates Roth, captivating his imagination and feeding his creative impulse. He will *not* be defeated; he will *not* turn to other matters, other worlds. Like Kafka before him he will turn the familial, communal, and cultural pressures facing him into the very substance of his art. The problems facing the artist become, in Roth's fiction, human problems to be faced by the hero; the "unreality" of American public life exercises a brutal power which the hero can attempt to conquer but cannot evade. Like the hero of Ellison's *Invisible Man*, whom Roth so admires, the Rothian hero must go out into the world — even if it is only to discover that he is a man without a country, invisible, homeless, a stranger to himself and his deepest beliefs — before he can go underground to wait for a new spring and the promise of hope.

3

Perhaps the best introduction into Roth's fictional world is to be found in Roth's very early "The Contest for Aaron Gold" and his very recent " 'I Always Wanted You to Admire My Fasting'; Or, Looking at Kafka." The former was published when Roth was only twenty-one years old, and the latter appeared in the *American Review* of May, 1973. The two stories serve as excellent parameters of Roth's artistry, suggesting not only the continuity of Roth's essential themes and hero types but also the subtle changes in Roth's artistic techniques, particularly his movement into the fantastic, his increasing reliance on autobiographical materials for his fiction, and his growing willingness, as he says in "Reading Myself," to be both subversive and perverse in his attack on traditional social values. Despite their differences, the two stories illustrate Roth's ongoing attempt to discover, in his own words, "a kind of passageway from the imaginary that seems real to the real that seems imaginary, a continuum between the credible incredible and the incredible credible."[14] And, as we shall see, the hero in each story brings with him not only the occupation but also the sensibility of the artist, one who is brought into direct confrontation with society.

"The Contest for Aaron Gold" focuses on the moral dilemma faced by Werner Samuelson, a Jewish artist driven from his studio in Austria by the Germans in 1940, who for the first time in fourteen years has left his Philadelphia ceramics shop for summer employment as a ceramics instructor at a boys' camp. The moral dilemma arises from Werner's growing interest in one of the campers, Aaron Gold, who "was about eight years old, bony, underfed, a little tired-looking." While the other boys take on handicraft projects that are less than distinguished ("snakes were the favorite, turtles a close second"), Aaron embarks on a warrior knight aiming a sword at a dragon. Difficulty arises when the aggressive, popular swimming instructor, Lefty Shulberg, lets it be known that he objects to Aaron's tardiness at swimming sessions — tardiness caused by Aaron's desire to finish his knight.

Werner's plight becomes more serious when the camp owner, Lionel Steinberg, places additional pressure on him:

> Look, Werner, let's get squared around. It's good you're taking your job seriously, looking after the kids and all. But if there's one thing we don't want here it's one-sided kids. That's what I tell the parents and that's what they want, an all-round camp, you understand? But if you're going to let one kid play potsy with clay all day, Werner, what the hell are his parents going to say to me?   (p. 44)

Lionel cannot understand why Aaron should be allowed extra time, despite the fact that Aaron's knight is much superior to the other boys' artistic efforts. In words that unconsciously parody the first of all creative acts, Lionel complains to Werner,

> For christ sake, we asphalted the whole entrance road, the whole thing, and the parking lot besides in seven days. Seven days, and you stand there and ask me why a kid shouldn't take forty hours to make a pair of goddam legs. Don't kid me, Werner.   (p. 45)

Werner's initial decision, preceded by four days of a cold, miserable rain that turns the lake into a murky brown (suggestive, perhaps, of Noah's flood), is as practical as the pragmatic Lionel could wish: He will ask the boys to speed up their work. "After all, Steinberg was his employer, paying the check, and he was the employee. This was just no summer to get fired." Aaron, however, upon hearing Werner's directive, cries that he cannot work quicker: "I can't finish by Sunday, Uncle Werner. I just can't!" Werner momentarily relents, but as the Sunday visitor's day approaches, he is faced once again with an irate Lionel. Clutching the unfinished knight in his hand, Lionel confronts Werner: "Wait'll Lefty hears about this goddam thing." Realizing that it is too close to visiting day for Steinberg to fire him, Werner turns his attention to Lefty. What *would* Lefty think?

> What he might think was that as far as the contest for Aaron Gold was concerned — for, apparently, that was what it had become to Lefty — he had lost. Lefty probably didn't like to lose, but Werner had had his way, and if that wasn't a loss, at best it was a tie. Ties probably wouldn't do for Lefty either. Maybe he would come over and punch him in the mouth. No, Lefty wouldn't settle up that way. It was too simple. No, but he would think of something. What? That didn't take too much pondering: probably Lefty would make Aaron Gold the most miserable kid in the world. He seemed capable.   (pp.48-49)

With Aaron's welfare clearly in mind, Werner takes on the task of completing Aaron's unfinished project, but when Aaron sees the result, he shouts angrily, "You ruined him, you did, you did" and runs out of the ceramics shop to the edge of the lake, "like a small wild animal who gets out of a blazing forest just as fast as he can." Werner, exhausted by the chain of events leading to the emotional confrontation with Aaron, flops into a chair to contemplate the knight.

> He set it upon the table before him, contemplating it as one might contemplate a rare piece of sculpture. He

stared a full minute, and then, like a mace, he pummeled his right fist down upon it. It shattered, but he pounded and pounded at it with his fist. He pounded until it was a mess, and even then he didn't stop. It was a better job than the dragon himself might have done.   (p. 50)

With the sound of Lefty Shulberg's jovial greetings to parents and visitors dinning in his ears, Werner washes his hands, packs his bags, and walks "along the hot, squirming road and out of the camp."

Although no critic has made mention of "The Contest for Aaron Gold," the story provides a clear index of Roth's early artistic intents and techniques. Like Neil Klugman of *Goodbye, Columbus*, Eli Peck of "Eli, the Fanatic," Nathan Marx of "Defender of the Faith," and Gabe Wallach of *Letting Go*, Werner is the unwilling hero, an essentially passive man who has a difficult moral choice suddenly thrust upon him. The choice — as is the case with other of Roth's early heroes — is not a clear-cut one, and the consequences of the choice are ambiguous. Werner is not merely torn between keeping his job and remaining loyal to Aaron Gold, for his final decision to destroy the knight he has wrongfully completed for Aaron comes after he realizes that his job is secure. The choice, rather, is a partially unwitting, or at least unarticulated, response to the crass middle-class values of Camp Lakeside, values that are embodied in the words and actions of Lefty Shulberg and Lionel Steinberg. As spokesmen for social "normalcy," Werner's two antagonists are the exponents of a suffocating, soul-numbing creed of expediency, against which the hero throws his uncertain power. This contest, I believe, describes the central conflict in Roth's fiction.

Lefty Shulberg, Werner's most immediate antagonist, is, like Ron Patimkin of *Goodbye, Columbus* a man to be respected because of his athletic prowess. His claims to fame are two: he had been a professional basketball player and he had once, in a Tarzan movie, fought an underwater battle with Johnny Weissmuller. Lefty and the other counselors live by the proposition that, as one of the boys says, "we gotta not play alone" because "it's no good for you." Lefty thinks that Aaron is "peculiar" because he does not like to swim, and as the contest for Aaron Gold continues, Lefty grows in the conviction that the relationship between Werner and Aaron is an abnormal one. It is clear that camp owner Steinberg knows of Lefty's suspicions (Steinberg tells Werner, "I'd hate like hell to tell you what he said about you and that kid") and comes to agree with Lefty ("Werner, I'm just about fed up. . . . What kind of game are you and that little queer trying to play anyhow!").

Lionel Steinberg, like Lefty Shulberg, is a subject for Roth's satirical eye. Like Lefty, Lionel is ruled by shallow middle-class values. Lionel believes in having all-around kids in an all-around camp because that is what parents want. Lionel warns Werner early in the story, "Every kid's going to have something finished by visiting day, Werner. Parents want something for their money." Lionel's other obsession is to have all the main arteries of the camp paved by visitor's day, after which, according to the construction supervisor, "we can start paving the goddam lake." The smell of asphalt and the roar of road machines supply an appropriate background for Lionel's notion of creativity — a creativity that is sterile, commercial and ugly in conception and fulfillment.

Over and against this backdrop is the uncertain voice of Werner the craftsman, speaking for the values of the artist. To an unimpressed audience on the first day of camp, Werner gives an explanation of the vessels made in ancient times with the potter's wheel:

> "The men"—whoever *they* were—"always tried to make these vessels more beautiful and shapely"—somebody

giggled. "They painted them red and gold, and blue and green, and they painted their sides with stories and legends. It took hundreds of years until men saw how much happier they could be if they surrounded themselves with beautiful—beautiful objects of art."   (pp. 39-40)

Armed with the conviction that "it takes time to learn what to do," Werner makes a reluctant crusade into the modern asphalt wasteland of Camp Lakeside. It is Werner who personifies Aaron's knight ("whose spindly legs wouldn't have done him much service against a good, fast dragon"); the dragon, on the other hand, is clearly symbolic of the Shulberg-Steinberg-Camp Lakeside values. Early in the story, Aaron pleads to be allowed to spend extra time to finish the knight's legs. Werner replies, "Of course — what do you think, I'm on the dragon's side?" Later, when Werner tries to implement Steinberg's speed-up policy, Aaron wants to know where Werner stands: "Whose *side* — me or the dragon?" At the end of the tale, when Werner realizes that in completing Aaron's unfinished knight he has capitulated to the Camp Lakeside values of Steinberg and Shulberg, he reverses the capitulation by becoming knight and dragon in one: "Like a mace, he pummeled his right fist down upon it," until the knight was shattered. "It was a better job than the dragon himself might have done."

The ironic twist involved in Werner's final decision to destroy the knight, the symbol of his own values, is characteristic of Roth's early fiction. In a world where normative social values hold sway, the actions of the hero sensitive to *human* values must often seem tinged with madness. To the public, represented by the parents who come on visitor's day, it is Lefty Shulberg, not Werner, who appears as the protective moral agent keeping watch over the children. In the last scene in the story, we see Lefty, who is about to give a special diving exhibition, welcoming visitors and campers with the aid of a megaphone:

> "How you doing, Mike. Sit your parents down right there. That a boy . . . Jeff-boy, what do you say, kid." The names snapped out like sparks, and then, a moment after Werner heard them, they were muffled in a wooly heat. "Artie, that a boy . . . Hey, Joe, how's my — Hey, what do you know! Goldy! How are you doing, Goldy — buddy! That your parents? Good, sit them right down front. What do you know!" Lefty waved his megaphone at Aaron Gold's parents. Mr. Gold, in white shirt and gray Bermuda shorts, waved back; Mrs. Gold nodded. Lefty was treating their boy all right.   (p. 51)

What do the parents know? They know that "Lefty was treating their boy all right" — a reasonable conclusion, after all, if one's vision is restricted to the smooth and artificial surface offered by Camp Lakeside.

One of Roth's most recent stories, " 'I Always Wanted You to Admire My Fasting': Or, Looking At Kafka," is, like "The Contest for Aaron Gold," a story about a Jewish artist who comes to America to confront its social forces; in this case, however, the artist is Franz Kafka and the setting is Newark, New Jersey, and the home of Philip Roth in 1942. The story is a strange blend of fact and fiction, reality and fantasy, which suggests how far Roth has come from the more traditional early techniques evidenced in "The Contest for Aaron Gold." After an introductory quotation from Kafka's "A Hunger Artist," the first part of this two-part story opens with the narrator, Roth, saying, "I am looking, as I write of Kafka, at the photograph taken of him at the age of forty (my age) — it is 1924, as sweet and hopeful a year as he may ever have known as a man, and the year of his death." The first section recounts the history of Kafka's anguished attempts, in his last years, to escape the pressures of home life, the domination of his father, and his own "habit of obedience and renunciation."

As a consequence of discovering some happiness with his mistress, Dora Dymant, Kafka, now in his fortieth year and away from Prague and his father's home, "seems at last to have been delivered from the self-loathing, the self-doubt, and those guilt-ridden impulses to dependence and self-effacement that had nearly driven him mad throughout his twenties and thirties." Roth reports, however, that it is also at this time that Kafka writes the unfinished story "The Burrow," the story of an animal "with a keen sense of peril whose life is organized around the principle of defense, and whose deepest longings are for security and serenity." But what if this Kafka who finally finds a tentative happiness in his women and his work should effect an escape of both literal and figurative death by fulfilling for himself the imagined journey of Karl Rossman, the journey, that is, to America?

It is, then, with this leap into fantasy that part two of the story begins. It is 1942, Roth is nine, and his Hebrew School teacher is Dr. Franz Kafka. Much to Roth's dismay, Dr. Kafka accepts an invitation to dine at the Roth home where Roth's father has arranged a match between Kafka and Aunt Rhoda, a spinster who works as an interior decorator at a large dry goods store ("The Big Bear") and whose aspirations are to appear on the stage. Roth's father is convinced that Kafka would "give his eye teeth to have a nice home and a wife," so he proceeds to "do a job" on Kafka ("Does he make a sales pitch for familial bliss!"). The affair between Kafka and Rhoda ends miserably, however, after Dr. Kafka apparently broaches the subject of sex. Aunt Rhoda returns to the Roth home from a weekend tryst with Kafka in Atlantic City (Kafka had wanted to see the famous board-walk and the horse that dives from the high board), and pours out her dismay in tearful scenes: "Have you ever?" says Aunt Rhoda, weeping. "Have you *ever*?" Kafka sends four letters to Rhoda in three days, but Rhoda's moral outrage remains. Everyone agrees with Roth's father when he says of Kafka, "Something is wrong with him all right." Kafka dies at the end of the tale, leaving behind no *Trial*, no *Castle*, no "Diaries." All that remains are four *"meshugeneh"* letters "accumulated in her dresser drawers by my spinster aunt, along with a collection of Broadway 'Playbills,' sales citations from 'The Big Bear,' and transatlantic steamship stickers."

> Thus all trace of Dr. Kafka disappears. Destiny being destiny, how could it be otherwise? Does the Land Surveyor reach the Castle? Does K. escape the judgment of the Court, or Georg Bendemann the judgment of his father? " 'Well, clear this out now!' said the overseer, and they buried the hunger artist, straw and all." No, it simply is not in the cards for Kafka ever to become *the* Kafka — why, that would be stranger even than a man turning into an insect. No one would believe it, Kafka least of all.   (p. 126)

What is the point of so bizarre a story? First of all, the story is clearly a continuation of one of the earliest thematic conflicts in Roth's fiction: the conflict between the sensitive man (quite often an artist, like Werner Samuelson, or a teacher-writer, like Kafka) and an insensitive society that constricts, stupefies, and maddens the would-be hero to despair. If you want to see why the artist becomes a "burrower," Roth seems to say, consider what would happen to Franz Kafka if he had to live in America, in Newark, in my home. "He's too quiet for Rhoda." Roth's mother says of Dr. Kafka, "I think maybe he's a little bit of a wallflower." "Don't worry," says Roth's father, "when the time comes I'll give him a little nudge." The banality, the tastelessness, the manipulative strategies (Aunt Rhoda had, in her younger days, put on puppet shows in which she did all the voices and "manipulated the manikins on their strings") combine to reduce Kafka to a shadow of a man, a "homeless K., but without K.'s willfulness and purpose, a homeless Karl, but without Karl's youthful spirit and resilience." Little wonder then that, after his "homey" experience in America, the homeless Kafka leaves no literary work behind — which is a way of suggesting that the artist in America experiences artistic starvation indeed.

A second point illustrated by the story (and emphasized by Roth's use of "Philip Roth" as narrator) is that Roth, like Kafka, does not hesitate to "burrow" inward and look backward, probing his own past experiences as Jew and writer for tensions that are given oblique and often ironic treatment in his fiction.[15]   Although the dangers of drawing parallels between an author's personal experience and his fiction are notorious, it is impossible to avoid observing that at times there is a proximity between Roth and his characters, between Roth's interests and those explored in his fiction (a point that is often made about Kafka's work as well). There is, of course, nothing unique about an author's utilizing his own experience in his fiction; nevertheless, Roth's candid and repeated admissions of his reliance on what is "close to home" underscores both his commitment to social realism and his willingness to explore some of his own responses to American culture through the focusing lens of fiction. Offering the suggestion that the writer "begins in a kind of assault upon his own conventional ideas, not upon the community's conventional ideas, and the assault is directed inwards" (*SDI*, p. 71), Roth says of his early fiction:

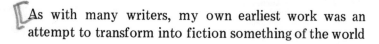

As with many writers, my own earliest work was an attempt to transform into fiction something of the world

Like the Roth and Kafka in " 'I Always Wanted You to Admire My Fasting': Or, Looking At Kafka," Roth's characters struggle to stay afloat in the dark, dangerous, inviting waters of the moral and psychological unknown — an area, Roth says, beyond "that barrier of personal inhibition, ethical restraint, and plain old conformism and fear."[20] And their struggle, not surprisingly, is often that of the artist, the sensitive man who is caught between seemingly inimical realms but who attempts to penetrate, to understand the mysteries surrounding his own life as well as those mysterious forces propelling him away from his own, his native land.

4

The religious issues raised by Roth's fiction have precipitated a battle of a different sort, yet one that Roth has entered aggressively. Jewish readers and literary critics alike have taken stands on the "Jewishness" of Roth's fiction, and one irate reader from the Jewish community, sure that Roth wrote only to chastise Jews, went so far as to claim that "Medieval Jews would have known what to do with him." (*WAJ*, p. 450) Praised as a Jewish moralist and condemned as a self-hating Jew, Roth has been offered, as David Baroff says, as a "kind of shibboleth for American Jews; they define themselves and other people in terms of how they react to Philip Roth." (*SDI*, p. 63) The controversies that swirl around the "Jewishness" of Roth's fiction have clouded, in most cases, the more essential questions of Roth's artistry: his affinities with social realism, his vision of human potential, his assault on American reality. It seems, however, that Roth has been called, ironically enough, to bear the standard in a dubious battle, while more fundamentally Jewish writers like Bernard Malamud and Saul Bellow have been allowed a graceful retreat behind university walls. Like one of his characters, Nathan Marx, Roth has become an about Judaism, a nay-saying that has aroused his public in unforeseen and unprecedented ways.

The complaints most often made against Roth's fiction by the Jewish community do not legitimately come under the heading of literary criticism in that such complaints do not derive from an analysis of the fiction. It is true, however, that the values that emerge from Roth's fiction often serve as a point of departure for charges of anti-semitism. After *Goodbye, Columbus* was published, many rabbis and other members of the Jewish community responded with letters and sermons denouncing Roth's fiction. For example, in *To Our Colleagues*, a journal supplying reform rabbis with usable quotations for sermons, Rabbi Saul Teplitz states, "Philip Roth, of 'Goodbye, Columbus' fame, constantly depicts the Jewish characters in his short stories and novels as depraved and lecherous creatures." Teplitz quotes Rabbi Theodore Lewis as saying, "The only logical conclusion any intelligent reader could draw from [Roth's] stories or books, is that this country — nay that the world would be a much better and happier place without 'Jews.' "[21]

Letters to the editors of *The New Yorker* and *Commentary* were prolific enough to spur Roth to write a defense of his fiction, which appeared in the December, 1963 *Commentary*. Roth opens his defense with a summary of critical reaction from the Jewish community:

Ever since some of my first stories were published in 1959 in a volume called *Goodbye, Columbus*, my work has been attacked from certain pulpits and in certain periodicals as dangerous, dishonest, and irresponsible. I have read editorials and articles in Jewish community newspapers condemning these stories for ignoring the accomplishments of Jewish life, or, as Rabbi Emanuel Rackman recently told a convention of the Rabbinical Council of America, for creating a "distorted image of the basic values of Orthodox Judaism," and even, he went on, for denying the non-Jewish world the opportunity of appreciating "the overwhelming contributions which Orthodox Jews are making in every avenue of modern endeavor...." Among the letters I receive from readers, there have been a number written by Jews accusing me of being anti-Semitic and "self-hating," or, at, least tasteless; they argue or imply that the sufferings of the Jews throughout history, culminating in the murder of the six million by the Nazis, have made certain criticisms of Jewish life insulting or trivial.

(*WAJ*, p. 446)

The charge of anti-semitism against a Jewish writer is not, of course, new. Saul Bellow, Leslie Fiedler, Herbert Gold, Babette Deutsch, Alfred Kazin, and Louis Untermeyer have all, at one time or the other, been accused of holding attitudes and beliefs inimical to the Jewish community, and Leslie Fiedler, in characteristic overstatement, congratulated Roth for having received the young Jewish author's initial accolade: the accusation of anti-semitism.[22] In Roth's case, however, charges of anti-semitism have extended beyond the stage of initial reaction, and the question of his Jewishness continues to occupy not only the Jewish community but also serious literary critics — both Jewish and non-Jewish.

If anything is clear about the controversies surrounding Roth's depiction of Jewish life, it is that there is no agreement among respected critics on just how traditionally Jewish Roth's values are. In his 1959 review of *Goodbye, Columbus* Irving Howe proposed the "saddening thought" that Roth

is one of the first American Jewish writers who finds, so far as I can judge, almost no sustenance in the Jewish tradition. Writers like Henry Roth, Daniel Fuchs,

Delmore Schwartz and Bernard Malamud have also dealt harshly with the life of middle-class American Jews, but to one or another extent the terms of their attack have been drawn from memories of Jewish childhood and family life, from the values of the Jewish tradition. Mr. Roth, however, finds little here to sustain him. . . . It is possible that this signifies the end of a tradition, the closing of an arc of American Jewish experience. [23]

In that same year another Jewish critic, Theodore Solotaroff, offered a very different opinion of Roth's relation to the Jewish tradition:

Throughout *Goodbye, Columbus* Roth works into his stories what he has seen and felt, fortifying it with his sense of traditional Jewish values and conduct. . . . Roth is so obviously attached to Jewish life that the charge of his being anti-semitic or a "self-hater" is the more absurd. The directness of his attack against arrogance, smugness, finagling and acquisitiveness should not obscure the perfectly obvious fact that he does so flying a traditional Jewish banner of sentiment and humaneness and personal responsibility. . . . [24]

In the years since the publication of *Goodbye, Columbus*, critics have placed themselves at various points between the two extremes represented by Howe and Solotaroff. Those who consider Roth's fiction as essentially Jewish in morality and values include Glenn Meeter, Dan Issac, Norman Leer, and Robert Detweiler. Meeter feels that "of the scores of Jewish writers in print since 1945, Malamud and Roth are . . . among the most 'Jewish' in character and setting";[25] Isaac, a rabbi, believes that Roth's fiction has the clear social vision of the prophecies of Jeremiah, and that rabbis who attack Roth "would do well to use his stories as sermon texts, and thereby attempt to alter through illustration and argument the faulty fabric of American Jewish life."[26] Norman Leer offers a similar argument:

> Roth's detractors chided him for drawing an unfavorable picture of American Jewish life. But they never bothered to ask whether the style of life that he portrayed was peculiarly Jewish, or whether it was a part of some larger American experience. And they never examined the values which Roth either implicitly or explicitly affirmed in his work.[27]

Had they made such an examination, Leer continues, they might have found "a frame of reference in Roth's stories based on traditional Jewish values."[28] Leer thinks it is possible to find in Roth's fiction themes that occur in Biblical, rabbinic, and contemporary Jewish thought. And Detweiler makes a convincing case for the thesis that Roth explores the human condition from an angle which tempers the Jewish heritage with the existential throught of Martin Buber.[29]

For a variety of reasons, other critics have hesitated to consider Roth's fiction as fundamentally Jewish in themes and values. Ben Siegel, for example, thinks that Roth, like Bellow, Malamud, Salinger and Gold, has a deep commitment to Judaic values, but "these values serve him only so far as they illuminate everyman's motivations and problems."[30] Joseph Landis maintains that although Roth makes use of the Jewish tradition, "he does not write about the problems that American Jewish life is deeply concerned with," nor does he "really deal with the complexities of the Jewish experience in America."[31] John Ditsky goes so far as to suggest that in Roth's fiction one finds "the early signs of a new post-Judeo-Christian moral orthodoxy, a stiffening of the grounds of situation ethics."[32]

The question of Roth's indebtedness to and reliance on Judaistic values and subject matter is beset with difficulties, and in his excellent book *The Jewish Writer in America* Allen Guttmann isolates the major one; he concludes, after citing many sociological studies,

> The main difference between Judaism and Christianity has been disavowed by contemporary Jews. When 56 per cent of the members of a Jewish country club in the Twin Cities area send Christmas cards *to each other*, when a rabbi announces that he is an "ignostic" who doesn't know what is meant by the term "God," there is something new under the sun. "There cannot be the least doubt that what the immigrant loses quickest in this country is his Judaism." This judgment by Solomon Schechter, one of the great leaders of Conservative Judaism, is quoted by Marshall Sklare and Joseph Greenbaum, who question on the basis of their studies the "long-range viability" of the contemporary pattern of Jewish adjustment. Irving Greenberg, writing as one committed to *Chalacha*, is even gloomier about the "terminal Jews" living on the residue of the past.[33]

It is paradoxical, perhaps, that at the very moment when, as Leslie Fiedler says, "everywhere in the realm of prose Jewish writers have discovered their Jewishness to be an eminently marketable commodity,"[34] Jewishness itself is marked by a crisis of identity and by impulses toward assimilation and secularism.

In confronting this paradox, different critics inevitably come to different conclusions about Roth's "Jewishness." Those critics who see themes of assimilation and secularism as central to Jewish-American fiction are likely to agree with Stanley F. Chyet: "It is for the most part only ideologically that the writers of the third generation are *hors de combat*.

Philip Roth, say, or Bruce Jay Friedman or Bellow or Malamud — these writers fight neither for nor against Judaism or Americanism."[35] On the other hand, those critics who attempt to isolate specific and unique Jewish character- istics (Jewish themes, Jewish values, Jewish symbols, and so on) are likely to feel uneasy and, I think, a bit perplexed about the fiction of Philip Roth. Irving Malin, for example, in his *Jews and Americans* and his introduction to *Break- through: A Treasury of Contemporary American-Jewish Fiction*, argues for an American-Jewish context, a " '*community of feeling' which transcends individual style and different genres*"[36] (the italics are Malin's). The com- munity of feeling is revealed, Malin believes, in common themes (exile, fathers and sons, time, head and heart, transcendence) and common forms (irony, fantasy, parable) used by Karl Shaprio, Delmore Schwartz, Isaac Rosenfeld, Leslie Fiedler, Saul Bellow, Bernard Malamud, and Philip Roth. Defining the Jewish experience as a series of moments in the search for God, Malin maintains that "we can begin with the premise that our writers present the Jewish Experience — which is social, religious and psychological. The center of this Experience is God. Our writers are trying in different ways to discover and name Him."[37] As interesting and as illuminating as this thesis is, Malin clearly runs into difficulties in accounting for Roth's fiction. Convinced that Jewish-American authors produce "powerful" and "sincere" art when they are concerned with Jewishness and "phony" and "imperfect" work when they are not, Malin concludes that just as Bellow is weaker in *Augie March* than in *Seize the Day*, so is Roth "weaker in *Letting Go* than 'Eli, the Fanatic' ";[38] what is meant by "weaker" is never made clear, however, and in any event few critics would agree with Malin's assessment of the comparative merits of Roth's works (to say nothing of Bellow's!). It should also be pointed out that of all the writers he examines Malin feels the least sure about Roth as a writer of Jewish-American fiction. He concludes that Roth "remains outside of the tradition, although he feels some kinship with Jews. . . ."[39]

Malin, Leslie Fiedler, Max Schulz, and William Freedman join in asserting that the American Jew is, in Fiedler's phrase, "in the process of being mythicized into the representative American."[40] These critics remind us that the alienation and suffering experienced by the Jew from the beginning of history have become today the symbols for the human condition, and hence, as Bernard Malamud has said, in a mythic or symbolic sense "all men are Jews." In addition to emphasizing the symbolic importance of the Jewish experience, each of the above critics finds special qualities associated with Jewish-American fiction — and each, for different reasons, either denigrates or dismisses Roth's accomplishments as a Jewish-American writer. Fiedler, for example, stresses the centrality of the assimilation theme in serious Jewish-American fiction but insists that the good Jewish-American writer will universalize the Jew's unique confrontation with the larger life in America; however, because he does not perceive symbolic and mythic elements in Roth's writings, Fiedler dismisses Roth as a "belated Forties writer,"[41] one whose nostalgic view of Jewish life is both "middle-brow" and provincial. Schulz sees Jewish-American fiction as growing out of both the Jewish and the American Romantic traditions, with particular reference to a "sophisticated" acceptance of unreconcilable opposites. He, like Fiedler, believes that Roth does not transcend the particularities of a "description of Jewish manners and [the] narration of the Jewish experience in America" and argues that Roth's stringent realism "militates against the suspension of judgment that characterizes radical sophistication."[42] Freedman, like Fiedler, identifies essential factors in serious Jewish-American fiction: "The patent emotionalism of Jewish fiction; its interest in the problem and experience of suffering; and its almost habitual embodiment of history and myth."[43] Freedman's criticism of Roth, however, is quite different from the objections offered by Malin, Fiedler, and Schulz. He believes that Roth is *overly* concerned with transcending the particularities of narration and detail: "In his eagerness to fulfill all the pre-determined requirements of Jewish fiction as a stereotyped form, to include all the standard themes of suffering, alienation and compassion, Roth spends too little time developing a fable which legitimately embodies these themes. . . ."[44]

I am not here merely trying to catch critics in contradictions; rather, I am suggesting that Roth and his fiction do not yield easily to Jewish-oriented theses about Jewish-American writers and their fiction, primarily because Roth is the most "marginal" of Jews. His reliance on Jewish materials and Jewish values is qualified by an essentially secular and skeptical perspective, a perspective that he has defended vigorously, even in the camp of the supposed enemy — in, that is, Jewish magazines like *Commentary* and Jewish symposia like the one held in Tel Aviv in 1963. His defense of himself is occasionally acerbic, in large part because of the intense and often heated attacks directed at him and his fiction by critics both inside and outside the Jewish community; his own point of view is, however, both consistent and illuminating, and thus serves as a helpful context for understanding his intentions and achievements as a Jewish-American writer.

5

Perhaps the most obvious and necessary observation that can be made is that Roth is very tentative about his relation to Judaism. He said in a recent symposium held by *Commentary* that "there does not seem to me a complex of values or aspirations or beliefs that continue to connect one

Jew to another in our country"; rather, Jews are held together by a disbelief in Jesus as Christ. Such a relationship is "enervating and unviable," for any religious, social, or moral community "springs not from disbelief, but faith and conviction." Roth feels that "neither reverence toward the tradition, nor reverent feelings about the Jewish past seem ... sufficient to bind American Jews together today," and he himself "cannot find a true and honest place in the history of believers that begins with Abraham, Isaac, and Jacob."[45] Roth put his tentative relation to Judaism more forcefully at a 1963 Tel Aviv symposium of Jewish intellectuals:

> I came all the way to Israel to find that writers think alike — which I knew in America — and that is, that one feels very little loyalty or obligation to organizations, to institutions; that a work of art is a work of intuition and you have to place your faith in this connection between intuition and experience. I do not only look outside the American Jewish community; I cannot think of any community that I think that I belong to, so why should I belong to the American Jewish community? The term has been used here over and again, but I do not even know what that means.   (*SDI*, p. 61)

This is not to say that Roth does not regard himself as a Jew. In fact, he says in the same symposium that he has a "good deal of feeling and ... a good deal of affection" for Jewish life.[46] (*SDI*, pp. 70-71) Roth feels, however, that the American Jew does not inherit a body of law and learning, but rather a psychological shell without clear historical, cultural or moral substance. Thus, Roth believes, "one had to, then, I think, as one grew up in America, begin to create a moral character for oneself. That is, one had to invent a Jew .... There was a sense of specialness and from then on it was up to you to invent your specialness." (*SDI*, p. 21) This challenge to invent moral responses and attitudes is for Roth both a blessing and a burden, for it provides one with unique obligations and a special perspective. He concludes, "If I can make any sense about my Jewishness and of my desire to continue to call myself a Jew, it is in terms of my outsideness in the general assumptions of American culture." (*SDI*, p. 39)

It is, of course, precisely this "outsideness in the general assumptions of American culture" that supplies much of the impetus to the satire found in Roth's fiction. Roth does not, however, bring a strong sense of Judaistic heritage to either his fiction or his view of himself as a writer. He makes a fine, but important, distinction when he says, "I am not a Jewish writer; I am a writer who is a Jew. The biggest concern and passion in my life is to write fiction, not to be a Jew." (*SDI*, p. 35) It is this distinction that Roth repeatedly insists on:

> My goal is not really to investigate Jewish life wherever it crops up and then to write fiction about it; I am interested in expression of human character and the mysterious connection between events and characters — who it is that causes what, and how it happened. This is not manifested only in Jewish life.   (*SDI*, p. 37)

Roth puts this idea in slightly different terms when he says, "I do not think that you have to love and revere Jewish life to write about it, but I can feel in its presence awe and wonder, which is what I do feel"; but, Roth goes on to say, "I have faith in a good deal of existence outside of Jewish community, outside the Jewish life." (*SDI*, p. 60)

From what Roth has said, we can see that he does not have a personal vendetta against the Jewish community; rather, he has a good deal of affection for Jewish life and the Jewish tradition. The difficulties of understanding one's role as a Jewish-American have provided Roth with a subject for his fiction, just as his memories of Jewish life in America have provided him with a context for his early novels and short stories. Roth insists, however, that as a writer and as a thinker his arena of interest is in no sense strictly Jewish, a point that is emphasized, to some degree, by the lack of attention to Jewish characters and to the Jewish milieu in "Novotny's Pain," *When She Was Good, Our Gang,* and *The Great American Novel.* He is, if anything, a humanist whose concerns are broadly moral and social, and whose artistic vision, though rooted in the particularities of Jewish life, extends outward to the common humanity shared by all men. In reply to a generalization by Leslie Fiedler, Roth emphasized the point his fiction starts from: ". . . I think that I write from a much narrower point of view than the critic later chooses to understand literature. That is, I do not think archetypally; I do not think in terms of myths; but I do think in terms of that which is close to me, . . . which is American Jewish life — the lives some Jews have led in America." (*SDI,* p. 61)

That Roth's concerns are broadly humanistic rather than narrowly Jewish is evidenced by his unwillingness, or at least his inability, to identify any uniqueness in Jewish values. In fact, Roth says that he is very often confused when the subject of Jewish values comes up; "when such values as social justice are cited, that seems to me to be a human value which has long since become everyone's." (*SDI,* p. 31) Roth carries his humanistic interests further — and there is certainly no contradiction in his use of Jewish materials here — when he admits, ". . . I am interested in situations which are not expressly Jewish. I'm not even interested, really, in attacking the Jewish community, though I don't mind saying what I don't like. But I'm interested in certain kinds of human situation." (*SDI,* p. 70) Certainly Roth's study of human character working through "moral and psychological obsessions" is related to his own Jewishness and that of his characters, but Roth insists that these obsessions do "not have to do specifically with the Jewish milieu." (*SDI*, p. 37) So much is Roth interested in the "human situation," in fact, that he feels no particular empathy for the Jewish characters in his first full-length novel, *Letting Go*; rather, the "distinction between Jewish characters and Gentiles was not always present in my mind. They existed as individuals, as people." (*SDI*, p. 80) Given Roth's humanism, his grounding of his fiction in particular experiences of Jewish life, and his hesitancy about the viability of Jewish values and the Jewish heritage, it is understandable that he says:

> I do not think of my work in terms of how much of the Jewish tradition is in it. There can only be that much of the Jewish tradition in it as in my character which has sifted down into me by way of all my attachments, particularly when I was a child. . . . I still find it hard to figure out what in my work is Jewish. (*SDI*, p. 74)

Roth has repeatedly answered his critics from the Jewish community by insisting that as a writer he has no obligation to write Jewish "propaganda." In a recent article, Roth took to task both Leon Uris and Harry Golden for feeding the stereotypes of the Jewish fighter and Jewish "warmth," respectively, at the expense of an honest and realistic portrayal of the Jewish condition. He concludes by saying, "I cannot help but believe that there is a higher moral purpose for the Jewish writer, and the Jewish people, than the improvement of public relations."[47] In regard to his own fiction, Roth strikes a similar note in responding to his critics. When, for example, Jews objected to Roth's depiction of a Jewish adulterer in one of his stories, Roth was quick to point out that adultery is not a uniquely Jewish but rather a human possibility; and when Jews objected to his depiction of a malingering Jewish soldier, Sheldon Grossbart in "Defender of the Faith," Roth responded, "He is not meant to represent The Jew or Jewry. . . . Grossbart is depicted as a single blundering human being." (*WAJ*, p. 449) Jewish critics, Roth maintains, confuse the purpose of the writer with the purpose of a public relations man. Jews feel that Roth is "informing" on Jews when he should be providing a picture of the positive aspects of Jewish life; Roth argues that he is indeed an informer, but all that he has told the gentiles is that "the perils of human nature afflict the members of our minority." (*WAJ*, p. 450)

A writer's evaluation of his own work is often of questionable validity; in Roth's case, however, the self-evaluation seems to be vigorously consistent. As a writer who is a Jew, Roth asks for a literary rather than a narrowly religious evaluation of his fiction; as a social realist, he takes as his domain the society that he has seen and known — which includes but is not limited to Jewish life; and as a humanist he is spurred by what Bellow calls "the legacy of humanism," "an idea of dignity which makes [one]. . . think a great deal of what he sees about him absurd."[48] An artist should be measured, Roth feels, by "the honesty of the portrayal, for the authenticity of [his] vision" (*SDI*, p. 76) — and not by the popularity of the portrayal or the good service done to the Jewish tradition and the Jewish community. In defense of his short story "Epstein," Roth clearly refutes the obligations so often foisted on him by Jewish critics and the Jewish community alike:

> The issue is not knowledge of one's "people." At least, it is not a question of who has more historical data at his fingertips, or is more familiar with the Jewish tradition, or which of us observes more customs and rituals. . . . The story of Lou Epstein stands or falls not on how much I "know" about tradition, but on how much I know and understand about Lou Epstein. . . . [One] has

every right to expect that I be close to the truth as to
what might conceivably be the attitudes of a Jewish
man of Epstein's style and history, toward marriage,
family life, divorce and fornication. The story is called
"Epstein" because Epstein, not the Jews, is the subject.

(*WAF*, pp. 447-448)

And in defense of "Defender of the Faith," he is quick to
note that, despite the objections of those who see the story
as anti-semitic, "the verisimilitude of the characters and
their situation was not what was called into question."
(*WAF*, p. 449)   *having merely the appearence of truth.*

From the point of view of literary criticism the inherent
rightness of Roth's stance makes us suspect the legitimacy of
the observations offered by some Jewish commentators.
Consider, for example, Baruch Hochman's complaint that
"one gathers that Roth does not really know Yiddish." [49]
Too, we might question a critic like Freedman when he tells
us of Roth's eagerness to fulfill all the predetermined
requirements of Jewish fiction as a stereotyped form. [50] And
Roth's remark that he does not think in archetypes and
myths is a thought-provoking rejoinder to critics like Irving
Malin and Leslie Fiedler. Roth himself isolates the danger of
Jewish-oriented approaches to his literature when he says of
certain readers:

> Not only do they seem to me often to have cramped
> and untenable notions of right and wrong, but looking
> at fiction as they do — in terms of "approval" and
> "disapproval" of Jews, "positive" and "negative" atti-
> tudes toward Jewish life — they are not likely to see
> what it is that the story is really about.   (*WAJ*, p. 446)

It is perhaps one of those interesting ironies that Roth, like
Kafka, is the most marginal of Jews who, nonetheless, must

fight the hardest against religious and communal pressures to deliver himself from his past into his future. If it is true that as a social realist Roth keeps his eye steadily on human character and heroic potential as it is developed in or defeated by communal life in America, it is equally true that his own potential and his own character have been tested by the community — and Roth has responded to the challenge openly and directly, not only in interviews and nonfictional essays but in his fiction as well. Clearly, however, if we would understand Roth's intentions and achievements as a writer of fiction, we must look at his central characters not as Jews in an ideological, traditional, or metaphorical sense, but as men yearning to discover themselves by swimming into dangerous waters beyond social and familial strictures: beyond the last rope. Only by so approaching Roth's fiction are we likely to see what it is that the stories are really about.

II

The Activist Hero in Roth's Fiction

Attempts to explain the popularity of Jewish-American fiction — its uniqueness of tone, theme, and style, on the one hand, and its tantalizing relation to the American literary tradition, on the other hand — have so far failed to supply valid and illuminating guidelines, particularly in the case of Philip Roth. Like other writers of Jewish-American fiction, Roth has defied easy categorization. After reviewing the Jewish-oriented criticisms offered by such critics as Fiedler, Malin, Schulz, and Freedman, one might ask, with Benjamin DeMott, whether in fact there *is* such a thing as Jewish literature in America:

> Is it not probable that the extraordinary influence of works by serious Jewish novelists signifies only that the voice of powerlessness speaking in situations of humiliation, nakedness, and weakness is the voice that speaks most directly to the *common* conviction about the nature of present experience? And if so, if there is no longer any special experience of Jewish powerlessness, what responsible critic would wish to single out Jewish

representations of this experience as special objects of attack?[1]

Whatever the answers to these questions may be, we must not lose sight of larger and more essential aspects of Jewish-American fiction — aspects that are grounded in artistic rather than in narrow religious considerations.

Certainly Jewish-American fiction has often fulfilled Henry James's single requirement for good fiction: it has been interesting, in the deepest sense of the word. One discovers in the fiction of Bellow, Malamud, Roth, and other Jewish-American writers an ultimate concern for what Malraux has called *la condition humaine* — a condition that is not the less human for being rendered through Jewish characters. Even Malamud, the most clearly Jewish of recent Jewish-American authors, strikes a note that joins him explicitly with Roth's and Bellow's humanistic interests: "My work," he declares, "all of it, is an idea of dedication to the human."[2] In attempting to investigate the human condition from the vantage point of Jewish characters, Jewish-American authors have worked into their fiction not only their own memories of their Jewish past but also their individual responses to influences from political, cultural, philosophic, and literary realms. From the subtle and complex interplay of both Jewish and non-Jewish influences has come a fiction whose flavor and frame of reference are often Jewish, but whose meaning extends through and beyond the confines of the Jewish experience. Because writers like Bellow, Malamud, and Roth are receptive to the rich materials of Jewish-American life and to the broader currents of the American experience, they are able to capture in their fiction something of the paradoxical condition of contemporary man in America. The hero who emerges from Jewish-American fiction brings with him the helplessness of man in the face of the forces of dehumanization, mechanization, and conformity, or the hopefulness, as futile as it may seem, of triumphing over these same forces. Between Bellow's Leventhal, the victimized hero of *The Victim*, and his Augie March, the self-asserting hero who refuses to be victimized, one finds the full range of heroic response possible to contemporary man, at least as it is imagined by our best contemporary authors, both Jewish and non-Jewish.

Bellow, Malamud, and Roth have presented heroes who have been caught on one or the other of these two horns of the now familiar existential dilemma: man victimized by a world he never made, and man yearning for transcendent power, for a privately satisfying sense of self.[3] Ihab Hassan's rebel-victim, his typical American fictional hero, combines in one paradoxical figure both the victimized hero and the self-asserting hero found so often in contemporary fiction and, most typically, in that of Jewish-American writers.

These two modes of existential response of central fictional characters best serve to illustrate the similarities and differences existing among Jewish-American writers of contemporary fiction. It is quite fashionable today to explain the presence of existential heroes in Jewish-American fiction by pointing to the merging of the Jewish plight and the existential plight: the suffering, the alienation, and the utter loneliness characterizing the Jew's experience for two thousand years become, in modern times, everyone's condition. With this phenomenon in mind, Leslie Fiedler speaks of the Judaization of the American culture and offers the Jew as a symbol of the modern predicament. Frederick J. Hoffman offers a similar observation, but one that emphasizes the self-assertion rather than the victimization of the hero:

> The Jewish situation is an existential one, within limits. The self-assertion in this circumstance is hedged by doubt, by a "comic self-consciousness," but ultimately

> the hero's decision is all but entirely his own; he has a tradition, but it demands that he act on his own initiative.[4]

The drawback to such explanations, however, is that they tend to exclude the possibility for influences from non-Jewish realms. Too, the presence of traditional Judaism in American fiction is not nearly so obvious as is often assumed. The assimilation theme, the merging of Jewish and American traditions, and the secular spirit of Jewish-American fiction point toward the riskiness of explaining the existential heroes in Jewish-American fiction solely in terms of the Jewish experience.[5] For example, Richard Boyd Hauck in his *A Cheerful Nihilism* has noted that existential heroes in American fiction by non-Jews have been generally characterized by a "comic self-consciousness" of their aspirations and limitations.

However much the Jewish experience lends itself to a dramatization of the modern plight, contemporary Jewish-American writers, particularly Philip Roth, are clearly responsive to more than the Jewish tradition in molding the heroes of their fiction. The passive victim-hero has his roots not only in the Jewish *shlimozel* and *lamedvavnik* but in American literary heroes extending back at least as far as Melville's Bartleby. The questing, self-asserting hero goes back equally as far in the American tradition, to Melville's Ahab. The two essential modes of existential response — active self-assertion and passive victimization — have come to represent the strongest hopes and deepest fears of contemporary American authors; and the potential for heroic response in the fictional character's encounter with his world has come to serve as a meaningful index of the sensibility of our most serious writers.[6]

The purpose of this chapter is to explore the first of these two modes of heroic response, active self-assertion, as it is found in some of Roth's fictional heroes. Roth's early fiction presents heroes who appear to conform to what Helen Weinberg, David L. Stevenson, and Albert J. Guerard have called the "activist mode." The term, as we shall see, is a very useful one for measuring both the uniqueness of Roth's early heroes and their similarity to other heroes of contemporary Jewish-American fiction. Furthermore, the particular modifications of active heroism demonstrated by Roth's early heroes indicate Roth's formative artistic concerns and the increasingly clear direction that his fiction takes. Only by observing the fate of the activist hero in Roth's early fiction can we understand the bitterness and the increasing absurdity that characterize the plight of the victim-hero in Roth's later fiction.

About one-third of the way through Roth's second novel, *Letting Go*, the central character, Gabe Wallach, describes his academic routine and his attitude toward it:

> So, for myself, I taught classes as diligently as I could, straining daily at being Socratic and serious; I marked all those weekly compositions with the wrath of the Old Testament God and the mercy of the New; I emerged bored but uncomplaining from endless, fruitless staff meetings; and every six months or so, I plunged into my grimy dissertation and mined from it another Jamesian nugget to be exhibited, for the sake of the bosses and their system, in some scholarly journal. But in the end I knew it was not from my students or my colleagues or my publications, but from my private life, my secret life, that I would exact whatever joy — or whatever misery — was going to be mine.
>
> (p. 230)

In turning away from public life and toward the private and secret life for self-fulfillment, Gabe aligns himself with other heroes in Roth's early fiction — Ozzie Freedman, Eli Peck, and Neil Klugman — and with the prototypal character that has often been called the activist hero.

The Activist Hero in American Fiction

Perhaps the clearest definition of the activist hero, who is in contrast to the victim-hero of absurdist fiction, is offered by David L. Stevenson. Stevenson says that a special kind of fiction has emerged since the Second World War, and

> a reasonably accurate label for it is "activist" fiction because its major concern is with the active self-consciousness, the active self-awareness, of characters full of high energy who are intellectual migrants from the norms of domestic morality and ambition in a closed, money-making society.... In substance, this activist fiction is almost wholly concerned with the details of a central hero's energetic quest. The peculiarity of this quest is that the hero, unlike his counterpart in more formal fiction, does not seek for conclusive, irreversible outcomes from specific predicaments. The activist hero is, rather, involved in a more nearly aimless search through the endless clutter of everyday existence for a sense of a privately satisfying identity or self.... His real concern is with his privately hoping, socially non-conforming, existential self.[7]

In her brilliant study entitled *The New Novel in America*, Helen Weinberg gives a similar definition of the activist hero: "He chooses, subjectively and irrationally, his self, his own being; he proposes the possibilities of his own being against the non-being of worldly schemes."[8] Albert Guerard explains that activist fiction is a valid response to the dullness and conformity of the Eisenhower period and that the activist hero is "tough," vigorous, amoral, non-conforming, energetic; above all, the activist hero rejects social fixity and responds "with a burning poetic consciousness to the ever-present novelty of life."[9]

Weinberg argues that the origins of the activist hero are to be found in Kafka's K. in *The Castle*, but, as the perceptive José Ortega y Gasset makes clear, the pitting of a self-image against the encroachments of worldly schemes and institutions is a basic conflict inherent in the very origins of the novel; that is, in *Don Quixote*:

> A similar phenomenon is unknown in the epic. The men of Homer belong to the same world as their desires. Here we have, on the contrary, a man [Quixote] who wishes to reform reality. . . . Doesn't he live off it, isn't he a consequence of it? How is it possible for that which is not — the project of an adventure — to govern and make up the harsh reality? Perhaps it isn't possible, but it is a fact that men exist who are determined not to be contented with reality. Such men aim at altering the course of things; they refuse to repeat the gestures that custom, tradition, or biological instincts force them to make. These men we call heroes, because to be a hero means to be singled out, to be oneself. If we refuse to have our actions determined by heredity or environment it is because we seek to base the origin of our actions on ourselves and only on ourselves. The hero's will is not that of his ancestors nor of his society, but his own. This will to be oneself is heroism.[10]

The "will to be oneself," to "base the origin of our actions on ourselves and only on ourselves," finds particularly strong expression in American literature and, indeed, in the American culture. Frederick J. Hoffman maintains that

"individualism, or self-assertion, or the ego's right of independence from excessive pressures of the 'other,' is so
firmly entrenched as a privilege and a characteristic of
American society that one would as soon attack motherhood
as deny it."[11]   Irving Howe speaks in similar terms when he
says, "American literature establishes its own tradition of
rebelliousness: it is steadily concerned with testing the
farthest reaches to which individualism — an individualism
assertive, willed, and often self-destructive — can be
driven."[12]   And in his *The Eccentric Design* Marius Bewley
has convincingly presented the thesis that the conflict
between the powers of the one and the powers of the many is
a central American preoccupation, one that is often reflected
in American literature.

It is not surprising, then, that our best contemporary
American writers have continued to explore the human
condition from the vantage point of the self-asserting hero.
The activist hero is not, however, the hero of the traditional
novel, nor is he the hero of nineteenth and early twentieth-
century American literature, even though he has many
affinities with these predecessors. His central concern is with
self-definition; he is highly conscious of the group pressures
that inveigh against his individualism; he has at times a
comic detachment from, at times a serious commitment
to the daily experiences that take on meaning as they
impinge upon his awareness of who he is and where he is
going; and, above all, he has an enduring courage, in the
face of the fragmented and often absurd world in which
he lives, to continue his quest for individual meaning and
personal freedom. Unlike the *isolato* in Melville's fiction,
the activist hero found in Jewish-American fiction is
willing, as Max Schulz says, "to accept the world on its
own terms," without "losing faith in the moral significance of human actions."[13]

The activist hero in Jewish-American fiction initiates his existential quest for freedom as the highest ideal for which he can strive. In Bellow's *Dangling Man*, Joseph voices the transcendent goal toward which the activist hero struggles in his process of becoming a spiritual self:

> If I had *Tu As Raison Aussi* with me today, I could tell him the highest "ideal construction" is the one that unlocks the imprisoning self.
>
> We struggle perpetually to free ourselves. Or, to put it somewhat differently, while we seem so intently and even desperately to be holding on to ourselves, we would far rather give ourselves away. We do not know how. So, at times, we throw ourselves away. When what we really want is to stop living so exclusively and vainly for our own sake, impure and unknowing, turning inward and self-fastened.
>
> The quest, I am beginning to think, whether it be for money, for notoriety, reputation, increase of pride, whether it leads us to thievery, slaughter, sacrifice, the quest is one and the same. All the striving is for one end. I do not entirely understand this impulse. But it seems to me that its final end is the desire for pure freedom. We are all drawn toward the same craters of the spirit — to know what we are and what we are for, to know our purpose, to seek grace.[14]

The activist hero in Bellow's fiction is best represented not by Joseph, who is a passive victim unable to undertake the spiritual quest he describes, but rather by Augie March in *The Adventures of Augie March* and Eugene Henderson in *Henderson the Rain King*. Each is a hero who actively attempts to define himself through his personal experiences, over and against worldly schemes. Augie, at the end of the novel, proclaims, "I am a sort of Columbus of those near-at-hand and believe you can come to them in this immediate *terra incognita* that spreads out in every gaze." This Columbus of the self travels through the *terra incognita* of his own existence in search of the "axial lines of life":

> I have a feeling . . . about the axial lines of life, with respect to which you must be straight or else your existence is merely clownery, hiding tragedy. I must have had a feeling since I was a kid about these axial lines which made me want to have my existence on them, and so I have said "no" like a stubborn fellow to all my persuaders, just on the obstinacy of my memory of these lines, never entirely clear.[15]

As Augie's words suggest, his heroism is defined not only by his goal of selfhood, but also by his stubborn resistance to outside forces that would deny him his quest. The goal itself is never entirely clear, but what is clear is that Augie has, as he says early in the novel, "a great desire to offer resistance and say 'No!' " This is not, however, Melville's cosmic "no in thunder," but rather a more limited and specific negation offered to the pressures of social conformity.

Another of Bellow's activist heroes, Henderson, is driven to Africa in an attempt to satisfy a voice from within him that continually cries, "I want. I want. I want." Like Augie, Henderson wants to add a spiritual quality to his life, a quality that cannot be answered by materialistic ends. As a millionaire, Henderson already has what money and position can offer. And like Augie, Henderson is never entirely clear about his goal, although he is quite sure that he must persevere in searching for it. As he explains to his native guide and friend, Romilayu, "Every man feels from his soul that he has to carry his life to a certain depth. Well, I have got to go on because I haven't reached that depth yet." Like Gabe Wallach, Henderson turns away from public life and toward a private life, for Henderson the fantasy world of Africa, for self-fulfillment. Augie, on the other hand, sifts through the experiences offered by Chicago (again like Gabe Wallach), Europe and Mexico in his attempt to find, as he often says, "a fate good enough."

Bellow's activist hero has had an enormous impact on the fiction and the fictional hero of Jewish-American writers. Surely Albert Guerard does not overstate the case when he says that *The Adventures of Augie March* "soon had a great influence — possibly the greatest influence exerted by any one book — on other novelists espousing activist attitudes. . . ."[16] Weinberg goes as far as to suggest that there is "The School of Saul Bellow," in which are included Mailer, Salinger, Malamud, Gold, and Roth. Of these writers Weinberg says, "That they are genuinely concerned with the problems of modern man's freedom and spirit, which the device of the activist hero has given them the opportunity to explore, does not lessen their indebtedness to Bellow for the first powerful presentation of such a hero in recent American fiction."[17] Weinberg is, I think, correct in her general assessment of the central concern of these writers, although she puts more emphasis on a direct influence of Bellow than is called for. Roth, for example, has been more influenced by Bellow's *The Victim* than by *Augie March* and *Henderson the Rain King*, and his activist hero is a reaction to rather than an imitation of Bellow's activist hero. Clearly, though, Roth and other Jewish-American writers do attempt to explore the problem and answer the question that Bellow puts so succinctly:

We have so completely debunked the old idea of the Self that we can hardly continue in the same way.

Perhaps some power within us will tell us what we are,
now that old misconceptions have been laid low.
Undeniably the human being is not what he commonly
thought a century ago. The question nevertheless
remains. He is something. What is he?[18]

The major Jewish-American writers have all created the
hero who has confronted exactly this problem: He is
something, but what is he? To discover his true being, the
activist hero often follows Mailer's prescription that the only
life-giving answer is "to divorce oneself from society, to exist
without roots, to set out on that uncharted journey into the
rebellious imperatives of self."[19] The hero may, like
Malamud's S. Levin, cut himself off from the tentacles of an
unfortunate past in order to begin a new life. He may, like
Salinger's Holden Caulfield, probe the borders of the closed
structure of society for an inaccessible salvation. And he
may, like Gold's Burr Fuller, drift through one experience
after another, cherishing experience for its own sake, only to
conclude with Fuller's last demand for additional experience:
"More. More. More! More! More!" In their quest for
"life-giving" answers, these heroes exist on the periphery of
society, where they can best make an unfettered exploration
of the meaning of their existence — where, that is, they might
best become, in Thoreau's phrase, experts in home cosmo-
graphy. Of the heroes of the activist novel, Stevenson says:

[They] are ontologists all, avid investigators into the
essential qualities of the events and the human relationships that chance their way. Unlike Hemingway's
Robert Jordan or Faulkner's Joe Christmas, who finally
surrender to fates imposed by the conditions of society,
the new activist hero remains to the end an intrepid
opportunist of the self. He is an eager, insatiable
explorer of his own private experience, always on the

alert, in Augie March's phrase, for "a fate good enough" to vindicate the energy spent on the exploration.[20]

Roth's Conception of the Activist Hero

Stevenson, Weinberg, and Guerard bring to their conception of the activist hero a perceptive insight into the pattern of much contemporary fiction. The fact that all three critics do not hesitate to include Roth among writers of activist fiction points to a literary — rather than religious — sensibility that Roth shares with other contemporary writers. With Mailer's "life-giving" answer clearly in mind, Weinberg gives the basis of this shared literary concern: "Bellow, Malamud, Salinger, Gold, Roth, all create heroes dedicated to the 'imperatives of self,' more or less rebelliously."[21]

It is my belief that Weinberg, Stevenson, and Guerard are responding to the right critical impulse in including Roth among writers of activist fiction, but that Roth's conception of the activist hero must be carefully qualified. Roth is not, in contrast to Weinberg's contention, imitative in his adaption of the activist mode. Rather, as an examination of his personal views and his fictional heroes will reveal, he brings to the activist hero a strong sense of the necessity of social engagement — a necessity that is generally absent in the writings of other "activist" authors. Roth does indeed create heroes who are dedicated to the "imperatives of self," but his heroes must make their quest through the recognizable social world. Thus with this qualification Roth separates himself from other writers of activist fiction.

In his essay "Writing American Fiction" Roth complained that many contemporary writers stylistically turn away from American public life by adopting a bouncy, self-indulgent language in their fiction, a language that veils the real world; this "bouncy" style is, in Roth's view, an indication of the writer's loss of the community as subject. Roth's observations about his fellow writers do not stop, however, with stylistic considerations. In speaking of the self-assertive, activist heroes of Bellow, Malamud, Salinger, and Gold, Roth clearly perceives the thrust of activist fiction, particularly its concern with the self as it is separated from the world. Roth views this inclination of activist fiction with disapproval:

> There is the world, but there is also the self. And the self, when the writer turns upon it all his attention and talent, is revealed to be a remarkable thing. First off, it exists, it's real. *I am*, the self cries, and then taking a nice long look, it adds, *and I am beautiful.*
>
> (*WAF*, p. 232)

Roth is not less interested in the self than are other activist writers, for he shares with Bellow, Malamud, Salinger and Gold an acute interest in the human condition; however, he does question the novelistic strategy of examining — and of celebrating — the socially excluded self.

We have seen that Roth is dedicated to certain kinds of human situations, and that he is interested in character and action rather than ethnocentric examinations of Jewish life. It is this interest that Alfred Kazin notes when he remarks, "The unusual thing, Mr. Roth's achievement, is to locate the bruised and angry and unassimilated self — the Jew as individual, not the individual as Jew — beneath the canopy of Jewishness."[22]   Roth is not satisfied, however, with merely locating the self. For Roth there is the self *and* the world, and one can understand the self only by taking the "world" into account. This, says Roth, is unfortunately what activist writers fail to do. Consider, for example, Roth's comment on *Henderson The Rain King:*

> . . . Saul Bellow's *Henderson the Rain King* is a book which is given over to celebrating the regeneration of a

man's heart, feelings, blood, and general health. Of course it is of crucial importance, I think, that the regeneration of Henderson takes place in a world that is thoroughly and wholly imagined, *but does not really exist.* That is, it is not a part of that reality which we all read about and worry over — this is not the tumultuous Africa of the newspapers and the United Nations discussions that Eugene Henderson visits. There is nothing here of nationalism or riots or *apartheid.*

(*WAF*, p. 232)

Roth's observation is revealing. Obviously he is reacting against that extreme aspect of activist fiction that Mailer underscores when he speaks of the necessity of divorcing oneself from society. Roth is very much aware that the absurdities of modern social life inveigh against the literary imagination and account for the creation of heroes who search for true being in imagined worlds. Nevertheless, it is exactly this inclination in various activist writers that Roth laments. However difficult the task may be, Roth believes that the writer should investigate the self as it exists in society, and therefore Roth puts himself behind a hero who moves in an environment different from that through which Augie March, Henderson, Holden Caulfield, S. Levin, and other activist heroes move. The hero, Roth believes, undertakes the most meaningful spiritual quest by confronting society, not by divorcing himself from it. Not surprisingly, several of his early heroes initiate their spiritual quests by going out into the heart of a realm often avoided by activist heroes: the community.

The Conversion of the Jews

"The Conversion of the Jews," a slight and in some ways flawed short story in Roth's *Goodbye, Columbus,* portrays the embryonic activist hero as Roth conceives of him. The central character, significantly named Ozzie Freedman, is a thirteen-year-old Jewish boy who brings a great deal of distress to his mother and to his rabbi by asking difficult questions about his religion. Rabbi Marvin Binder has twice summoned Ozzie's mother to the Hebrew School because of Ozzie's seeming impertinence during so-called "free-discussion" period. Now Rabbi Binder must summon Mrs. Freedman again, for Ozzie has questioned the rabbi's explanation that the Immaculate Conception is quite impossible. Ozzie explains his own position to his friend, Itzie Lieberman, by pointing to the omnipotence of a God who could create the world in six days: "I asked Binder if He could make all that in six days, and He could *pick* the six days He wanted right out of nowhere, why couldn't He let a woman have a baby without having intercourse."

Previously, Ozzie had earned the rabbi's displeasure by asking how Binder could call the Jews "The Chosen People" if the Declaration of Independence claimed all men to be created equal. Too, Ozzie had dared to ask why some of his relatives considered a plane crash a tragedy only because eight of the fifty-eight victims were Jewish. Ozzie's question about the Immaculate Conception is, it seems, too much for the rabbi and Mrs. Freedman to bear. When Ozzie tells his mother that she must once again see Rabbi Binder, she hits Ozzie across the face with her hand. And when Rabbi Binder forces Ozzie to participate in "free-discussion" in the following class meeting, Ozzie's contribution ("You don't know anything about God!") results in the rabbi's slapping Ozzie squarely on the nose.

The rabbi's slap precipitates a fast-paced response. Ozzie twice calls Rabbi Binder a "bastard" and then races to the roof of the school, with the rabbi and the other students in close pursuit. He successfully escapes his pursuers by locking the only door to the roof, and then pauses to consider his actions:

A question shot through his brain. "Can this be *me*?" For a thirteen-year-old who had just labeled his religious leader a bastard, twice, it was not an improper question. Louder and louder the question came to him — "Is it me? Is it me?" — until he discovered himself no longer kneeling, but racing crazily towards the edge of the roof, his eyes crying, his throat screaming, and his arms flying everywhichway as though not his own.

"Is it me? Is it me Me Me Me Me! It has to be me — but is it!"   (p. 106)

After a few moments, however, "his self-examination began to grow fuzzy." He peers at the street below, where a crowd has begun to form. From the midst of the crowd comes the commanding voice of Rabbi Binder, "a voice that, could it have been seen, would have looked like the writing on scroll." Rabbi Binder, standing in the attitude of a dictator, points a menacing finger at Ozzie and orders him to come down from the roof immediately:

Ozzie didn't answer. Only for a blink's length did he look towards Rabbi Binder. Instead his eyes began to fit together the world beneath him, to sort out people from places, friends from enemies, participants from spectators. In little jagged starlike clusters his friends stood around Rabbi Binder, who was still pointing. The topmost point on a star compounded not of angels but of five adolescent boys was Itzie. What a world it was, with those stars below, Rabbi Binder below. . . . Ozzie, who a moment earlier hadn't been able to control his own body, started to feel the meaning of the word control: he felt Peace and he felt Power.   (p. 107)

Below, various members of the assembled crowd try to get Ozzie's attention. Firemen attempt to get Ozzie to jump into a net; Ozzie's mother, having just arrived for her conference with Binder, pleads for her "martyr" to come down, and, "as though it were a litany," Rabbi Binder repeats her words: "Don't be a martyr, my baby. Don't be a martyr"; the other children, however, misunderstanding the word, join in singing "Be a Martin, be a Martin." At first Ozzie is confused about his choice. "Yearningly, Ozzie wished he could rip open the sky, plunge his hands through, and pull out the sun; and on the sun, like a coin, would be stamped JUMP or DON'T JUMP." Soon, however, he asserts his new-found power by demanding that everyone below kneel in the gentile posture of prayer. He follows this command with another: they must tell him, first individually and then all together, that God can do anything, that He can make a child without intercourse, and that they all believe in Jesus Christ. He concludes with a final demand:

> "Promise me, promise me you'll never hit anybody about God."
>
> He had asked only his mother, but for some reason everyone kneeling in the street promised he would never hit anybody about God.
>
> Once again there was silence.
>
> "I can come down now, Mamma," the boy on the roof finally said. He turned his head both ways as though checking the traffic lights. "Now I can come down. . . ."   (p. 114)

Thirteen-year-old Ozzie Freedman is doubtless the youngest spiritual activist hero in contemporary fiction. Like Augie March, he says *no* to all his persuaders, and like Joseph in *Dangling Man*, he is drawn by a desire to be, as his last name suggests, a freed man — to know who he is and what he is for. Of course he is only dimly aware of the impulse that drives him, and his final pronouncement that "you should never hit anybody about God" sets the limits of his spiritual insight. Nevertheless, Ozzie displays several attributes of spiritual activism as it is defined by Weinberg, Stevenson, and Guerard. His quest for spiritual truth is indeed genuine — so much so that he is willing to suffer the indignities of social disapproval to achieve his end, a disapproval that is dramatized by the slaps administered by his mother and his rabbi. Ozzie sifts through his home life and his religious training for spiritual truth, but he is thwarted at every turn.

At home Ozzie is confronted with a mother whose spiritual sensitivity is limited to lighting candles for the Sabbath and for her dead husband:

> When his mother lit the candles . . . her eyes would get glassy with tears. Even when his father was alive Ozzie remembered that her eyes had gotten glassy, so it didn't have anything to do with his dying. It had something to do with lighting the candles.   (pp. 102-103)

Ozzie perceives the importance of the ritual for his mother, as is demonstrated by his muffling the phone to his breast after it rings during the lighting of the candles. "When his mother lit candles Ozzie felt there should be no noise." At other times she did not look like a chosen person, but when she lit candles "she looked like something better; like a woman who knew momentarily that God could do anything." The moment passes all too quickly, however; immediately afterwards she strikes Ozzie when he tells her that she must see Rabbi Binder after school. It seems that, after all, Mrs. Freedman is no more convinced that God can do anything than is Rabbi Binder.

At the Hebrew School Ozzie is confronted with a rabbi who is as spiritually empty as Mrs. Freedman. Rabbi Binder can offer only clichéd theological responses about cultural unity and historical evidence in replying to Ozzie's questions. "What Ozzie wanted to know was always something different." Rabbi Binder "binds" Ozzie to the letter of theology, and by so doing he fetters the spiritual quest that Ozzie unconsciously wishes to take:

> When it was Ozzie's turn to read aloud from the Hebrew book the rabbi had asked him petulantly why he didn't read more rapidly. He was showing no progress. Ozzie said he could read faster but that if he did he was sure not to understand what he was reading. Nevertheless, at the rabbi's repeated suggestion Ozzie tried, and showed a great talent, but in the midst of a long passage he stopped short and said he didn't understand a word he was reading, and started in again at a drag-footed pace. Then came the soul-battering. (p. 104)

Rabbi Binder inhibits the religious experience by insisting upon a doctrinaire and literal theology when he is exposed to the naive but nonetheless spiritually "right" impulses of his students. His religious sense seems no more fully developed than Mrs. Freedman's, and his ability to see beneath the surface of his religion is as restricted as that of the seventy-one-year-old custodian of the school, Yakov Blotnik. Blotnik, a projection of the young rabbi in future days, spends his time aimlessly polishing the artifacts and mumbling to himself, unaware of the time and of the day.

> To most of the students Yakov Blotnik's mumbling . . . made him an object of wonder, a foreigner, a relic, towards whom they were alternately fearful and disrespectful. To Ozzie the mumbling had always seemed a monotonous, curious prayer; what made it curious was that Old Blotnik had been mumbling so steadily for so many years, Ozzie suspected he had memorized the prayers and forgotten all about God. (pp. 103-104)

Binder, Mrs. Freedman, and Blotnik come to represent the narrow and sterile religiosity from which Ozzie wishes to escape. The religious sensibilities of Binder and Mrs. Freedman are no more meaningful to Ozzie than Blotnik's mumblings, and rabbi and mother unknowingly embrace Yakov's view of life. "For Yakov Blotnik life had fractionated itself simply: things were either good-for-the-Jews or no-good-for-the-Jews." The smug self-righteousness of such a view assaults Ozzie from every direction, and "the soul-battering that Ozzie Freedman had just received" has "imposed its limitation." Ozzie's flight to the roof is initially an attempt to escape this limitation ("he had just run to get away"), but from his new perspective on the roof Ozzie is momentarily given an insight into his own spiritual and, ironically, communal power. For a moment, Ozzie becomes Christ, saint, and martyr in one, offering his life serio-comically for his followers, who kneel in a "whole little upside down heaven" below him. Believing that he has accomplished the conversion of the Jews through a spiritual revitalization, he concludes, "Now I can come down," and he re-enters the community by hurling himself from spiritual as well as physical heights into "the yellow net that glowed in the evening's edge like an overgrown halo."[23]

"The Conversion of the Jews" has often been cited as an example of Jewish self-hatred writing — a thoughtless charge, for, as Ben Siegel says, "Certainly Ozzie Freedman's innocent heresies come closer to Orthodox Judaism's core than do the rabbinical clichés."[24] Even more important for this study of Ozzie Freedman is the observation of Irving and Harriet Deer: "What has been violated in him is not so much his logic as his sense that as an individual he has the right to ask questions, even of religion. He is protesting his individuality rather than his theology."[25] It should be added, however, that Ozzie works within the community that oppresses him, rises above the community only as a last desperate action, and symbolically as well as literally leaps back into the community at the end of the tale. Ozzie struggles for a sense of self (in an undefined and unarticulated way that befits his age, to be sure) in the best tradition of the activist hero. His quest does not take him into the imagined world of Henderson, however, but merely to the roof of the Hebrew School in which he is to receive his Bar Mitzvah. Ozzie travels no further from the community than does Malamud's Angel Levine, with whom Ozzie has much in common.

Eli, the Fanatic

Ozzie's quest should be viewed in light of the quest of another activist hero, Eli Peck, the central character in Roth's "Eli, the Fanatic." This story, which appears in the *Goodbye, Columbus* collection along with "The Conversion of the Jews," describes a different type of Jewish conversion, for at the end of the story Eli returns to the letter *and* the spirit of the traditional Judaism that Yakov Blotnik dimly remembers in "The Conversion of the Jews." Although they differ in the direction of their spiritual quests, both Ozzie and Eli share in the search for spiritual selfhood in the arid realms of modern society.

At the opening of the story, we see that Eli Peck is a lawyer who has been hired to rid Woodenton, a modern New York community, of a recently established Yeshivah school of Orthodox Jews, headed by Leo Tzuref and consisting of eighteen children and a mysterious "greenie." It seems that the secularized Jews of Woodenton, who regard themselves as progressives, feel threatened by the presence of Orthodox Jews who dress in strange clothes, practice strange rituals, and mutter a strange language. Particularly offensive to the modern Jews is the appearance in town of the "greenhorn," an Old Country rabbi who is the epitome of all that the Woodenton Jews despise about the Displaced Persons. Eli has been selected as Woodenton's envoy to the Yeshivah DP's, and his message is one of compromise and conciliation. Early in the story Eli conveys his message *via* a letter to Leo Tzuref:

> I don't think there's any reason for us not to be able to come up with some sort of compromise that will satisfy the Jewish community of Woodenton and the Yeshivah and yourself. It seems to me that what most disturbs my neighbors are the visits to town by the gentleman in the black hat, suit, etc. Woodenton is a progressive suburban community whose members, both Jewish and Gentile, are anxious that their families live in comfort and beauty and serenity. This is, after all, the twentieth century, and we do not think it is too much to ask that the members of our community dress in a manner appropriate to the time and place.   (p. 189)

Eli has expressed, diplomatically, the fear that the modern Jewish community feels. Others among the modern Jews are not so gentle in their remarks. Harry Shaw fears that someday "it's going to be a hundred little kids with little *yamalkahs* chanting their Hebrew lessons on Coach House Road"; Ted Heller fears that "pretty soon all the little Yeshivah boys'll be spilling down into town," and "next thing they'll be after our daughters"; even Eli's wife, Miriam, has strong feelings on the subject:

> All she wanted really was for Eli to send Tzuref and family on their way, so that the community's temper would quiet, and the calm circumstances of their domestic happiness return. All she wanted were order

and love in her private world. Was she so wrong? Let the
world bat its brains out — in Woodenton there should be
peace.   (pp. 188-189)

It is because the newcomers threaten the peace of
Woodenton that Eli is sent to Leo Tzuref. The Yeshivah Jews
too painfully remind the secularized Jews of the past —
Nuremburg, Warsaw, Brownsville, indeed the *Heilsgeschichte*,
the entire redemptive history of a people's suffering. Eli's
encounter with Tzuref is, however, less than successful, for
Tzuref's conception of law is somewhat different from that
of the Woodenton lawyer: "What you call law, I call shame.
The heart, Mr. Peck, the heart is law! God!" Beside Tzuref's
pronouncement, Eli Peck's conception of law is shallow and
self-serving. He has attempted to evict the members of the
Yeshivah on the basis of zoning laws, and he suggests that the
"greenhorn" should replace his traditional black vestments
with offerings from the local Robert Hall store in order to
satisfy the legal terms of the compromise. Eli is unable to
understand that wearing the clothes of a despised creed is the
only affirmation that the "greenie" can make, in that he has
been deprived of wealth, family, even his manhood by Nazi
terrorism. Nor can Eli fathom Tzuref's terse defense of the
"greenie's" garb: "The suit the gentleman wears is all he's
got."

If the presence of the Yeshivah school disturbs the Jewish
townspeople, it mystifies Eli. Tzuref counters Eli's legal
arguments with Talmudic wisdom that, for Eli, is mere
doubletalk. When, for example, Eli brings to Tzuref's
attention that he is living in the twentieth century, Tzuref
replies, "For the goyim, maybe. For me the Fifty-eighth."
And when Eli tries to disengage himself from the pressures
that the community is bringing to bear, Tzuref hits home
once again by replying, "They are you." When Eli replies, "I
am me. They are them. You are you," Tzuref's rejoinder is

equally baffling to Eli: "You talk about leaves and branches. I'm dealing with under the dirt." Coupled with the mystifying words is Tzuref's habit of appearing suddenly from behind one of the pillars in front of the school. Eli, in fact, wonders if Tzuref might live there. The pillar, as a symbol of the God who led the Jews from Egypt in a pillar of cloud by day and a pillar of fire by night (Exodus 13: 21-22), is associated with Tzuref and the "greenie"; it suggests that these two men are true spokesmen for a religious spirit that, in Woodenton, has been lost. Too, the Yeshivah children flee from Eli whenever he appears, as if they cannot allow an unbeliever to view their ritualistic games and dances. To the sensitive Eli the Yeshivah brings sensations and wonderment that are inaccessible to the modern Jews whom he has been representing.

Eli fights for a while against the spiritual stirrings generated by his encounter with the Yeshivah. He dimly perceives that the members of the Yeshivah share in his own dilemma: the loss of spiritual identity amid the forces of modernism. At home Eli is oppressed by the soul-batterings given to him by Miriam, who believes that Eli's spiritual disquietude will disappear if he will only subject himself to psychoanalysis. Miriam has brought to the marriage nothing more than "a sling chair and a goddam New School enthusiasm for Sigmund Freud." As Eli sleeplessly anguishes over his problem, he is aware that if Miriam were awake, "she would set about explaining his distress to him, understanding him, forgiving him, so as to get things back to Normal, for Normal was where they loved one another."

With Freud on one side of him and the Jaycees on the other, Eli misguidedly tries to solve his conflicts by giving the "greenie" one of his own Brooks Brothers suits. At night — the very night that Miriam is taken to the hospital to have their baby — Eli packs the suit in a Bonwit box, takes it to the Yeshivah, and sets it upon the steps. Now he sees the "greenie" for a second time, and now he first confronts the spiritual ache within himself. The "greenie"

> was facing Woodenton and barely moving across the open space towards the trees. His right fist was beating his chest. And then Eli heard a sound rising with each knock on the chest. What a moan! It could raise hair, stop hearts, water eyes. And it did all three to Eli, plus more. Some feeling crept into him for whose deepness he could find no word. It was strange. He listened — it did not hurt to hear this moan. But he wondered if it hurt to make it. And so, with only stars to hear, he tried. And it did hurt. Not the bumble-bee of noise that turned at the back of his throat and winged out his nostrils. What hurt buzzed down. It stung and stung inside him, and in turn the moan sharpened. It became a scream, louder, a song, a crazy song that whined through the pillars and blew out to the grass. . . .   (p. 203)

The following day brings the surprising fulfillment of the vague quest for selfhood that Eli had first realized on the preceding night. The day begins with telephone calls informing Eli that the greenie has been seen in town and that, incredibly, he is wearing Eli's suit and looking like the very image of Eli. Soon, however, Eli receives a greater surprise, for the "greenie" appears at Eli's doorstep, leaving there a box containing his own black garb. In a dreamlike sequence of events, Eli dons the "greenie's" suit and races to the Yeshivah to confront the "greenie," who is found painting the base of a pillar that "glowed like white fire." Eli stares at the "greenie" with "the strange notion that he was two people." After asking the "greenie" what he should do now, Eli gets the "greenie's" response:

> He raised one hand to his chest, and then jammed it, finger first, towards the horizon. And with what a pained

look! As though the air were full of razors! Eli followed
the finger and saw beyond the knuckle, out past the
nail, Woodenton . . . .

Suddenly the greenie made a run for it. But then
he stopped, wheeled, and jabbed that finger at the
air again. It pointed the same way. Then he was
gone.

And then, all alone, Eli had the revelation. He did
not question his understanding, the substance or the
source. But with a strange, dreamy elation, he
started away.   (pp. 210-211)

Perceiving the territory in which he must make his spiritual
affirmation, Eli makes his way down Coach House Road, the
main street of Woodenton. The townspeople first think that
the "greenie" has changed back to his own clothes; shortly,
however, "everybody in Coach House Road was aware that
Eli Peck, the nervous young attorney with the pretty wife,
was having a breakdown." Knowing that it is not enough to
walk on one side of the street, Eli crosses and recrosses Coach
House Road, greeting everyone he sees with "Sholom"; his
spiritual test requires that he confront the entire community,
it seems. He proceeds to the hospital, where he is once again
subjected to a psychoanalysis by his distraught but "understanding" wife: "Oh, Eli, sweetheart, why do you feel guilty
about everything? Eli, change your clothes. I forgive you."
Finally, he stands in front of his new-born son. Soon,
however, his spiritual and physical transformation conclude
in the only logical result: men in white coats, alerted by Ted
Heller, come to take him away.

. . . He rose, suddenly, as though up out of a dream, and
flailing his arms, screamed: *"I'm the father!"*

But the window disappeared. In a moment they tore
off his jacket — it gave so easily, in one yank. Then a
needle slid under his skin. The drug calmed his soul, but

did not touch it down where the blackness had
reached.   (pp. 215-216)

Like "The Conversion of the Jews," Roth's "Eli, the
Fanatic" explores the possibilities for spiritual freedom,
but those possibilities are examined as they exist *within*,
not outside, the community. Eli is intelligent, as is
attested to by his profession, and he is sensitive, as is
affirmed by his two "nervous breakdowns." He is not,
however, on the lookout for spiritual freedom in the
sense that Augie March, Henderson, and S. Levin are.
Rather, his sensibility is initially restricted by the powerful forces of the society of which he is all too much a
part. Eli is, for understandable reasons, attracted to the
security and peace that the secularized Jews of
Woodenton want to preserve. As he takes his new suit to
the "greenie," he pauses to consider the lifestyle that he
will soon give up:

> Here, after all, were peace and safety — what
> civilization had been working toward for centuries.
> For all his jerkiness, that was all Ted Heller was
> asking for, peace and safety. It was what his parents
> had asked for in the Bronx, and his grandparents in
> Poland, and theirs in Russia or Austria, or wherever
> else they'd fled to or from. It was what Miriam was
> asking for. And now they had it — the world was at
> last a place for families, even Jewish families. After
> all these centuries, maybe there just had to be this
> communal toughness — or numbness — to protect
> such a blessing. Maybe that was the trouble with the
> Jews all along. Sure, to live takes guts . . . . (p. 202)

In his meditation, Eli is both right and wrong; Eli comes to
understand that communal toughness is indeed what is

needed, but that it is the members of the Yeshivah, not the
Jews of Woodenton, who have fortitude, precisely because
they can live without peace and safety. The "numbness"
invoked by the Woodenton Jews leads ultimately to a
secularized community insensitive to the pain of spiritual
activism, to the sacrifices needed for the existential affirmation. Eli has been pushed, despite himself, to the point of
decision that Kierkegaard, in speaking of Eli's ancestor,
Abraham, calls the moment of "either/or": Either "the
individual is able to stand in an absolute relation to the
absolute (and then the ethical is not the highest)/or Abraham
is lost — he is neither a tragic hero, nor an aesthetic hero."[26]

The secularized Jews of Woodenton deny spiritual absolutism by fanatically opposing religious fanaticism, replacing
it with the soul-numbing ethics of moderation. Anything that
smacks of absolutism is desperately avoided by the
Woodenton Jews. Abraham's heroism is, in Woodenton's
view, absurd. Ted Heller unwittingly speaks for the religious
sensibility of the secularized Jews when he complains to Eli:

> Sundays I drive my oldest kid all the way to Scarsdale
> to learn Bible stories . . . and you know what she comes
> up with? This Abraham in the Bible was going to kill his
> own *kid* for a sacrifice. She gets nightmares from it, for
> God's sake! You call that religion? Today a guy like that
> they'd lock him up. This is an age of science, Eli. I size
> people's feet with an X-ray machine, for God's sake.
> They've disproved all that stuff, Eli, and I refuse to sit
> by and watch it happening on my own front lawn.
>
> (p. 200)

Ted Heller and the other secularized Jews are for common
sense and moderation, precisely the affliction that has
attacked Eli's spirit (Eli says to his wife, "I do *everything* in
moderation. That's my trouble"). It is only by the most

radical commitment to his spiritual quest, a commitment that strikes the townspeople as an insane act, that Eli is able to discover his quintessential self. As Eli, dressed in the garb of the "greenie," walks along Coach House Road, he is beset by townspeople who stare at him with curiosity and call his name:

> He began to walk slowly, shifting his weight down and forward with each syllable: E-li-Peck E-li-Peck E-li-Peck. Heavily he trod, and as his neighbors uttered each syllable of his name, he felt each syllable shaking all his bones. He knew who he was down to his marrow — they were telling him.   (p. 212)

In the view of the townspeople, Eli has suffered another nervous breakdown, but Eli knows differently. His act has been consciously selected, and, in Eli's words, "if you chose to be crazy, then you weren't crazy. It's when you didn't choose." From this point of view it is the townspeople who are "crazy," not Eli, for the townspeople have accepted their ethical and social stance without examination and, we are led to believe, without conscious choice.

If Eli is insane, then it is the insanity of the truly spiritual man that Kierkegaard describes in *Fear and Trembling:* "He knows very well where he is and how he is related to men. Humanly speaking, he is crazy and cannot make himself intelligible to anyone."[27] To the wooden sensibilities of the secular Jews of Woodenton, Eli's actions are indeed unintelligible, for Eli has not acted with reason and common sense. Just as the secularized Jews wish to neutralize a threat to their placidity by expelling the members of the Yeshivah, and just as Miriam would neutralize Eli's bizarre behavior by subjecting him to psychoanalysis, so, in the final scene, do the doctors at the hospital attempt to tranquilize the "new" Eli out of existence. In pulling Eli away from his son, in stripping him of his jacket, and in drugging "his soul," the doctors ironically re-enact the persecutions visited upon the Jews of history, the Jews of the Yeshivah, and, most specifically, the "greenie." But, we are told, the drug "did not touch [his soul] down where the blackness had reached."

In "Eli, the Fanatic" Roth presents us with a hero who is in certain respects aligned with the prototypal spiritual activist hero. Eli is drawn to what Joseph in *Dangling Man* calls the craters of the spirit; after a faltering start he dedicates his actions to "the imperatives of self"; and he conforms to Weinberg's definition of the activist hero in that "he proposes the possibilities of his own being against the non-being of worldly schemes." In part, then, Eli possesses qualities of spiritual activism. In other respects, however, Eli is outside the range of qualities associated with the activist hero. He does not begin his quest with a conscious commitment to the self; in fact, the reverse is true, for Eli is initially a spokesman for social conformity. More importantly, he finds his identity not by divorcing himself from society but by immersing himself in it. In pointing toward the horizon, toward Woodenton, the "greenie" has left no room for debate about where Eli's spiritual quest must be undertaken. Finally, it should be noted that Eli's actions are irreversible, conclusive, final. Whereas the open structure of activist fiction typically allows for further exploration of a selfhood not realized within the experiences encountered in the fictional work, "Eli, the Fanatic" is a closed-structured tale. In the course of the story Eli discovers his spiritual essence, and "he would walk forever in that black suit, as adults whispered of his strangeness and children made 'Shame . . . shame' with their fingers."

The single most important quality of the activist hero is his condition of living only for the present and the future, in "radical innocence" of the past, in boisterous and energetic disregard for society as a real and actual force. As has been mentioned, it is precisely this quality that Roth does not admire in the heroes of activist writers. Eli finds selfhood only by feeling in the marrow of the bone his deep affinity with the past, with traditional Judaism. James R. Hollis is certainly correct when he says, "Eli Peck is not overtly the hero type, and yet one may see in his effort to come to terms with his ancestral 'homeland' a spiritual quest of heroic dimensions."[28]   Rather than shedding the past, Eli painfully and willfully resurrects memories of Jewish history that he and the modern Jews have been all too willing to repress beneath the soul-numbing rationality of the secular age. Through Eli, Roth provides an unequivocal answer to Kierkegaard's question, "Does the age really need a ridiculous exhibition by a religious enthusiast in order to get something to laugh at, or does it not need rather that such an enthusiastic figure should remind it of that which has been forgotten?"[29]   Given the choice between the apparent absurdities of traditional Judaism and the even greater absurdities of a pastless secularism, Roth clearly, in "Eli, the Fanatic," sides with the former.

Goodbye, Columbus

In "The Conversion of the Jews" and "Eli, the Fanatic" Roth explores two types of "community" that generate the need for existential response. Ozzie Freedman asserts his individuality in the face of a religious community that does not respond to his spiritual need; Eli, on the other hand, lives in a social community that so frowns on individualism that he is driven to religious fanaticism. In both cases, however, Roth dramatizes the difficulty of spiritual activism in conformist systems, whether they be religious or social. And in both cases these two heroes remain outside the boundaries of the spiritual activist hero in that they find a resolution to their spiritual quests, and in their quests they confront

society head on. In contrast to these two heroes is Neil
Klugman, of *Goodbye, Columbus*, who is more clearly within
the activist mode. Whereas Ozzie and Eli make specific and
morally responsible choices in the context of communal
values, Neil is characterized by an intellectual commitment,
amoral and indeterminate, to his present and future personal
fulfillment. Neil is, in some respects, much closer to the
activist hero than are Ozzie and Eli. Ultimately, however, we
cannot accept Stevenson's assertion that *Goodbye, Columbus*
is "wholly within the activist formulations."[30]

Neil Klugman is a twenty-three-year-old adventurer after
experience *and* social advancement. So much is this the case,
that one critic, Ben Siegel, concludes:

> Neil's flaw is that he is determinedly uncommitted. His
> lack of purpose prevents his accepting, rejecting or
> defining either his Jewishness or his social role. He is
> content to remain a seeker — or to apply the title
> metaphor — an explorer, without a destination. His
> feelings toward life are tentative, ambivalent.[31]

A philosophy major and a graduate of Newark Colleges of
Rutgers University, Neil works in a library and lives with his
Aunt Gladys and Uncle Max in a lower-middle-class Newark
neighborhood. He has effectively cut himself off from his
parents and his religion (when asked if he is orthodox or
conservative, he replies, "I'm just Jewish"), yet he has deep,
though divided, feelings about the city in which he has grown
up. On one occasion, while sitting in a park, Neil "felt a deep
knowledge of Newark, an attachment so rooted that it could
not help but branch out into affection." More typically,
however, Newark too painfully reminds Neil of the social
fixity that has restricted his dream of the rich life — of a life
that carries with it the potential for economic, intellectual,
and spiritual fulfillment.

Access to this fuller life is offered by Brenda Patimkin, daughter of the wealthy Patimkins of Short Hills. To Neil Brenda is an angel of deliverance: "There were two wet triangles on the back of her tiny-collared white polo shirt, right where her wings would have been if she'd had a pair." When Neil first embraces Brenda, his hands upon her shoulder blades, he senses

> a faint fluttering, as though something stirred so deep in her breasts, so far back it could make itself felt through her shirt. It was like the fluttering of wings, tiny wings no bigger than her breasts. The smallness of the wings did not bother me — it would not take an eagle to carry me up those lousy hundred and eighty feet that make summer nights so much cooler in Short Hills than they are in Newark.   (p. 10)

His affair with his "angel" finally proves unsuccessful, however, for like Tommy Wilhelm in Bellow's *Seize The Day*, Neil does not know how to reach the consummation of his heart's ultimate need.

Just as Augie March dreams of a place of his own where "all noise and grates, distortion, chatter" are "passed off like something unreal," so does Neil participate in the vision of a young Negro boy who daily visits the "heart section" of the library (the unintentional pun is significant) to look at a "silent" Gauguin painting of "three native women standing knee-high in a rose-colored stream." For Neil, however, the luxuriant vision of Tahiti is fulfilled by the wealth and luxury of the Patimkins: "I sat at the Information Desk thinking about Brenda and reminding myself that that evening I would have to get gas before I started up to Short Hills, which I could see now, in my mind's eye, at dusk, rose-colored, like a Gauguin stream."

As Neil sifts through the experiences offered him by Brenda and her family, he is constantly amazed by the exotic lushness that their wealth provides. Fruit — tropical fruit that is in contrast to the rotten oranges stored in the refrigerator of his Aunt Gladys — becomes the index of the Patimkins' claim to a Tahitian paradise. On one occasion, Neil examines the contents of an old refrigerator in the Patimkins' pine-paneled basement:

> I opened the door of the old refrigerator; it was not empty. No longer did it hold butter, eggs, herring in cream sauce, ginger ale, tuna fish salad, an occasional corsage — rather it was heaped with fruit, shelves swelled with it, every color, every texture, and hidden within, every kind of pit. There were greengage plums, black plums, red plums, apricots, nectarines, peaches, long horns of grapes, black, yellow, red, and cherries, cherries flowing out of boxes and staining everything scarlet. And there were melons — cantaloupes and honeydews — and on the top shelf, half of a huge watermelon . . . . Oh Patimkin! Fruit grew in their refrigerator and sporting goods dropped from their trees!
>
> (pp. 30-31)

As Neil's involvement with Brenda becomes more serious, he increasingly surrounds himself with the luxuries spilling from the Patimkin *cornu copia* — and Brenda herself becomes, unobtrusively but inevitably, another Patimkin luxury for Neil to enjoy: "When we went back to Brenda's we filled a bowl with cherries which we carried into the TV room and ate sloppily for a while; and later, on the sofa, we loved each other and when I moved from the darkened room to the bathroom I could always feel cherry pits against my bare soles."

What Neil discovers is that involvement incurs responsibilities that he is not ready to accept. Brenda, who first appeared to Neil to be "a sailor's dream of a Polynesian maiden," wishes to impose upon Neil normal conventional demands as they are conveyed to her through her parents: marriage, then a job in her father's business of manufacturing kitchen and bathroom sinks. Although he is attracted to Brenda and to the Patimkin wealth, Neil is not ready to commit himself, especially to a family like the Patimkins. Brenda's father, Ben, is a generous but coarse man; her mother is an overbearing, insensitive matriarch who mindlessly flaunts her money and her Jewish orthodoxy (when Neil asks Mrs. Patimkin if she is familiar with Martin Buber, she can only reply, "Is he *reformed*?"); Brenda's younger sister, Julie, is a spoiled and pampered eleven-year-old who always insists on having her way; and her brother, Ron, is a former Ohio State basketball player who entertains himself by listening to his "Goodbye, Columbus" record, a record that nostalgically recounts the glories of Ohio State. To counter the crude power of these Brobdingnags (as Neil calls them) and to escape the marriage that all the Patimkins expect, Neil suggests an alternative to Brenda: she can buy a diaphragm.

In suggesting that Brenda buy a diaphragm, a symbol of the sterility of the relationship, Neil brings to the surface his previously repressed understanding that Patimkin wealth does not hold "fruitful" rewards for his spiritual selfhood. While he waits for Brenda to be fitted for the contraceptive device, he enters St. Patrick's Cathedral, where he perceives for the first time just how far his desire for the rich life has led him away from his spiritual quest:

It wasn't much cooler inside the church, though the stillness and the flicker of the candles made me think it was. I took a seat at the rear and while I couldn't bring myself to kneel, I did lean forward onto the back of the bench before me and held my hands together and closed my eyes. I wondered if I looked like a Catholic, and in my wonderment I began to make a little speech to myself. Can I call the self-conscious words I spoke prayer? At any rate, I called my audience God. God, I said, I am twenty-three years old. I want to make the best of things. Now the doctor is about to wed Brenda to me, and I am not entirely certain this is all for the best. What is it I love, Lord? Why have I chosen? Who is Brenda? The race is to the swift. Should I have stopped to think?

I was getting no answers, but I went on. If we meet You at all, God, it's that we're carnal, and acquisitive, and thereby partake of You. I am carnal, and I know You approve, I just know it. But how carnal can I get? I am acquisitive. Where do I turn now in my acquisitiveness? Where do we meet? Which prize is You?

It was an ingenious meditation, and suddenly I felt ashamed. I got up and walked outside, and the noise of Fifth Avenue met me with an answer:

Which prize do you think, *schmuck*? Gold dinnerware, sporting-goods trees, nectarines, garbage disposals, bumpless noses, Patimkin sink, Bonwit Teller —

But damn it, God, that *is* You!

And God only laughed, that clown.   (pp. 71-72)

The shame that Neil feels for his "ingenious meditation" is due to a conscious recognition that Patimkin wealth is not the answer, finally, to his vague yearnings for paradisiacal peace and serenity. Earlier, Neil has a dream that foreshadows both his revelation in St. Patrick's Cathedral and his ultimate rejection of Brenda and the Patimkins. Neil dreams that he is the captain of a ship, and on board with him is the little Negro boy who so admires the tranquility of the Gauguin painting of the Tahitian women:

> For awhile it was a pleasant dream; we were anchored in the harbor of an island in the Pacific and it was very sunny. Upon the beach there were beautiful bare-skinned Negresses, and none of them moved; but suddenly we were moving, our ship, out of the harbor, and the Negresses moved slowly down to the shore and began to throw leis at us and say "Goodbye, Columbus ... goodbye, Columbus ... goodbye ..." and though we did not want to go, the little boy and I, the boat was moving and there was nothing we could do about it. . . .   (p. 53)

At the end of the novel, Neil's dream is, in effect, realized: he argues with Brenda (significantly, the argument centers around the diaphragm, which Brenda has, wittingly or unwittingly, allowed her parents to discover), and Neil says a final farewell to her. As Dan Isaac says, "Neil refuses to pay the price. He will not sacrifice his moral integrity for a comfortable position in the Patimkin household, even if it means losing Brenda."[32] Neil's rejection of Brenda and her way of life is not a painless one, however, for he realizes that the experience has taken its toll. In rejecting Brenda, he has lost a dream and gained a sad insight into the shallowness of his quest. The refrain of "goodbye, Columbus" and the meaning of Neil's last name in Yiddish ("sadfellow") bring to mind the cry of the Jewish immigrant, cursing the unkept promises of the new world: *A klug zu Columbusn* ("Woe to Columbus"). In making himself, even in making God, over in the Patimkin image, he has lost sight of larger intellectual and spiritual goals, goals symbolized by the Newark Public Library, "whose long marble stairs . . . led to Tahiti."

In the final scene, Neil stands before the Lamont Library, above Harvard Yard, and thinks about the person he has become. In the glass front of the building he sees his own reflection:

Suddenly I wanted to set down my suitcase and pick up a rock and heave it right through the glass, but of course I didn't. I simply looked at myself in the mirror the light made of the window. I was only that substance, I thought, those limbs, that face that I saw in front of me. I looked, but the outside of me gave up little information about the inside of me. I wished I could scoot around to the other side of the window, faster than light or sound . . . to get behind that image and catch whatever it was that looked through those eyes. What was it inside of me that had turned pursuit and clutching into love, and then turned it inside out again? What was it that had turned winning into losing, and losing — who knows — into winning? . . . I looked hard at the image of me, at that darkening of the glass, and then my gaze pushed through it, over the cool floor, to a broken wall of books, imperfectly shelved.   (pp. 96-97)

With this image in mind, Neil returns to his old job at the Newark Public Library, where he begins work on the first day of the Jewish New Year.

Neil Klugman is, with some qualifications, within the activist mode. He is, like Augie March, a "sort of Columbus of those near-at-hand," and Neil searches for his own "axial lines" by turning, misguidedly, to the gilded ghetto of Short Hills. Like other activist heroes, Neil does not search for irreversible, conclusive outcomes to particular predicaments. When Brenda asks Neil if he plans to make a career of his library job, Neil truthfully replies, "Bren, I'm not planning anything. I haven't planned a thing in three years." Neil simply lives for the present, taking each experience for the satisfaction that it offers. He does not commit himself to any particular set of values, although he knows what he dislikes about both the Patimkins (upper class) and his Aunt Gladys (lower class). Like Augie, he perseveres in waiting for a "fate good enough," although he is not at all sure what that fate will be. He comes to realize, however, that the Patimkin way of life is not the answer he has been searching for. As Joseph C. Landis asserts, "The return to work is Neil's own goodbye, Columbus, a goodbye to the sad values and empty lives that are normal in America. . . . That his renewal of himself should take place on the New Year is symbolically appropriate."[33] Unlike "The Conversion of the Jews" and "Eli, the Fanatic," *Goodbye, Columbus* utilizes the open structure of the activist mode. At the conclusion, we are left with a character who is still in the process of "becoming" a fully-realized self.

Although Neil has most of the qualities associated with the activist mode, *Goodbye, Columbus* is clearly concerned with more than Neil's heroic quest. The novel examines social values with a rigor not found in activist fiction.[34] Like Ozzie Freedman and Eli Peck, Neil does not conform to Stevenson's criterion that activist heroes "are intellectual migrants from the norms of domestic morality and ambition in a closed, money-making society."[35] On the contrary, Neil's quest for self takes him into the very heart of a closed, money-making society that has a strong attraction for him. Although Kazin is incorrect in saying that Neil is defeated by this society, he is certainly right in emphasizing the impact that the social values have on Neil's personal and romantic notions of selfhood. It is true enough to say that Roth is generally concerned with Neil's possibilities for an existential affirmation of self, but, characteristically, Roth places his activist hero not on the periphery of society, but at its very center.

Letting Go

Ozzie Freedman, Eli Peck, and Neil Klugman have all contributed, in different ways, to Roth's conception of

Gabriel Wallach in *Letting Go* (a novel that Weinberg calls "the history of an activist hero"). From Ozzie Freedman Gabe inherits a sincere, and at times naive, resentment of limitation; from Eli Peck Gabe inherits a keen awareness of society's expectations for conformity, a nervous indecisiveness, and a final courage to exert his individuality despite the consequences; and from Neil Klugman Gabe inherits an intellectual awareness of moral issues and a misguided yearning for wealth and social advancement. Like Neil, Gabe discovers that human encounter exerts a burden on the human spirit, and, like Neil, Gabe's experiences lead only to the promise, not to the realization, of spiritual fulfillment. At the end of the novel we find Gabe in Europe, still trying to "make some sense of the larger hook I'm on."

Letting Go is a story of human relationships. The novel follows Gabe Wallach through his graduate school days at Iowa University, where he first meets Paul and Libby Herz, a Jewish graduate student and his gentile wife. The Herzes are beset with marital problems ranging from poverty to estrangement from their parents, and their marriage is an unhappy one. Gabe, who is economically secure, is attracted to the Herzes's plight, and, feeling an uncertain love for Libby, he involves himself with their problems.

After his graduate work, Gabe takes a job at the University of Chicago. He continues to help the Herzes by wangling a job there for Paul. He tries to heal the estrangement between Paul and Paul's parents in Brooklyn, an estrangement caused by Paul's marrying a gentile. Finally, when Paul and Libby decide that adopting a child might help their marriage (Libby had been pregnant earlier, but Paul insisted on an abortion), Gabe arranges for a private adoption. He brings them a daughter, the illegitimate child of Theresa, a married Catholic girl, and later tries to overcome the resistance raised by Theresa's husband, Harry Bigoness. In a desperate attempt to placate Bigoness, Gabe takes the child, Rachel, from her crib and drives to the Bigoness residence, where he attempts to enlist their sympathy. In violently arguing with Harry, Gabe collapses. In the last scene of the novel, Gabe flees to London in an attempt to recuperate, to re-evaluate his experiences, and to sever all ties with the past.

Gabe has several other painful involvements in the novel. He is constantly beleaguered by a loving, doting father. Dr. Wallach, a dentist, is a lonely widower who makes excessive demands on his son's affections. Gabe's most serious romantic involvement is with Martha Reganhart, a divorcée with two small children, Cynthia and Mark. Martha, Dr. Wallach, and the Herzes all contribute to the tension existing between Gabe's ideal of an ordered, peaceful existence and the actual demands of interpersonal relationships — a tension that builds to Gabe's breakdown at the end of the novel. Like Paul Herz, Gabe finally comes to an existential crisis in his life, a crisis that provides a horrifying but necessary insight into the darker aspects of human existence.

Throughout the novel, Gabe is beset by indecision:

> He is better, he believes, than anything that he has done in life has shown him to be. . . . He has the malaise of many wealthy but ordinary young men: he does not exactly know what to do with himself. . . . He has an income, he has perfect health, and he believes not only in the pursuit, but the catching by the tail and dragging down into the clover, of happiness. Unfortunately, all these beliefs don't got too much in the way of his actions. If his own good fortune were inevitable, he should not have so much trouble making up his mind. For an optimist, he is very nervous and indecisive.   (p. 69)

Gabe *wants* to pursue the "imperatives of self," as he makes clear on several occasions. In the first scene of the novel, for example, Gabe reads a deathbed letter from his mother (she confesses that she has always been "Very Decent to People," so that she "could push and pull at people with a clear conscience"), after which Gabe promises himself, "I would do no violence to human life, not to another's, and not to my own." He wonders if his cloying father can understand "that I was not prepared to surrender my life to his." After Paul Herz is offered a job at the University of Chicago through Gabe's manipulations, Gabe wants to make it clear to himself "that if the Herzes should come to Chicago he could manage to have an active life of his own, independent of theirs." Returning from an attempt to reconcile Paul with his family, Gabe "spent much of the day looking for some door that would lead me back into the simple life."

It is a desire for a simple life that impels many of Gabe's actions and occupies many of his thoughts. He recognizes that the involvements with his father, Martha Reganhart, and the Herzes have blurred his own sense of self, and he is tantalized by the possibilities of giving himself over to his own personal strivings. One evening, after a particularly painful encounter with the Herzes, Gabe battles with the alternatives of "letting go" of the Herzes or involving himself more deeply in their poverty-stricken lives:

> My life, what is it? My life, where has it gone? One moment I knew myself to be justified and the next vindictive; one moment sensible and the next ignorant and cruel. The battle raged all night, and through it my bruised sense of righteousness, flying a big red flag reading I AM, kept rushing forward — my patriot! my defender! my own self! It cried out that I had every right to be cruel, every right to be through with the Herzes. With everybody. It raised a question that is by no means new to the species: How much, from me!   (p. 368)

In characteristic indecisiveness, however, Gabe cannot put into action his desire to divorce himself from "everybody." His applications for teaching positions in Greece and Istanbul remain uncompleted on his desk — even though "in filling out the applications he would at least have begun to make a plan for departing."

Gabe cannot, in Mailer's phrase, divorce himself from society and set out into the imperatives of self, for he is caught in a net of responsibilities incurred by his relationships with his father, with Libby and Paul, and with Martha Reganhart. Gabe is continually confronted with responsibilities that he cannot handle, and, as Gabe says at one point, "I was furious with myself for having thought again that I could simplify life." Martha demands from him a mature relationship based on more than sex; his father's loneliness is a fact that he cannot forget; and the Herzes, especially, weigh heavy upon his mind.

These responsibilities to others have an enervating and paralyzing effect on Gabe's ability to act. When Harry Bigoness refuses to recognize the legality of the adoption proceedings that Gabe has initiated for the Herzes, Gabe is finally forced into a personal decision that changes his life. Through his involvements he has come to a tentative conclusion about himself:

> The same impulse that had led him to want to tidy up certain messy lives had led him also to turn his back upon others that threatened to engulf his own. He had finally come to recognize in himself a certain dread of the savageness of life. Tenderness, grace, affection: they struck him now as toys with which he had set about to hammer away at mountains. (p. 529)

Gabe sees that he has used other people, used his quest for the simple life, used his withdrawal from social and personal commitment to avoid a confrontation with the "savageness of life." In a last desperate act to assert himself, to throw off the indecisiveness that has protected him from a genuine self-exploration, Gabe grabs Rachel from her crib and begins his journey to Gary, Indiana, where he intends to confront Harry Bigoness:

> He clutched her to himself as though she *were* himself. . . . He had passed beyond what he had taken for the normal round of life, beyond what had been kept normal by fortune and strategy. Tears would only roll off the shell of him. And every reason had its mate. Whichever way he turned, there was a kind of horror.
>
> (p. 599)

The ensuing argument with Bigoness leads to Gabe's nervous breakdown, but it also leads him into a new life. In becoming "the mad crusader" (which is the title of the section of the novel that depicts Gabe's moment of decision), Gabe finally penetrates the shell of normalcy and self-protection that he has so carefully devised. His moment of decision brings about, as Gabe says, the "dissolution of character, of everything," but he cannot — in the name of the future, perhaps — accept forgiveness for my time of strength."

Gabe Wallach's affinity with other activist heroes is apparent enough. Like other activist heroes, Gabe strives for a fate good enough to fulfill, in Stevenson's words, a sense of privately satisfying identity or self. As previously noted, Gabe commits himself to exactly this quest in the novel: "In the end I knew it was not from my students or my colleagues or my publications, but from my private life, my secret life, that I would exact whatever joy — or whatever misery — was going to be mine." Too, it appears that Gabe, unlike Eli Peck and Ozzie Freedman, is a "hero-in-process," continually defining himself through his experiences. In this respect he embodies the vision of existence supported by the activist mode:

> That there is no single, certain way of the self; that the self in its striving must embrace uncertainty and paradox . . .; that it is in the striving that the self exists and not in the end, not in the realized goal; that man is a becomingness and not a beingness and that in this fact lie his hopefulness and his freedom.[36]

Perhaps the most common feature shared by activist heroes is that they long for a place of rest and peace, where the quest for selfhood can be finally realized. This desire is the activist writer's modification of the dream of Utopia found in the writers of the thirties, especially Dreiser, Dos Passos, Steinbeck and Farrell. The political utopian dream of the thirties becomes, for the activist writers, a dream of personal fulfillment. For Holden Caulfield, it is the dream of being a catcher in the rye, a preserver of youthful innocence; like Holden, Augie March wants to "start in lower down, and simpler," and so he holds to the dream of opening a school for children. S. Levin, who calls herself a "conscientious becomer," holds to a pastoral vision of the Pacific Northwest, the idyllic but unfulfilled promise of the mythical state of Cascadia; for Neil Klugman it is the vision of tranquility represented by the Gauguin painting of the three Tahitian women. In their own ways these activist heroes yearn for the simple life that Gabe Wallach yearns for, a life free from commitments, free from the entanglements of the past, free from the pressures of society.

Although Gabe Wallach is clearly within the activist mode, it seems equally clear that the informing theme of *Letting Go* is a reaction against rather than an extension of literary activism. The novel has been attacked as a failure precisely because, I think, critics have not distinguished between the intentions of the activist writers and the intentions of Philip Roth. Baruch Hochman's response typifies critical reaction to the novel:

> The odd thing about *Letting Go* is that everyone in it is perplexed most of the time, but the reader never clearly perceives what it is they are perplexed about. They are all very busy trying to be good, to do the right thing by others and by themselves, but they are perpetually sloshing in the agitated (if shallow) waters of selfhood. This contributes to the sense of childishness that pervades the novel.[37]

Arthur Mizener's complaint is more serious. He complains that Roth cultivates a sense of life that is "almost exclusively personal"; further, he believes that Roth, like other writers of his generation, is guilty of shying away from public life as "an unjustifiable, inexplicable — if immovable — obstacle to the realization of the private self."[38] Weinberg makes a quite different observation. After asserting that *Letting Go* is clearly within the activist mode, she argues that Gabe Wallach fails as an activist hero. The basis for her complaint is that Gabe "does not desert his past for the sake of the present but uses it as an integral part of his investigation into the meaning of his life." She goes on to say that Gabe's "habit of looking backward while supposing himself to be moving forward has a curious effect, making of Gabe a whining and ineffectual hero with whom the reader is supposed to sympathize in spite of his unattractiveness."[39] Hochman and Mizener object that Gabe is too much concerned with his personal life. Weinberg takes an opposing view in suggesting that Gabe is unable to give himself wholly to his personal quest because he is too engaged with the past.

Roth's strong commitment to the necessity for examining the public life, the "social being's private life," and the impact of the community on personal self-assertion, qualifies severely his conception of the activist hero. Hence, one might well question the bases of the criticisms offered by Hochman, Mizener, and Weinberg. It is evident, I think, that in *Letting Go* Roth is exploring the genuine difficulties of active self-assertion *within* the community. Hochman is correct in maintaining that Gabe's search for selfhood is an agitated, childish, and perhaps shallow one. But Roth suggests that so it must be if such a quest takes place within the complexities of social life. Roth's social view is colored by a bitterness that borders on the absurd (we recall that in Roth's view American reality stupifies, sickens and infuriates, with the result that the "tug of reality" may repel the writer), and it is precisely this view that is illustrated in *Letting Go*. Mizener is certainly not far wrong when he maintains that in Roth's novel public life is an obstacle to the realization of the private self, but his assertion that Roth cultivates an exclusively personal sense of life is not entirely accurate, nor is it very consistent with his observation about "public life" in Roth's fiction. Weinberg, on the other hand, is too much under the sway of her own generalizations. She assumes that Roth is attempting to imitate Bellow's (and Kafka's) conception of the activist hero when in fact Roth hesitates to accept Bellow's two activist heroes, Augie March and Eugene Henderson, as fully realized characters. Weinberg's complaint is, I think, based on a reading of the story that is biased by her incorrect understanding of Roth's conception of the activist hero. She makes the mistake of transferring Gabe's activist intentions to Roth:

> One might argue that Roth's novel in its inability to create viable alternatives to the nihilism which informs modern life is existentially faithful to the way-it-is. But in Gabe's protests we inevitably read a larger (finer) intention. . . .[40]

Roth's statements about the purpose of fiction, coupled with his distinctive conception of the activist hero, go far toward suggesting that the criticisms of Hochman, Mizener, and Weinberg are wide of the mark. Hochman and Weinberg complain that Gabe is a whining, ineffectual, childish hero with whom the reader cannot sympathize — exactly the charge that is often leveled at Neil Klugman; Roth's reply, however, is that he is indeed being faithful to the way-it-is. He says of his characters, "The crucial thing . . . is not to empathize with them but to try to understand them" (*SDI*, p. 81) — to understand, that is, how difficult is self-assertion *within* the community and how complex is the self's confrontation with familial and social pressures. The unattractiveness and ineffectualness of Neil and Gabe — in marked contrast to Augie and Henderson — should leave little doubt that Roth's intentions, values, and attitudes are not to be equated with those of Bellow; Weinberg and Mizener, however, do not allow for the obvious differences between Bellow's and Roth's vision of human potential, nor do they account for the greater emphasis that Roth places on social and family pressures.[41] The implicit assumption in their charges is that both Roth and Bellow are committed to an exclusively personal sense of life, but that Roth does not convey such a vision so clearly and unequivocally as Bellow does.

In Roth's early fiction, his unique presentation of the activist hero underscores his basic attitudes and concerns. From this early fiction we may derive insights that are fundamental to Roth's vision of the human condition, a vision that in later fiction becomes darkened by a pessimism that is implicit in the earlier stories. What we discover in "The Conversion of the Jews," "Eli, the Fanatic," *Goodbye, Columbus*, and *Letting Go* is to some extent, I think, a working out of commonly held convictions about the self within the context of Roth's own convictions about the

American public life. On one level, at least, Roth's early fiction is a testing ground for certain hypotheses about the human condition. This is not to say that Roth has replaced the interests of fiction with those of religion, philosophy or sociology; rather, Roth uses the fictional medium, much as Bellow does, to investigate what Lionel Trilling calls "the dangers of the moral life itself."[42] Roth's conclusions, however, are quite different from Bellow's.

It should be stressed that, in contrast to many of the activist writers and in contrast to Mizener's observations, Roth is very much concerned with man in society. Irving and Harriet Deer emphasize this important point when they say that Roth lines up behind a hero "who realizes the confusion and absurdity of modern (American) society but who, instead of rejecting that society, is determined to discover a truthful way of acting in it."[43] As Ozzie Freedman, Eli Peck, Neil Klugman and Gabe Wallach learn, such a discovery costs dearly, for what one comes to discover is that there may be no truthful way to act. Perhaps the only way to survive in the world as Roth envisions it is to follow the advice of Paul Herz's Uncle Asher:

> Things come and go, and you have got to be a receptacle, let them pass right through. Otherwise death will be a misery for you, boy. I'd hate to see it. What are you going to grow up to be, a canner of experience? You going to stick plugs in at either end of your life? Let it flow, let it go. Wait and accept and learn to pull the hand away. *Don't clutch!* (p. 83)

In clutching to a false ideal of self-fulfillment Neil Klugman has turned love inside out. Nor can we forget Roth's description of Neil as he views his reflection in the glass of the Lamont Library, wishing that he could "get behind that image and catch whatever it was that looked through those eyes." Ozzie Freedman's question ("It has to be me — but is it!") is basically the same question that Neil, as well as other of Roth's characters, asks. But in desperately grabbing for answers one may discover (as Gabe discovers in clutching young Rachel to him) that there is a kind of horror beneath the surface. When personal deceptions are swept away, when social absurdities are penetrated, one may find not a beatific realization of self, but a turbulent and chaotic storm. It is precisely this insight that finally comes to Paul Herz as he stands by his father's grave and receives his mother's embrace:

> . . . And now he closed his eyes and opened his arms and what he saw next was his life — he saw it for the sacrifice that it was. Isaac under the knife, Abraham wielding it. *Both*! While his mother kissed his neck and moaned his name, he saw his place in the world. Yes. And the world itself — without admiration, without pity. Yes! Oh yes! . . . He kissed nothing — only held out his arms, open, and stood still at last, momentarily at rest in the center of the storm through which he had been traveling all these years. For his truth was revealed to him, his final premise melted away. What he had taken for order was chaos. Justice was illusion. Abraham and Isaac were one.   (p. 452)

Paul's realization, like Gabe's, is an existential one, within limits. And, as Robert Detweiler points out, this realization, like Gabe's, "takes place within and through the community."[44] For a moment he is filled with strength, and "he felt himself under a wider beam," but at the end of the novel Paul's life has not visibly improved. He has, however, learned to accept the absurdities of life without clutching for final answers.

It is perhaps not surprising that, in his "Writing American Fiction," Roth rejects the activist heroes of Salinger, Bellow,

Malamud and Gold — for these heroes are not willing to confront the storms of social, familial and religious pressures; rather, they affirm life in fantastic and imagined worlds. More honest, Roth implies, is the hero of Ralph Ellison's *Invisible Man*, who in the end is left only "with the simple stark fact of himself." Ellison's hero, however, chooses to go underground only after he has "gone out into the world; he has gone out into it, and out into it, and out into it." (*WAF*, p. 233) Ellison's hero is, like Roth's activist hero, one who tries to live in a world not to his liking. A gaining of identity, a struggling toward spiritual fulfillment, and a commitment to one's self are meaningless if not undertaken in the recognizable terrain of community, Roth feels; but that community foists upon the quester the weight of the past, the obligations of the family, the banalities of shallow social and religious values — and the obsessions and deceptions that derive therefrom.

The possibilities for spiritual activism are, for Roth, so circumscribed by social and psychological realities that, finally, even for the hero who opens himself to the flow of life, there is no cause for celebration. In varying degrees, Ozzie Freedman, Eli Peck, Neil Klugman, and Gabe Wallach have been able to strike through the forces that undermine the hero's active quest for spiritual selfhood. In each case, however, Roth shows us that the forces of normalcy present snares and obstacles of awesome proportions. Roth suggests, however, that a genuine quest for pure freedom must proceed, as Bunyan knew, through the vanities and treacheries of the recognizable social world. And when Roth's attention turns not upon the self but upon the world through which it travels, his hopes for the individual are darkened by the absurdity, by the pathetic emptiness of what he sees.

In his early fiction Roth examines the possibilities for active self-assertion within, rather than outside, the community. His conclusions are tentative, reserved, and less than optimistic. Perhaps true freedom is an illusion, perhaps not, but in any event a clutching for freedom, a commitment to the imperatives of self, does not necessarily and inevitably bring productive results. Perhaps, as Wallace Stevens says in "Aesthetique du Mal" (which serves as an epigram to *Letting Go*), it may be that one life is a "fragmentary tragedy / Within the universal whole." It is, I think, this possibility that underlies both the comic quest of Ozzie Freedman and the deadly earnest one of Gabe Wallach, a possibility that increasingly informs Roth's artistic vision. Even in his earliest fiction, Roth's assessment of the human condition encompasses the social landscape through which the self struggles — like an usher with a dim flashlight in a darkened theater. And even in his earliest fiction Roth's attention is claimed by the dark forces that the activist hero keeps at bay only with a desperate act of will — or self-deception. Increasingly, in Roth's fiction, the uncertain success of the activist hero gives way to the more certain failure of a hero who succumbs to the forces of social absurdity and psychological compulsion, the activist hero's alter ego and secret sharer: The Victim.

III

The Victim-Hero in Roth's Fiction

After examining Malamud's *The Assistant,* Gold's *The Man Who Was Not With It,* Salinger's *The Catcher in the Rye,* and Bellow's *The Adventures of Augie March* and *Henderson the Rain King,* Irving Howe concluded:

> Though vastly different in quality, these novels have in common a certain obliqueness of approach. They do not represent directly the postwar American experience, yet refer to it constantly. They tell us rather little about the surface tone, the manners, the social patterns of recent American life, yet are constantly projecting moral criticism of its essential quality. They approach that experience on the sly, yet are colored and shaped by it throughout. And they gain from it their true subject: the recurrent search — in America, almost a national obsession — for personal identity and freedom.[1]

Howe's observation is a telling one. Certainly the novels that we have termed *activist* have presented heroes who have given themselves to the possibilities for personal identity and freedom; it is also certain that such an inquiry has been characterized by an obliqueness of approach, a circumvention of surface tone, manners, and social patterns of recent American life. The activist hero divorces himself from society in order to follow the imperatives of self, to pursue a new life of the spirit, to quest after a "fate good enough" — rejecting, in the process, the landscape of nightmare, limitation, and absurdity that characterizes the recognizable social world. One finds in heroes like Augie March and Eugene Henderson a paean to the unfettered human spirit. According to Weinberg, such a hero "chooses to sustain his alienation in order to assert his own subjective truth and to seek for himself a wonderful, improbable, transcendent self, an authentic identity he has created for himself, a self that refuses to participate in the schemes of a maddeningly reasonable world's failures and successes."[2] In essence, activist fiction is a response to the pervasive modern conviction that, as Galloway contends, "orthodox 'systems' can offer at best only a superficial reassurance"[3] and that at worst such systems destroy the human spirit. As Weinberg says, activist novelists "implicitly acknowledge that value resides in or in relation to an undefined, often undefinable, spiritual region, *not in or in relation to society*"[4] (italics mine). Hence it is virtually inevitable that activist fiction is in some respects "oblique" in its approach to social patterns of recent American life.

Roth's inquiries into the possibilities for personal identity and freedom have taken a route different from that followed by Bellow, Malamud, Salinger, and Gold. The schemes of a maddeningly reasonable world engage the attention of the most "spiritually active" of Roth's heroes, for in Roth's view personal freedom and identity are revealed to the hero through the actions he takes in the social world — and through the actions the social world performs on the hero. Despite Roth's affinities with the activist impulse, his interest in his early fiction is divided between the self and the public realm in which the self moves, and he is, one suspects, too much committed to social realism in his fiction to give himself over completely to the post-Romantic self celebrated in activist fiction. Heroes like Ozzie Freedman, Eli Peck, Neil Klugman, and Gabe Wallach do indeed quest after spiritual selfhood, but even here Roth is as much concerned with the social aspects of the quest as he is with the metaphysical aspects. It is, in fact, the social concerns in Roth's fiction that distinguish him from other activist writers, particularly Bellow. Bellow himself has correctly said that in Roth's fiction the public realm encroaches on the private and reduces the power of the individual — a brief but accurate assessment not only of Roth's fiction but of Bellow's own early works, especially *Dangling Man* and *The Victim*.[5]

For Roth the social world is a composite of institutions, attitudes, expectations and values particularized in his fiction by readily identifiable spokesmen who are sustained by empty and meaningless customs, beliefs, and traditions. Roth, for the most part, nervously views social attitudes that have the stamp of middle-class normalcy, a normalcy sanctioned by television, newspapers, popular magazines, businessmen's clubs, popular novels, churches and synagogues, and politicians. Significantly, Roth opens his essay "Writing American Fiction" with a long account of social absurdities communicated, even propagated, by the mass media. His first example is of two teenage girls who had been murdered in Chicago; the absurdities involved include one newspaper running a weekly contest entitled "How Do You Think The Grimes Girls Were Murdered?," a song in honor of the murderer becomes popular, and a businessman presents the mother of the murdered girls with a new kitchen. Roth concludes, "The daily newspapers then fill one with wonder and awe: is it possible? is it happening? And of course with sickness and despair. The fixes, the scandals, the insanities, the treacheries, the idiocies, the lies, the pieties, the noise. . . ." Even popular novels like *Cash McCall*, *The Man in the Gray Flannel Suit*, *The Enemy Camp*, and *Advise and Consent* are written by writers who "just don't seem able to imagine the corruptions and vulgarities and treacheries of American public life any more profoundly than they can imagine human character — that is, the country's private life." (p. 225) With the vigor and outrage of the social satirist, Roth seizes upon the absurdities of "normal" life in the American public but not, as is often thought, for the sheer delight of making fun of assimilated Jews. In Roth's fictional realm normalcy is a real and present danger, one that, either comically or tragically, circumscribes the ability of the individual to act in morally or spiritually satisfying ways. Increasingly in such fiction the hero sets about to discover a "fate good enough," only to discover that he has become a victim of worldly absurdities.

The purpose of this chapter is to examine some of these victims of worldly absurdities in Roth's fiction. It is my contention that in the course of Roth's fiction there is a subtle but significant shift from the activist to the absurdist mode; that Roth's fiction increasingly dwells upon the irritants and absurdities of the world; and that the dangers of victimization are evident in both the early and late fiction of Philip Roth.

The Victim-Hero in American Fiction

In his illuminating study of the American novel, Ihab Hassan says, "The victim, broadly conceived, is the representative hero of our time," and "his condition is simply the test case of our moral and aesthetic life."[6] Professor Hassan has given a detailed and perceptive explanation of the prevalence of the victim-hero in modern American literature, tracing the atrophy of the hero as a process determined by complex cultural, philosophical, psychological, and religious factors, and it is not my purpose to recount these factors here;[7] what is important to note is that, whatever the causes may be, "the deep and disquieting insights revealed to us by modern literature often require that we project ourselves into the predicament of victims."[8] Northrup Frye speaks of the typical victim as the *pharmakos* or scapegoat, and goes on to say, "The *pharmakos* is neither innocent nor guilty. He is innocent in the sense that what happens to him is far greater than anything he has done provokes. . . . He is guilty in the sense that he is a member of a guilty society, or living in a world where such injustices are an inescapable part of existence."[9] The inescapability of injustice, guilt, and help-lessness is, most observers agree, the dominant and pervasive problem confronting the modern self, a problem that Wylie Sypher poses as central to modern man's existential pre-dicament: "Under the dominion of apparatus, the self acts, but acts do not express the self or lead to any assertion of the self or any sense of self-fulfillment. . . . To adapt the self to the new realities of power is to feel a new kind of dread, to sense a new kind of guilt, to be weighted by a new kind of helplessness. . . ."[10] The twin aspects of guilt and helpless-ness oppress and baffle the ordinary man who yearns for self-fulfillment, who faces up to the "new realities" of his condition only to discover that he has become a victim.

The victim-hero is, as Hassan suggests, a relatively new figure in American fiction, particularly because the victim is a figure who is most often found in realistic literature; as Richard Chase makes clear, American literature has been essentially romantic, and "Romance does not plant itself . . . solidly in the midst of the actual.[11] Saul Bellow puts the matter in different terms when he says of his own novel, *The Victim*,

> I think that realistic literature from the first has been a
> victim literature. Pit any ordinary individual — and

realistic literature concerns itself with ordinary individuals — against the external world and the external world will conquer him, of course. Everything that people believed in the nineteenth century about determinism, about man's place in nature, about the power of productive forces in society, made it inevitable that the hero of the realistic novel should not be a hero but a sufferer who is eventually overcome. So I was doing nothing very original by writing another realistic novel about a common man and calling it *The Victim.*[12]

It is true that realistic and naturalistic *fin de siècle* writers like Stephen Crane, Jack London, Theodore Dreiser, and Frank Norris have outlined the figure of the victim, and that social writers of the 1930's like Steinbeck, Dos Passos, and Farrell have investigated the paralysis of will amid the powers of society. Realistic literature has not, however, been particularly congenial to American writers, and hence the victim-hero in American fiction has been, until recently, an atypical figure.

In contemporary fiction, however, the face of the victim has become, as Hassan says, a familiar one. So much is this the case that Saul Bellow recently commented, "On the whole, American novels are filled with complaints over the misfortunes of the soverign Self . . . . The Self is asked to prepare itself for sacrifice, and this is the situation reflected in contemporary American fiction."[13] In Bellow's view, and he is by no means alone in this, America is now in the grip of "a dark literature, a literature of victimization, of old people sitting in ash cans waiting for the breath of life to depart."[14] Bellow points out, with some despair, that

. . . the latest work of writers like James Jones, James Baldwin, Philip Roth, John O'Hara, J.F. Powers, Joseph Bennett, Wright Morris, and others shows the individual under a great strain. Laboring to maintain himself, or perhaps an idea of himself (not always a clear idea), he feels the pressure of a vast public life, which may dwarf him as an individual while permitting him to be a giant in hatred or fantasy. In these circumstances he grieves, he complains, rages, or laughs. All the while he is aware of his lack of power, his inadequacy as a moralist, the nauseous pressure of the mass media, and the weight of money and organization, of cold war and racial brutalities.[15]

What Bellow has described is, of course, the victim-hero of contemporary American fiction, a hero who is variously called the "non-hero," the "rebel-victim," and the "anti-hero." He is a figure who appears at the center of absurd fiction — fiction, that is, that explores the dwindling potential of the individual to achieve spiritual harmony and self-fulfillment (which Camus calls "intention") in the recognizable social world (which Camus calls "reality"). Weinberg, in giving the general characteristics of the absurdist mode of fiction, says that this mode

has at its center the victim of worldly circumstances. The victim, whether innocent (guileless and unaware of the worldly circumstances which ensnare him) or guilty (cognizant of and in complicity with worldly ways), is caught in the absurd situation of trying to deal simply (if he is innocent) or rationally (if he is guilty) with a variety of worldly circumstances which pretend to represent objective truths but are in fact totally divorced from objective truth (if there is any) or from an ultimate ideality (if there is one). The world view of the absurdist novel sees the complete disjunction between the social-political systems of men in the world and a system of higher being: the focus of this novel's world view is on this disjunction. To live acquiescent to the terms of this world is to be passive; to allow the nonbeing of worldly routines and reasons to encroach upon the life of the self and its possibilities for true being is to become a victim.[16]

Weinberg goes on to say that "the passively guilty victim-hero, trapped in an absurd situation and unable to extricate himself by rational means ... would seem to be the proto-type for the hero of many self-enclosed stories in recent American fiction;"[17] thus she makes essentially the same point as Bellow: absurdist fiction portraying victim-heroes tends to be characterized by a "more or less realistic surface, with somewhat surrealistic elements. Realism of detail ... underscores the madness of the world, its grotesque comedy."[18]

Hassan has given one of the chapters of *Radical Innocence* the suggestive and ominous title "Contemporary Scenes: The Victim With a Thousand Faces," a title that underscores the prevalence of a wide variety of victims in recent literature. Contemporary American fiction has portrayed the victim as saint (Salinger's Holden Caulfield), as martyr (Malamud's Frank Alpine), as fool (Bellow's Tommy Wilhelm), as madman (Heller's Yossarian), as picaro (Bellow's Joseph). The victim may, like Malamud's Yakov Bok, suffer the indignities of an unjust imprisonment; he may, like Ellison's "invisible man," turn to strategies of withdrawal and retreat; or he may, like Baldwin's Giovanni, turn to strategies of violence to combat a loveless world. If, as Hassan suggests, the "encounter between the new ego and the destructive element of experience ... lies at the dramatic center of the modern novel in Europe and America,"[19] the victim becomes the index of how desperate the conflict has become, how destructive the experience can be. Overwhelming guilt, unaccountable aggression, empty laughter, and impotent rage are, it would seem, the modes of response available to the man who does not divorce himself from society. Whether passive or active, guilty or innocent, the victim finds himself ensnared by ironies and absurdities that underscore the disparity between the whisperings of his inner voice and the reality which he encounters, the absurd disparity, as Camus says, "between the mind that desires and the world that disappoints."[20]

Roth's Conception of the Victim-Hero

Philip Roth's conception of the victim-hero has been nourished, in part, by his artistic inclinations toward social realism. Certainly Irving and Harriet Deer are right in saying that Roth shows "the ways in which the modern American, Jew or non-Jew, is struggling to gain a sense of self: a sense that is true to his character as a whole and not merely to some fragment of it;"[21] it is precisely this attention to the self that has led to Roth's inclusion in the circle of activist writers headed by Bellow. It is equally true, however, that Roth's concern with the social world — particularly, as Bellow noted, in terms of the encroachment of the social world on the powers of the self — has led him to write fiction whose focus is on the disjunction between social-political systems of men and a system of higher being; fiction, that is, that approaches the absurdist mode. Activist writers have consciously turned away from the "real" world ("the world that disappoints," as Camus has said) to explore the potential of the self, a novelistic strategy that Roth, as a writer of social realism, specifically repudiates. In Roth's view, the absurdities of American society should severely qualify the note of affirmation and celebration found in activist fiction:

> If the world is as crooked and unreal as I think it is becoming, day by day; if one feels less and less power in

the face of this unreality, day by day; if the inevitable end is destruction, if not of all life, then of much that is valuable and civilized in life — then why in God's name is the writer pleased? Why don't all of our fictional heroes wind up in institutions like Holden Caulfield, or suicides like Seymour Glass? Why is it, in fact, that so many of our fictional heroes — not just the heroes of Wouk and Weidman, but of Bellow, Gold, Styron, and others — wind up affirming life? For surely the air is thick these days with affirmation, and though we shall doubtless get this year our annual editorial from *Life* calling for affirmative novels, the plain and simple fact is that more and more books by serious writers seem to end on a note of celebration. Not just the tone is bouncy, but the moral is bouncy too.   (*WAF*, p. 231)

It should be pointed out that Roth's comment is directed more toward the absurdities of American life than toward specific activist writers. He is concerned that modern writers celebrate the self that is excluded from society or the self that exists in worlds of fantasy and myth, but he is equally concerned with another problem: "What can the writer do with so much of the American reality as it is?" (*WAF*, p. 227) What Roth should have added is that the loss of community as subject is a problem of particular importance to a writer whose artistic inclinations are toward social realism. It is exactly this point that Roth makes in replying to a flurry of hostile letters that poured into *Commentary* after the publication of "Writing American Fiction." In the September, 1961 edition of *Commentary* Roth defended himself by saying,

The purpose of my essay was to make some suggestions as to how and why [writing American fiction] is arduous today, *and particularly so for the writer whose concerns are social and whose talent and instinct lead*

> *him to write in the mode of realism . . . .* I was not
> asking . . . any other writer to share whatever concern
> for "time, place, and class" I may have displayed in
> certain stories of my own. Rather I intended to examine
> the relationship between our experience and our art,
> and perhaps to come up with some reasons to explain
> the discomfort so many contemporary writers feel —
> myself included — with realism, and with satire too,
> where one sometimes winds up doing less than one
> intended (italics mine).[22]

One suspects that Roth's disclaimer about wanting other
artists to share his concerns is less than truthful, but the
important point to be made is that Roth is keenly aware of
social absurdities in the American public life, absurdities that
place severe limitations on the artist's imagination. Particularly is this so for the writer like Roth whose interest is in a
realistic portrayal of the struggles of the self *in* society. "The
actuality is continually outdoing our talents, and the culture
tosses up figures almost daily that are the envy of any
novelist. Who, for example, could have invented Charles Van
Doren? Roy Cohn and David Schine? Sherman Adams and
Bernard Goldfine? Dwight David Eisenhower?" (*WAF*, p.
224) Despite the difficulties confronting the social realist,
Roth has continued to explore the problem of the self in
America, and he has continued to ask the question that is
often on the lips of the victim: "Our world is cockeyed:
okay. Now what does it *feel* like to have it be cockeyed?
How human or inhuman does its cockeyedness make me?"[23]

Victimization in Roth's fiction takes many forms. The
hero may, like Novotny ("Novotny's Pain") and Milton
Lippman ("On the Air"), be victimized by the grotesque and
overwhelming force of social systems; he may, like Lucy
Nelson (*When She Was Good*), Paul and Libby Herz (*Letting
Go*), and Alexander Portnoy (*Portnoy's Complaint*), be

victimized by faulty self-conceptions. At times the victimization is the comic one of Epstein, at times the tragi-comic one of Portnoy, at times the pathetic one of Lucy Nelson. With the exception of Paul Herz, Portnoy, and David Kepesh, however, Roth's victim-hero does not come to the liberating awareness of the absurd man as described by Camus in *The Myth of Sisyphus*; rather, Roth's victim-heroes only dimly perceive that they live in what Camus calls the "unreasonable world," where there is a "disproportion between his intention and the reality he will encounter, . . . between his true strength and the aim he has in view."[24] Of all of Roth's victim-heroes, Portnoy is best able to articulate a recognition of his absurd condition, and for him there is no Sisyphusian joy in the awareness. Caught in the crossfire of social conformity and individual desire, languishing in "nothing but *self*! Locked up in *me*," slaving under the ridiculous disproportion of the guilt," Portnoy alone concludes with the "pure howl" of outrage implicit in other heroes, and, one is tempted to say, in Roth himself.

In Roth's fiction — even in his activist fiction — the sting of social absurdity is always present. Of "Eli, the Fanatic" Roth said, ". . . It seems to me what happens in that story happens in other stories of mine — and that is, an attempt on the part of a hero to be heroic in a world in which passions, including his own, seem to be diminished; to attempt to be more than he once imagined himself to be." (*SDI*, p. 70) The world of diminished passions — a world that assaults the imagination of the individual — is, of course, the world of the absurd, or, as Roth would say, the world of normalcy. Like the townspeople, Eli's wife compulsively wants "to get things back to Normal," but normalcy in "Eli, the Fanatic" embraces a variety of attitudes that are vapid, meaningless, and absurd. There is, for instance, Ted Heller's normalcy, which would expel the truth of Abraham and replace it with X-ray machines for measuring feet; there is the normalcy of

Harriet Knudson, who, it seems, has a penchant for painting the rocks in her lawn pink. And there is the normalcy of Coach House Road, which to Eli "seemed paved with chromium." As Eli enters Coach House Road to begin his ordeal of spiritual affirmation, his eye takes in the brittle exterior of Woodenton, a modern-day whited sepulchre:

> On Coach House Road, they were double-parked. The Mayor's wife pushed a grocery cart full of dog food from Stop N' Shop to her station wagon. The President of the Lions Club, a napkin around his neck, was jamming pennies into the meter in front of the Bit-in-Teeth Restaurant. Ted Heller caught the sun as it glazed off the new Byzantine mosaic entrance to his shoe shop. In pinkened jeans, Mrs. Jimmy Knudson was leaving Holloway's Hardware, a paint bucket in each hand. Roger's Beauty Shoppe had its doors open — women's heads in silver bullets far as the eye could see. Over by the barbershop the pole spun, and Artie Berg's youngest sat on a red horse, having his hair cut; his mother flipped through *Look*, smiling.
>
> (p. 211)

Eli, Ozzie Freedman, Neil Klugman, and Gabe Wallach have all been subjected to absurdities of the social world, and they have all actively, and to some degree successfully, asserted the rights of the self. Other of Roth's fictional heroes — Lou Epstein, Paul and Libby Herz, Lucy Nelson, Alexander Portnoy — have been less fortunate. These heroes, in various ways victims of worldly circumstance, represent Roth's most abiding conviction about the human condition: that in America "there's a kind of public insanity — human feelings, human desires and needs often seem the last concern of the people with power"[25] — and that man's essential condition in America is that of the victim.

Epstein

"Epstein," one of Roth's earliest stories, initially appeared in *The Paris Review* and was later included in the *Goodbye, Columbus* collection. The central character, Lou Epstein, the fifty-nine-year-old owner of a paper bag company, is, from all appearances, a socially successful man. He had come to America when he was seven years old, at which time he was unceremoniously deloused with kerosene. With this antiseptic baptism, Lou was initiated into a life noted for its exemplary tidiness. He worked hard, and, as he explains to his nephew, Michael, "all my life I tried. I swear it, I should drop dead on the spot, if all my life I didn't try to do right, to give my family what I didn't have." Life has not, however, been particularly kind to Epstein. Herbie, his son and only possible heir to Epstein Paper Bag, died at the age of eleven. The thought of a stranger taking over the company depresses Epstein, for "he had built the business from the ground, suffered and bled during the Depression and Roosevelt, only, finally, with the war and Eisenhower to see it succeed."

Equally depressing is the family with which Epstein has been saddled. His wife, Goldie, has suffered the ravages of time. "What once could be pinched, what once was small and tight, now could be poked and pulled. Everything hung." More exasperating, however, is Goldie's fetish for cleanliness: "My Goldie, that such a woman should become a cleaning-machine. Impossible." His only child, Sheila, once a pink-skinned baby, has turned out to be a one-hundred-sixty-pound socialist. Epstein wonders, "What year, what month did those skinny ankles grow thick as logs, the peaches-and-cream turn to pimples? That lovely child was now a twenty-three-year-old woman with 'a social conscience'!" Sheila is nicely complemented by her fiance, Marvin, a "chinless, lazy smart aleck whose living was earned singing folksongs in a saloon." The only family member who is at all attractive is Michael, the son of Lou's brother Sol: "A Gregory Peck," says Goldie, "and a regular gentleman."

For some time Epstein has been vaguely aware that he has missed personal satisfaction and fulfillment in life. His thoughts on this subject are crystalized one evening; as he lies in bed he becomes irritated by noises of zippers and hard breathing in the living room below — noises that he has heard before:

> He tensed and waited for the noises — it didn't take those Socialists long. At night the noise from the zipping and the unzipping was enough to keep a man awake. "What are they doing down there?" he had screamed at his wife one Friday night, "Trying on clothes?" Now, once again, he waited. It wasn't that he was against their playing. He was no puritan, he believed in young people enjoying themselves. Hadn't he been a young man himself? But in 1927 he and his wife were handsome people.   (pp. 146-147)

When he descends the stairs, he discovers that the noise is being caused not by Sheila and Marvin, but, surprisingly, by Michael and Linda Kaufman, the girl from across the street. "Epstein tingled; he did not dare move, he did not want to move. . . ."

The experience has shaken Epstein considerably. He realizes that what he has been deprived of is a joyous inner life, an emotional freedom whose outward sign is sexual involvement. Shortly thereafter, he begins an affair with Linda Kaufman's recently widowed mother, Ida.

> Once or twice Epstein had tipped his hat to her, but even then he had been more absorbed in the fate of Epstein Paper Bag than in the civility he was practicing. Actually then, on that Monday morning it would not

have been unlikely for him to have driven right past the bus stop. It was a warm April day, certainly not a bad day to be waiting for a bus. . . . But the woman at the bus stop wore a thin dress and no coat, and Epstein saw her waiting, and beneath the dress, the stockings, the imagined underthings he saw the body of the girl on his living room rug. . . . So Epstein pulled slowly to the curb and, stopping for the daughter, picked up the mother.   (p. 150)

Ida, Lou discovers, is all that his wife is not: lusty, sensuous, and adventurous. As a foreshadowing of things to come, however, Epstein's indiscretion earns him society's disapproval: one traffic ticket for running a red light and two other tickets for speeding.

The *coup de grâce*, however, is delivered by Mother Nature herself, for after his affair with Ida has progressed to some short trips to the beach, Epstein awakes one morning with a suspicious-looking rash. Is it perhaps prickly heat? "Prickly heat is what Herbie always had — a child's complaint. Was it possible for a grown man to have it?" Is it perhaps a sand rash? "A rash. That's a crime?" asks Epstein. To the slowly comprehending Goldie, it is a crime indeed:

> She stepped up closer and reached out her hand, not to touch but to point. She drew a little circle of the area with her index finger. "A rash, there?"
>
> "Why not there?" Epstein said. "It's like a rash on the hand or chest. A rash is a rash."
>
> "But how come all of a sudden?" his wife said.
>
> "Look, I'm not a doctor," Epstein said. "It's there today, maybe tomorrow it'll be gone. How do I know! I probably got it from the toilet seat at the shop. The *shvartzes* are pigs—"
>
> Goldie made a clicking sound with the tongue.

"You're calling me a liar?"

She looked up. "Who said liar?" And she gave her own form a swift looking-over, checked limbs, stomach, breasts to see if she had perhaps caught the rash from him. She looked back at her husband, then at her own body again, and suddenly her eyes widened. "You!" she screamed.

"Shah," Epstein said, "you'll wake Michael."

"You pig! Who, who was it!"

"I told you, the *schvartzes*—"

"Liar! pig!" Wheeling her way back to the bed, she flopped onto it so hard the springs squeaked. "Liar!" And then she was off the bed, pulling the sheets from it. "I'll burn them, I'll burn every one!"   (pp. 153-154)

What follows is highly comic. Epstein and Goldie engage in a tug-of-war with the sheets, Epstein protesting that he is innocent and "clean," Goldie repeatedly crying, "Don't come near me, you filthy pig! Go touch some filthy whore!" and bemoaning the misfortune that has come to "my sheets, my nice clean sheets." In the midst of battle Sheila, Marvin, and Michael break into the bedroom, where they view with moral indignation the emblem of Epstein's fall from virtue. Goldie demands a divorce and Epstein is ordered to Herbie's room as punishment for his sins.

The ostracism continues the next morning. No one speaks to Epstein, and Marvin takes over Epstein's Sunday ritual of going for the newspaper and the lox. An outcast in his own home, Epstein leaves the house. Across the street he sees Ida Kaufman, who is wearing shorts and a halter and hanging her daughter's underwear on a clothesline. "Ida saw him and smiled. Growing angry, he stepped off the curb and, passionately, began to jaywalk." Soon thereafter a siren is heard in the Epstein home. After much confusion, Goldie, Sheila, and Marvin discover that the ambulance has come to

the Kaufman home, and that the cause of the alarm is none
other than Epstein, who has had a heart attack. With fear and
apprehension, Goldie climbs into the ambulance to see her
stricken husband:

> "It's your wife, Lou," the doctor said. Epstein
> blinked his eyes. "He knows," the doctor said. "He'll be
> all right. All he's got to do is live a normal life, normal
> for sixty."
>
> "You hear the doctor, Lou. All you got to do is live a
> normal life."
>
> Epstein opened his mouth. His tongue hung over his
> teeth like a dead snake. . . .
>
> "Don't you talk," his wife said. "Don't you worry
> about anything. Not even the business. That'll work out.
> Our Sheila will marry Marvin and that'll be that. You
> won't have to sell, Lou, it'll be in the family. You can
> retire, rest, and Marvin can take over. He's a smart boy,
> Marvin, a *mensch*.
>
> . . . Suddenly she gripped his hand. "Lou, you'll live
> normal, won't you? *Won't you*?"   (pp. 164-165)

For Epstein, living "normal" means living a life of external
success and internal misery. Cleanliness becomes the
symbolic quality of the ordered life of spotless appearance —
a life that is antiseptic, sterile, unfulfilling. It is of course
Goldie, the spokesman for normalcy, who represents this
ordered life. Epstein complains to Michael, "She cleans? That
deserves a medal? One day I should come home and the
house should be a *mess*. I should be able to write my initials
in the dust, somewhere, in the basement at least." For
Epstein, "after all these years that would be a pleasure," but
the pleasure of etching his identity in something other than
cleanliness is not in Goldie's plans for him. While Lou cavorts
with Ida, Goldie "ran one hand across a slat, checking for

dust while she awaited her husband's homecoming." Only once in the past had Goldie indulged Lou's "itch" for the underside of life — the very night, according to Epstein, that their son Herbie was conceived:

> "And that night we took pictures, photos. I set up the camera — it was in the old house — and we took pictures, in the bedroom." He stopped, remembered. "I wanted a picture of my wife naked, to carry with me. I admit it. The next morning I woke up and there was Goldie tearing up the negatives. She said God forbid I should get in an accident one day and the police would take out my wallet for identification, and then oy-oy-oy!"
>
> (pp. 157-158)

Epstein's desire to identify himself through an exploration of vague sexual longings is rebuffed on every side by worldly circumstances. When did his irritation with a normal life begin? Did it begin with Herbie's death? Or with seeing Michael and Linda Kaufman on the living room floor? "Or, Epstein wondered, was it that night fifteen years ago when instead of smelling a woman between his sheets he smelled Bab-O? Or the time when his daughter had first called him 'capitalist' as though it were a dirty name, as though it were a crime to be successful?" Time, family, and society have conspired in inhibiting Epstein's desires, at the same time finding him guilty of something, he does not know what. "He was innocent! Unless what made him guilty had nothing to do with some dirty bug. But either way the doctor would prescribe for him. And then the lawyer would prescribe. And by then everyone would know...." Against the ubiquitous forces that confine him Epstein is an ineffectual opponent, one who knows he has been victimized but who has only one course of retaliation:

When they start taking things away from you, you reach out, you *grab* — maybe like a pig even, but you grab. And right, wrong, who knows! With tears in your eyes, who can even see the difference!   (p. 158)

Epstein's "grabbing" — like the ill-advised clutching of Neil Klugman and Gabe Wallach — is not, however, a successful answer to his longings for fulfillment. In the eyes of the social world, Lou's grabbing is indeed a crime, and he has been punished accordingly — first gently, with traffic tickets, then more severely with ostracism by his family, and finally nature itself punishes his *crime passionnel* with the most appropriate of sentences: a heart attack. The rash, clearly symbolic of the wages of Epstein's "sin," becomes a sign of Epstein's folly in thinking that he can escape society's sentence upon him, the sentence of living the "normal" public life. But what society gives, society can also take away. Epstein's version of the scarlet letter can, after all, be removed. In the last scene in the story, Goldie turns her attention away from the stricken Epstein and toward the doctor who has just entered the ambulance:

> She asked, softly, "Doctor, you have something that will cure what else he's got — this rash?" She pointed.
> The doctor looked at her. Then he lifted for a moment the blanket that covered Epstein's nakedness.
> "Doctor, it's bad?"
> Goldie's eyes and nose were running.
> "An irritation," the doctor said.
> She grabbed his wrist. "You can clean it up?"
> "So it will never come back," the doctor said, and hopped out of the ambulance.   (p. 165)

Epstein, like Eli, lives in a world of diminished passions, and like Eli, he has attempted to be more than he once imagined himself to be. His "piggishness," a losing rear-guard action, is a response to the sterility of his "Bab-o-ized" life — but so powerful are the forces against him that his most effective retaliation does not extend much beyond passionate jaywalking. In the end, normalcy wins out, and Epstein has the less than comforting thought that he must now return to his cleaning machine of a wife, Goldie, who has suggested that they go to the mineral baths in Saratoga (for additional purgation?) while Marvin the folksinger takes over Epstein Paper Bag; and through the wonders of modern medicine, Epstein has the dubious assurance that his irritation will "never come back."

In his *Advertisements for Myself* Norman Mailer said, "I still feel rage at the cowardice of our time which has ground down all of us into the mediocre compromises of what had been once our light-filled passion to stand erect and be original."[26] It is this rage that underlies Roth's comic treatment of Epstein, a man who is a mediocre compromise of what he originally might have been. Epstein is victimized by his instincts, which are only imperfectly realized in the absurd world that he inhabits. His business, his family, even his Jewishness contribute to the worldly circumstances that press an assault against his all too human desires. Roth says of Epstein, "The fact that this man was Jewish was not a problem; it caused me great delight because the absurdity of his situation became even more clear. His sense of what he was, was in part defined by his being Jewish; and certainly the sense his wife has of who he is, is defined by what she thinks a Jewish husband should do." (*SDI*, p. 71) In another article Roth said that he wrote the story because "I seem to be interested in how — and why and when — a man acts counter to what he considers to be his 'best self,' or what others assume it to be, or would like for it to be. . . . It may

be that *life* produces a melancholy middle-aged businessman
like Lou Epstein.... I myself find Epstein's adultery an
unlikely solution to his problems, a pathetic, even a doomed
response, and a comic one, too, since it does not even square
with the man's own conception of himself and what he
wants." (*WAJ*, p. 447) In part, "Epstein" addresses the
problem that Dr. Tamkin outlines for Tommy Wilhelm, the
victim-hero of Bellow's *Seize the Day*: "I want you to see
how some people free themselves from morbid guilt feelings
and follow their instincts. Innately, the female knows how to
cripple by sickening a man with guilt. It is a very special
*de*struct, and she sends her curse to make a fellow impotent."
For Epstein, as for Wilhelm, there is no way to follow his
instincts to gain a happy resolution. And at the end of *Seize
the Day*, Wilhelm is left, like Epstein, with the perplexity and
sorrow of knowing that he has not reached "the consummation of his heart's ultimate need."

Novotny's Pain

Sickness and "crippledness" are, of course, the dramatic
metaphors used by authors to underscore the emotional and
psychological victimization suffered by their heroes. In
"Novotny's Pain," a short story that appeared in *The New
Yorker* less than three years after *Goodbye, Columbus* was
published, Roth explored the use of these metaphors in a
unique way. The depth of Novotny's emotional victimization
is revealed through a mysterious physical pain incurred
during his tour of duty in the army. The military (as Kafka in
"In the Penal Colony," Heller in *Catch-22*, and Bellow in
Dangling Man demonstrate) is the epitome of irrational
worldly schemes. Roth couples the army regimen with the
physical crippledness of Novotny to give a portrait of the
victim's helplessness in the face of such "schemes." On one

level, the story is a joke, for army life gives Novotny a pain "directly above the buttock"; for Novotny (as for Portnoy), however, the pain of living in an absurd world is no joking matter.

Novotny is a passive victim, one whose upbringing and personal inclinations lead him to be acquiescent in the face of worldly routines:

> Though there was much of Army life that he had to grit his teeth to endure, he did not have to work at getting up on time; it simply happened to him. When it was necessary to grit his teeth, he gritted them and did what he was told. In that way, he was like a good many young men who suffered military life alongside him or had suffered it before him. His sense of shame was strong, as was his sense of necessity; the two made him dutiful.   (p. 46)

The mysterious pain, the result of a K.P. accident, is accepted by Novotny uncomplainingly, for a while. Although Novotny has been drafted into the army, he "believed in fighting for freedom," primarily because his parents expect such a belief from him. Nonetheless, "what he himself wanted most from any government was that it should let him alone to live his life." Complaining, Novotny realizes, would fulfill neither the expectations of his parents ("his mother had never had any reason not to be proud of Novotny's behavior") nor of the government ("When he had been drafted, he had vowed he would do whatever they told him to do, no matter how much he might resent it").

Despite his resolve, Novotny finally drags himself to the infirmary — where he is not allowed to see a doctor. A medical orderly puts three inches of tape around Novotny's middle, and he is sent back to duty. After repeated efforts, Novotny is permitted to see the doctor, but X-rays reveal nothing. Novotny is ordered back to duty once again, but, to his own surprise, he refuses to go. He is shuttled off to the colonel, who informs him that he will have to appear at a summary court-martial. With the aid of some medical texts that he has read, however, Novotny convinces the doctor to put him in traction, but "when they put him in traction, he had further premonitions of his court-martial and his subsequent internment in the stockade. He, Novotny, who had never broken a law in his life."

In attempting to explain his pain to himself, Novotny turns to every avenue of explanation, even to his sexual involvement with his sweetheart, Rose Ann. After having read about psychosomatic illnesses, Novotny wonders:

> Was he being punished for being so happy with her? Were they being punished for all that sex? Unlike his mother, he was not the kind of Catholic who believed in Hell; he was not the kind who was afraid of sex. All he wanted was his chance at life. That was all.   (p. 53)

Novotny is sent to the psychiatrist, where he breaks down, admitting that he has a fear of death and a hatred for the army; his frankness results in the psychiatrist's labelling him a "passive-aggressive," which, in the eyes of the colonel, is "just another kind of coward." The colonel, firmly convinced that Novotny is using an imaginary pain to get out of the army, explains that his discharge will be a dishonorable one, and he "made it clear that such a discharge followed a man through life." The ending is, however, a happy one, for after his discharge Novotny marries Rose Ann, and over the years the pain subsides in severity. Only occasionally does a twinge remind him of his experience, and only occasionally does he awaken at night "to worry in the dark about the future."

Novotny is the most passive victim in Roth's fiction. The story is a tentative exploration of heroic potential in an absurd environment, an exploration that is more fully undertaken in *When She Was Good* and *Portnoy's Complaint*. Roth's own observation about Novotny is suggestive:

> . . . He gets a backache and everybody tells him why he has it, but there is no adequate physiological explanation. So then people invent explanations and he must invent an explanation to be discharged from the army — and once discharged, he loses the pain. By making him a Jew I would have become involved in a lot of other problems, like the typical notion of the Jewish malingerer. . . . If in my story I had made the guy a Jew, it would have been to shift the concern. My concern was really with the mystery of his pain and the world of condemnation, self-doubt that grew up out of his mysterious pain. To make him a Jew would have been to introduce a completely different interest in the story. It would have seemed that his problem was perhaps particularly Jewish.   (*SDI*, p. 75)

One notes that once again Roth emphasizes his interest in human, rather than specifically Jewish problems; more importantly, however, Roth suggests that his interest in the story is with the impact of reality on the individual. The victimization of Novotny begins when he is quite young. His parents had demanded from him absolute fidelity to an external code of behavior, so much so that as a child he "had always collected articles having to do with how to act at parties, or dances, or on the job." With recourse only to a vague private feeling that he would like to be free of the absurdities that surround him, Novotny can only say of his new-found pain, "How unfair — for he *had* been a good son."

Novotny's victimization is of some interest, for it prepares the way for later victim-heroes in Roth's fiction. Like Lucy Nelson in *When She Was Good*, Novotny is a non-Jewish Midwesterner; like Paul and Libby Herz in *Letting Go*, Novotny is a passive victim of inexplicable miseries and absurdities; and like Portnoy, Novotny registers an ineffectual complaint. Most significant, however, is the process of victimization through which Novotny, like later heroes in Roth's fiction, is led. Novotny's sensitivity to viable modes of escape from absurdity has been deadened by a hide-bound and superficial code of morality and values imposed upon him from his earliest youth; and because his inner resources have not developed, the absurdities of society lead the hero to an even greater absurdity: self-victimization. In attempting to understand character in American society, Roth concludes that character "grows out of the reality. . . . But it is not essentially the reality around us that counts; it is the one we invent." (*SDI*, p. 75) Given this persuasion about reality, it is understandable that Roth refuses to consider the self apart from the recognizable social world — for the invented reality of the self arises from the reality of the external world, its mores, taboos, customs, traditions, and values. In Novotny's anguish, he turns, as do Lucy Nelson and Portnoy, to his past for explanation and vindication: "What had he done in life to deserve this? What had he done, from the time he had grown out of short pants, but do everything that was asked of him?" At the end of the tale, as Novotny waits to receive his dishonorable discharge, he comes close to penetrating the "invented reality" with which he has victimized himself. The solace that his thoughts bring him partially mitigates his misfortune, but he remains a self-pitying victim whose questions reveal the shallowness of his character:

All he had done was answer people and tell them the truth, and what had it got him? What good was it, being good? What good was it, especially if at bottom you were bad anyway? What good was it, acting strong, if at bottom you were weak and couldn't *be* strong if you wanted to? With the colonel glaring across at him, the only solace Novotny had was to think that nobody knew any more about him than he himself did.   (p. 56)

Novotny's crucial question — "what good was it, being good?" — is the question that virtually all of Roth's heroes attempt to answer. It is the question that, in Roth's fictional realm, arises from the exact point of conflict between the expectations of society and the desires of the self. Epstein, Paul and Libby Herz, Lucy Nelson, and Alexander Portnoy have become victims of "goodness," and they have discovered, in the perverse logic of the nursery rhyme as it is acted out by Lucy Nelson, that when they are good they are horrid, miserable, or baffled beyond belief.

Letting Go

The image of the hero victimized by society and himself has been an increasingly dominant one in Roth's fiction. Werner Samuelson, in "The Contest for Aaron Gold," and Lou Epstein have seen their private lives invaded by the forces of an absurd society. In "Defender of the Faith" (which, like "Epstein," appeared in the *Goodbye, Columbus* collection) Nathan Marx, an embattled Jewish sergeant, is victimized by another Jew, Private Sheldon Grossbart. Grossbart plays upon their shared Jewishness to get special favors from Marx. Only at the end of the story does Marx overcome his victimization by re-assigning Grossbart to the much-feared battle area in the Pacific; hence, the victim becomes victimizer. "Novotny's Pain" is based on a similar motif, with two important differences: Novotny is not

Jewish, and his victimization undergoes no dramatic reversal. In *Letting Go*, which appeared in the same year (1962) as "Novotny's Pain," Roth continued his exploration of the victim-hero in his presentation of Paul and Libby Herz, as well as in several skillful vignettes involving minor characters. The victims in *Letting Go* bear out Theodore Solotaroff's contention that victimization in Roth's fiction develops out of human relationships, "sometimes sought by [the hero] but, as often as not, inflicted upon him, with the distinction tending to become lost as a relationship develops: the seeker becoming the victim or vice versa."[27]

Libby Herz is, like Epstein, a caged self. Gabe Wallach says Libby is plagued by "yearning and misery and impotence. . . . She was like something in a cage or a cell — that was my first impression." Estranged from her unloving husband, Libby "felt like one of those old movies — tied to the railroad tracks with the train coming." Libby has turned to every available channel — her parents, a flirtation with Wallach, her job as a secretary, pregnancy, adoption, a psychiatrist, even a conversion to Judaism (shortly after marrying Paul she had undergone a *mikvah* bath at the Ann Arbor Y.M.C.A. in her "old blue Jantzen" swimsuit) to find order, direction, and, most of all, happiness in her life. Suckled on creeds that are empty and sterile if not outworn, Libby can do no more than scrape at the surface of her despair. Like Lucy Nelson, she sees her life as a melodrama, but, as Gabe says of her, "Libby did not need to be rescued, or was impossible to rescue."

The overwhelmingness of Libby's victimization is suggested by her last desperate attempt to bring a happily-ever-after ending to her tormented relationship with Paul. Faced with the failure of her attempts to make Paul's life happy, she finally submerges herself in *The Wonder of Life*, a book subtitled "Suggestions for the Jewish Homemaker":

> What she had always taken for granted about Jewish life
> was the warm family environment. And what an irony!
> Look at Paul's parents; Paul himself. In the most
> Protestant household in America there could be no
> more coldness than had surrounded her first five years
> of marriage. But perhaps the fault was partly hers.
> Perhaps there was one final way out of all this mess that
> was not psychoanalysis, or money in the bank, or
> carnality, or self-pity, or madness: Religion. . . . Not
> even a belief in God necessarily; . . . something warm,
> sacred, worthwhile: *Traditions and ceremonies, holy
> days and holidays and customs.*   (pp. 354-355)

Falling back upon the externals of religion, Libby feverishly
grates potatoes for lutken, her right hand "pulsing, *aching*,
with the effort to bring a little religion into her house";
nevertheless, as she grates she sheds tears, "because finally
she no longer believed in the restorative powers of anything
or anyone." Her attempts to restore religion to her house
reveal, comically and pathetically, her helplessness to escape
the invented, stereotypic reality that has victimized her
throughout the novel.[28]

Paul Herz is, like his wife and Gabe Wallach, a victim of
false ideals. Throughout his tortured marriage with Libby he
has struggled to reconcile his duties to wife and family with
his vague commitments to personal freedom, love, and
self-fulfillment. Toward his parents he feels a filial duty that
he hopes will gain him access to the "great world beyond the
family to which he aspired, a world of order and decency,
which, if he had not as yet experienced, he had fully
imagined." Toward Libby, however, he feels not love, but
rather the same duty that he believes he owes his family.
Libby has brought to the marriage a frail and sickly body, an
overwhelming collection of woes, and an oppressive set of
circumstances — so much so that Paul complains at one

point, "It's just how long can we keep being the victims of everything. I'm starting to think there's some conspiracy going."

Late in the novel, Paul comes to some understanding that not only circumstances but also his false image of himself has created his misery:

> Of course he had been miserable. Between the preten-
> sion and the fact, what's invented and what's given,
> stands one's own tortured soul. Paul Herz had been
> pretending all these awful years that he was of another
> order of men. It occurred to him now . . . that, no, he
> was not a man of feeling; it occurred to him that if he
> was anything at all it was a man of duty. And that when
> his two selves had become confused — one self, one
> invention — when he had felt it his duty to be feeling,
> that then his heart had been a stone, and his will,
> instead of turning out toward action, had remained a
> presence in his body, a concrete setting for the rock of
> his heart.   (p. 408)

With this recognition, Paul can begin to reconstruct a more honest, non-victimized life. He convinces himself that he must "start making a life not on the basis of what he dreamed he was, or thought he was supposed to be, or what literature, philosophy, friends, enemies, wife, parents told him he must be, but simply in terms of his own possibilities." Finally grasping the truth of his Uncle Asher's assessment ("You are a victim, my friend, of circumstantial thinking"), he works his way toward the realization that is dramatically revealed to him at his father's graveside: Abraham and Isaac, victim and victimizer, are one, and his own life has been a sacrifice to realities that are, in fact, illusionary.[29]

In *Letting Go* Roth gathers together a full range of characters who struggle to "let go" of social and personal absurdities that have been victimizing them. Gabe Wallach is at least partially successful in his attempts to break away; Paul Herz comes to the essential knowledge of his imprisoned condition, but at the end of the novel his life is still steeped in misery; Libby's solution is least successful, for her response is a neurotic escape into irrational and superficial solutions. On one level, the novel is, I think, a reaction against the activist impulse to celebrate the glorious possibilities of the self. Roth had examined such possibilities with guarded optimism in *Goodbye, Columbus*;[30] In *Letting Go*, however, the complexity of the entanglements, the power and nastiness of external circumstances, and the bleakness of outlook reinforce a suspicion that Roth is increasingly pessimistic about the chances for the self in society. In his essay "Some of the Talent in the Room" Norman Mailer speculated that the depressiveness in *Letting Go* had to do with the working out of an obsession. I think this is so, and, although Mailer does not elaborate, it seems to me that the obsession partly deals with Roth's firm conviction that heroic response is severely restricted by external forces beyond the hero's control. The depressiveness of *Letting Go* is, from one point of view, a rejoinder to the "bouncy" and optimistic note of affirmation struck by such activist writers as Bellow and Gold — exactly that note of affirmation that Roth attacked in "Writing American Fiction," an essay published one year before the publication of *Letting Go*.

When She Was Good

The milieu explored by *Letting Go* is essentially academic, Jewish, and metropolitan. In his next novel, *When She Was Good*, Roth turns to an altogether different milieu, that of the small town, Protestant Midwest. In part, *When She Was Good* picks up on some non-Jewish elements introduced in

Letting Go. In *Letting Go* Roth had engaged briefly some non-Jewish characters, particularly Gabe's first mistress, Marge Howells by name, Libby Herz's Catholic parents, and an old widow, Mrs. Baker. Marge, a "sweet, empty-headed girl" who is in revolt against Kenosha, Wisconsin, latches on to Gabe Wallach because she views him as a "delicious specimen of Hebraic, Marxist exotica." When Gabe turns the tables by asking her how it feels to be a Protestant in America, what she tells him is "very dry and very typical." Libby's father, Mr. DeWitt, appears in the novel only through the letter he sends to Libby in response to her request for money. The narrow-minded self-righteousness of his reply foreshadows Roth's treatment of moral and religious issues in *When She Was Good*: "My obligations, Mrs. Herz, are to sons and daughters, family and Church, Christ and country, and not to Jewish housewives in Detroit. . . . You have defied your father, your faith, and every law of decency, from the most sacred to the most ordinary." The religious shallowness of the DeWitts is paralleled by the social shallowness of Mrs. Baker, who trusts in old-fashioned conventions ("the husband chooses the wife, he gets down on bended knee . . . and then he's got the duty to stand by her") and the fraternal order of Masons ("I had two fine husbands, both of them Masons, . . . men's men, who had the respect of their neighbors and knew their duty to their wife"). Mrs. Baker's address to Gabe Wallach reveals the essence of her values:

> Now I wouldn't try to convince you of anything, Mr. Wallach. I'm only saying I think you might give it some thought. You know what they say: "Once a Mason, always a Mason." I was married to two men, both Masons and both fine men, Mr. Wallach, respected in the community and in the home as well. They were stern men, and maybe they didn't wipe the dishes like some husbands do, but they knew right from wrong. . . . You

talk to the top professors and you see if they're not
Masons — the top professors, and deans, and so on.

(pp. 392-393)

Respectability, duty, "right and wrong" involve social
values that Roth explores in all his fiction. In *When She Was
Good*, however, he examines these values as they exist within
the Midwestern Protestant community, and, more particularly, within the novel's heroine, Lucy Nelson. Lucy has been
anticipated by some of Roth's earlier heroes and heroines:
she has Brenda Patimkin's concern for social appearance and
prestige; she has Libby Herz's baffled yearning for love and
understanding; she has Novotny's ill-conceived notions of
duty and "goodness." Like other characters in Roth's fiction,
Lucy struggles to find a peaceful existence amid the
brutalities of the social world, only to discover, as Gabe
Wallach has, that beneath the veneer of conventional society
and morality there is a kind of savagery and horror. But
unlike other central characters in Roth's fiction, Lucy is
sustained by a demonic rage to reshape the conditions of her
life by "holding on" to her provincial Midwestern convictions
of moral goodness — convictions that unfortunately are as
superficial and narrow-minded as those of Marge Howells, the
DeWitts, and Mrs. Baker.

The action of *When She Was Good* spans three generations
and is set in the small country town of Liberty Center,
Illinois. The name of the town is both ironic and symbolic,
for, we discover, no genuine liberty is to be had in Liberty
Center. Lucy's grandfather, Willard ("Daddy Will") Carroll,
had migrated to Liberty Center to escape the cruelty of an
ignorant father and the barbarity of the northern woods:
"Not to be rich, not to be famous, not to be mighty, not
even to be happy, but to be civilized — that was the dream of
his life. . . . He knew for sure what he didn't want, and that
was to live like a savage." These words, with which the novel

opens, provide the central irony on which the theme of the story rests, for the "civilized" lives of Willard, his daughter Myra and son-in-law Whitey, and his granddaughter, Lucy Nelson, are continually assaulted by a savageness that is all the more horrifying for its being cloaked by a thin gauze of respectability. In large part the story is a refutation of the notion that civilized society and conventional morality have either liberating or curative effects for what ails the self — a notion that is implicit in the attitudes of virtually every character in the story. The victimization of Lucy Nelson, a direct result of the "civilized" life, is itself a tragic and ironic rejoinder to the guileless observation of one of Lucy's friends who has recently moved to Chicago: "I wish I were right back here in Liberty Center, where at least you don't get all that hatred and violence."

Hatred and violence are precisely those qualities reflected in Lucy Nelson's character. What Lucy hates most, it seems, is the weakness and selfishness she sees in all those who surround her. In Lucy's eyes, Daddy Will is an ineffectual and misguided Good Samaritan; her mother, Myra, is a sniveling, weak-minded sentimentalist; her husband, Roy, is an immature dreamer; and her father, Whitey, is a drunken, parasitic ne'er-do-well who is unwilling to accept the responsibilities of a father. Against these crippled bumblers Lucy throws the full weight of her sense of moral superiority:

> Eventually, must not the truth prevail? Oh, it had not been in vain then that she had sacrificed and struggled! Oh yes, of course! If you know you are in the right, if you do not weaken or falter, if despite everything thrown up against you, despite every hardship, every pain, you oppose what you know in your heart is wrong; if you harden yourself against the opinions of others, if you are willing to endure the loneliness of

pursuing what is good in a world indifferent to good; if you struggle with every fiber of your body, even as others scorn you, hate you and fear you; if you push on and on and on, no matter how great the agony, how terrible the strain — then one day the truth will finally be known.   (p. 273)

One sees that Lucy is by no means a passive victim. Like Salinger's Holden Caulfield and Seymour Glass, Lucy perceives the corruptions of the world, but, unlike Holden and Seymour, she defiantly pits herself against a world indifferent to good. With the suffering of a martyr and the rigor of a saint, she carries the battle to extremes, at infinite cost to herself and her family, Roth, in recalling his initial thoughts about the novel, underscores the particular nature of Lucy's victimization:

> As I remember it, what most intrigued me at the outset was the utter victimization of this girl, whose misfortune it was to have been born into a world to which she believed herself morally superior. What it took me nearly four years to discover and articulate was not only the exact price, in pain and deprivation, that the girl whom I called Lucy Nelson would have to pay for the circumstances of her youth, but the price that she would make others pay in return.[31]

Lucy's victimization is, as Roth suggests, the central issue in the novel. Her moral outrage is hurled against members of her family and community with such indignation that one critic declared her actions to be a "vendetta against human nature, at least in its characteristic American manifestations."[32]

Lucy Nelson's story begins as an account of a normal young girl of the 1950's (in fact, her husband calls her

"Typical American Girl"). Lucy and her parents live with "Daddy Will" in what passes for a conventional, civilized family. Lucy's father, Whitey, has never recovered from the Depression, and he relies on occasional odd jobs and an incessant dream of a new life in Florida to keep him going. Lucy is horrified by her father's shiftlessness, his sporadic drinking bouts at Earl's Dugout, and his thoughtless treatment of his wife, who passively accepts his failures. Daddy Will is, as Lucy perceives, a well-meaning but ineffectual mediator of family difficulties that grow increasingly intolerable for Lucy.

Lucy's first response is to turn away from "despising herself and her narrow Protestant background" by turning toward Catholicism. Under the tutelage of Father Damrosch and Sister Angelica, Lucy finds a temporary balm for her free-floating anger. Particularly appealing to her is Saint Teresa of Lisieux, whose patient suffering and self-denial have been captured in Lucy's favorite devotional text, *The Story of a Soul*. One evening, Whitey returns from Earl's Dugout and, in frustration and despair, kicks over a pan of water in which Myra has been soaking her feet. Lucy responds with an action that indicates the measure of her hatred for her father. "After calling upon Saint Teresa of Lisieux and Our Lord — and getting no reply — she called the police." Sainthood is no answer for Lucy, for "she hated suffering as much as she hated those who made her suffer, and she always would." The police, at least, can offer immediate results. From this moment on, Lucy becomes a mad crusader against all imprudent, indecisive men, against all men, that is, who do not do their "duty" as it is conceived by Lucy.

At the age of eighteen, Lucy becomes pregnant by Roy Bassart, a young ex-serviceman, and marries him even though she is aware that he is a weak and immature man, one who snacks on Hydrox cookies and milk and compulsively watches the high school football team, the band, and cheerleaders practice for Saturday's game. Constantly Roy dreams of becoming successful and important, and he had returned from the service with the thought of his "whole life ahead of him. A whole future, in which he could be and do anything he wanted." In marrying Lucy, however, he finds that his fantasies of success must co-exist with harsh reality; he is forced to take a job as photographer's assistant, which, however, sets him dreaming more than ever.

Against Roy's dreams Lucy throws the full force of her moral righteousness. Disliked and distrusted by her husband's relatives, she tells herself that "I am their superior in every single way! People can call me all the names they want — I don't care! I have nothing to confess, because I am right and they are wrong and I will not be destroyed!" Increasingly Lucy becomes entrapped by a paranoic martyrdom that leads her to suspect Roy's Uncle Julian and Aunt Irene of plotting against her, and she becomes furious with Roy for not sharing in her beliefs: "You're blind to how awful people are! How rotten and hateful they are! They tell you I'm lower class and don't have ordinary emotions, and you believe them!" It appears that Lucy's brush with Saint Teresa has had some impact, for she comes to see herself as a martyred savior with no worthy followers ("You can't be saved. You don't even want to be," she tells her husband). To Uncle Julian, however, Lucy's sainthood is neither redemptive nor regenerative: "that's the saint you are, kiddo — Saint Ball-Breaker." To Lucy, the observations of Uncle Julian and others are unintelligible. "Why were they against a family, and a home, and love? Why were they against a beautiful life, and for an ugly one? Why did they fight her and mistreat her and deny her, when all she wanted was what was right!"

Lucy, now a victim and victimizer in one, drives her husband to flee with their son Edward to Uncle Julian's. In a furious encounter, Lucy faces Roy and Uncle Julian with the news that she is once again pregnant, and demands that Roy

and Edward return with her. She is forcibly expelled from
the house and taken to her grandparents' house, where she
turns her fury on Daddy Will: "What are you going to do
about it? The world is full of fiends and monsters, and you
do absolutely nothing, and you never did!" In a final
confrontation with her mother, whom Lucy finds reading a
letter from Whitey (now in prison), Lucy lashes out at her
father for the last time. " 'Mother, *he* is who destroyed our
lives.' She grabbed the letter from the bed. '*Him*!' she cried,
shaking it over her head. '*This*!' " Lucy grabs the letter and
heads toward the police station, which for her has become
the only form of authority that can produce results. Her
sense of persecution, however, is too overwhelming to allow
her to continue:

> ... She knew what it would mean to continue on to
> the police station, she knew what Julian Sowerby would
> try to do; she knew the use to which such a man would
> put this opportunity, how he would seize it to destroy
> her, once and for all. Yes, because she knew right from
> wrong, because she saw her duty and did it, because she
> knew the truth and spoke it, because she would not sit
> by and endure treachery and betrayal, because she
> would not let them steal her little boy, and coddle a
> grown-up man, and scrape out of her body the new life
> beginning to grow there — they would try to make it seem
> that *she* was the guilty party, that *she* was the criminal!
>
> (p. 303)

Realizing that she has no one to turn to ("it was now as it
had always been — the one to save her was herself"), Lucy
flees through the snow to Passion Paradise, the lovers' lane
where her involvement with Roy had begun. There her body
is found three days later, with Whitey's letter frozen to her
cheek.

No mere summary of plot can do justice to the victimization that Lucy endures. Certainly one must agree with Richard Gilman's assertion that Lucy "grows up with a rising compulsion to insert her own strength into the vacuum," and "as it turns out, her strength is really a species of vindictive, hysterical fury."[33] The key words here are *vacuum* and *compulsion*, for Lucy's fury is a response to the meaninglessness and emptiness of so-called civilized life in Liberty Center. Lucy has been victimized by the banal normalcy of the Protestant Midwest ethic, and she has simply nothing with which to combat the banality of her existence, other than a misguided and ineffectual outrage. Perhaps for this reason Lucy can write with sympathy about Shelley's "Ozymandias" in one of her college essays:

> "Even a great king," her paper began, "such as Ozymandias apparently had been, could not predict or control what the future, or Fate, held in store for him and his kingdom; that, I think, is the message that Percy Bysshe Shelley, the poet, means for us to come away with from his romantic poem 'Ozymandias,' which not only reveals the theme of the vanity of human wishes — even a king's — but deals also with the concept of the immensity of 'boundless and bare' life and the inevitability of the 'colossal wreck' of everything, as compared to the 'sneer of cold command,' which is all many mere mortals have at their command, unfortunately." (p. 183)

In Liberty Center Lucy perceives herself to be surrounded by the wreckage of social normalcy. She acts out the drama of the absurd, which Camus describes as the "confrontation between the human need and the unreasonable silence of the world,"[34] but she lacks the vision of the absurd man that would allow her to find solace and happiness in her condition. In the face of the world's silence, Lucy repeatedly commands from others a moral goodness and a sense of responsibility that she herself cannot define:

> Oh, how absurd this all was! How unnecessary! Why must they force her always to the extreme? Why must they bring this down upon themselves when the simple and honorable solution was always and forever at hand? If only they did their duty! If only they would be men!
>
> (p. 298)

How simple the solution is, for Lucy! Even her last words, cut short by death, convey her simplistic notion of life: "For they are wrong, and you are right, and there is no choice: the good must triumph in the end! the good and the just and the true *must*—." Lucy's trust in human power is countered by her fate, however, for her burning fury leads her to a frozen death in Passion Paradise. The irony is compounded by Lucy's dying with her father's letter frozen to her cheek — a letter that contains Whitey's conviction that "there is a point where punishment becomes corrective. Beyond that, it becomes destructive." Unable to grasp the complexity of the human condition, Lucy Nelson has initiated a mad crusade to bring instant goodness into the world. Convinced of her own innocence and equipped with the most shallow of moral codes, Lucy launches her own attack against the evils of the world, where "nothing changes, nothing ever changes." Perhaps the greatest irony of all is that, in Roth's view, Lucy's observations about the meaninglessness of her social life and the weakness of the people surrounding her are essentially correct. Roth's interest, however, is with the naive and misguided response of Lucy, a response that Roth sees as pervasive among many "average" Americans. Roth says that in Lucy's character and behavior there is

> much that American readers will find altogether ordinary and recognizable. For it has always seemed to me

> that though we are, to be sure, not a nation of Lucy
> Nelsons, there is a strong American inclination to
> respond to life *like* a Lucy Nelson — an inclination to
> reduce the complexities and mysteries of living to the
> most simple-minded and childish issues of right and
> wrong. How deeply this perverse moralistic bent has
> become embedded in our national character and af-
> fected our national life is, I realize, a matter for debate;
> that it is even "perverse" is not a judgment with which
> everyone will readily agree. What destroys Lucy (some
> readers may hold) has nothing whatsoever to do with
> the rest of us. I am of a different opinion. [35]

Through the experiences of Lucy Nelson, Roth explores
psychological and moral obsessions arising from a cultural
predicament that is, in Roth's view, more or less pervasive.[36]
Roth implies that, just as American life produces a melancholy character like Epstein or a passive character like
Novotny, so does it produce a character like Lucy, whom
Roth calls a "puritanical, haunted heroine."[37] The themes of
guilt and persecution, their causes and their effects on human
character, are themes that Roth treats in deadly earnest in
Letting Go and *When She Was Good*. Some critics have been
understandably irked by the unrelenting somberness of these
two novels, but, as Theodore Solotaroff has pointed out, the
somberness of the novels is indeed an accurate reflection of
the Midwest milieu that Roth experienced while he lived in
Chicago, a milieu that in a real sense is the protagonist —
what Hoffman calls "the landscape as assailant" — in
Letting Go and *When She Was Good*. Solotaroff says that

> what Roth was mainly drawing on, I felt, was a certain
> depressiveness that had been in the air. . . . Mostly this
> depressiveness was caused by the self-inflicted burdens
> of private life, which in this age of conformity often

seemed to serve for politics, art, and the other avenues
of youthful experience and experiment. One of the
principal occupations in Hyde Park seemed to be
difficult marriages: almost everyone I knew was locked
into one. This penchant for early marriage and child-
rearing, or for only slightly less strenuous affairs, tended
to fill the vacuum of commitment for sophisticated but
not especially stable young couples and fostered a rather
pretentious moralism of duty, sacrifice, home therapy,
experiment with domestic roles — often each other's —
working things out, saving each other.[38]

Through the characters of Nathan Zuckerman and
Peter Tarnopol in *My Life As A Man*, Roth continued
to explore, in somber, realistic prose, the "depressive"
social milieu of the fifties and its impact on the
possibilities for self-assertion and self-fulfillment. *When
She Was Good* represents, however, a turning point in
his artistic interests. Although Roth did not turn away
from themes of guilt and persecution, he did find with
the completion of *When She Was Good* a kind of
liberation from the darker aspects of these themes, a
liberation that resulted in his writing *Portnoy's Complaint*. Roth himself gives an illuminating extended
comment on this shift in his attitude toward these
themes:

At the time I was beginning to play around with the ideas
for what turned out to be "Portnoy's Complaint," I was
teaching a good deal of Kafka in a course I gave once a
week at the University of Pennsylvania; when I look back
now upon the reading I assigned that year I realize that the
course might have been called "Studies in Guilt and Persecution" — "Metamorphosis," "The Castle," "In the
Penal Colony," "Crime and Punishment," "Notes from

Underground," "Death in Venice," "Anna Karenina" .... My own previous two novels, "Letting Go" and "When She Was Good," were about as gloomy as the gloomiest of these blockbusters, and fascinated, obviously, as I still was by these dark books, I was actually at that time looking for a way to get in touch with another side of my talent. Particularly after three arduous years spent on "When She Was Good," with its unfiery prose, its puritanical, haunted heroine, its unrelenting concern with banality, I was aching to write something extravagant and funny. It has been a long time between laughs. ... Now, the road ... to "Portnoy's Complaint" was more winding and eventful than I can begin to describe here; there is certainly a personal element in the book, but not until I had got hold of guilt, you see, as a *comic idea*, did I begin to feel myself lifting free and clear of my last book, and my old concerns. [39]

In coming to a recognition that excessive guilt and punishment have their comic aspects, Roth was able to provide a wider perspective on and a more inclusive vision of his essential themes — precisely what he had not been able to do in *Letting Go* and *When She Was Good*. As Roth says, he came to the recognition that "it was all so *funny*, this morbid preoccupation with punishment and guilt. Hideous, but funny." [40] The result of Roth's attempt to get in touch with another side of his talent is a victim-hero who finds his situation not "hideous but funny" but rather the other way round: superficially funny but in essence hideous indeed. That character is, of course, Alexander Portnoy.

Portnoy's Complaint

In *Portnoy's Complaint* Roth's interest in moral and psychological obsessions arising from the conflict between public life and private life is given its most forceful — and most exasperated — expression. Like other victim-heroes in Roth's fiction, Portnoy desperately wants to get in touch with the life-sustaining qualities of personal joy, harmony, and peace, but he is torn between conflicting loyalties to the public self and the private self. Portnoy is, as Roth says, "a man speaking out of an overwhelming obsession: he is obscene because he wants to be saved. An odd, maybe even mad, way to go about getting saved; but, nonetheless, the investigation of this passion, and the combat it precipitates with his Conscience, is what's at the center of the book."[41]

In essence, *Portnoy's Complaint* is a compendium of conflicts and themes that Roth had treated previously in his fiction. Like Lucy Nelson, Portnoy is overwhelmed by the expectations of social morality (when a friend inquires about what he does for a living, Portnoy asks himself, "Doesn't everyone know I am now the most moral man in all of New York, all pure motives and humane and passionate ideals? Doesn't he know that what I do for a living is I'm *good*?"). Like Libby Herz and Novotny, Portnoy asks when "we can leave off complaining how sick we are — and go out into the air, and live!" Like Paul Herz, Portnoy is, as he says, "shackled and fettered" by his sense of public duty, which has produced in him an "icebox heart." Like Epstein, Portnoy combats the sterility of "normal" and "public" expectations by "piggishly" grabbing for sexual pleasure ("So what's the crime?" Portnoy asks. "Why, why can I not have some pleasure without the retribution following behind like a caboose! Pig? Who, *me*?"). And like the Roth and the Kafka of "I Always Wanted You to Admire My Fasting," Portnoy is "impaled again upon the long ago, what was, what will never be." He is a victim-hero whose "complaint" embraces a wide range of debilitating, paralyzing forces imbedded in Jewish and gentile cultures, in communal and familial values, in public and private expectations. "Torn by desires that are repugnant to my conscience, and a conscience repugnant to my desires,"

Portnoy acts out the absurd drama of the *pharmakos* living in a world where injustice is a sadly comic, absurdly inescapable part of existence.

Portnoy's Complaint takes the form of a long monologue delivered by Alexander Portnoy to a New York psychiatrist, Dr. Spielvogel. Progressing through what Roth calls blocks of consciousness, Portnoy brings to the surface the pleasures and pains of childhood, his daily battles with his mother and father, his masturbatory fantasies, his sexual adventures in high school and college, his unsatisfying love affairs undertaken while he holds the post of Assistant Commissioner of the New York Commission on Human Opportunity, and his frenetic flight to Israel in a fruitless quest for salvation. Like Kafka's Joseph K., Portnoy labors under a heavy sentence imposed by a mysterious tribunal, with the result that he sees his life as a monstrous trick played upon him by his parents, by his community, by his religion, and, ironically, by himself. Portnoy confronts his psychiatrist with the problems, the questions, and the demands that have driven him to the analyst's couch:

Doctor Spielvogel, this is my life, my only life, and I'm living it in the middle of a Jewish joke! I am the son in the Jewish joke — *only it ain't no joke*! Please, who crippled us like this? Who made us so morbid and hysterical and weak? . . . Doctor, what do you call this sickness I have? Is this the Jewish suffering I used to hear so much about? Is this what has come down to me from the pogroms and the persecution? from the mockery and abuse bestowed by the *goyim* over these two thousand lovely years? Oh my secrets, my shame, my palpitations, my flushes, my sweats! The way I respond to the simple vicissitudes of human life! Doctor, I can't stand any more being frightened like this over nothing! Bless me with manhood! Make me brave! Make me strong! Make me *whole*! Enough being a nice

Jewish boy, publicly pleasing my parents while privately pulling my putz! Enough! (pp. 39-40)

Portnoy himself locates the basic cause of his victimization in his parents. His father, Jake, is a beleaguered, ineffectual, permanently constipated *schlemiel* whose greatest fear is that he will die before Alexander gives him a grandson. In Alexander's eyes, Jake is completely dominated by his wife, by WASPS, and by a recalcitrant sphincter:

Oh, this father! this kindly, anxious, uncomprehending, constipated father! Doomed to be obstructed by this Holy Protestant Empire! The self-confidence and the cunning, the imperiousness and the contacts, all that enabled the blond and blue-eyed of his generation to lead, to inspire, to command, if need be to oppress — he could not summon a hundredth part of it. How could he oppress? — he *was* the oppressed. How could he wield power? — he *was* powerless. (p. 43)

His mother, Sophie, has the qualities of the stereotypical Jewish mother: forceful, self-righteous (she confides to a neighbor, "You know what my biggest fault is, Rose? I hate to say it about myself, but I'm too good"), generous ("the patron saint of self-sacrifice," Alex calls her), and fearful of life's hazards. Together Jake and Sophie have contributed, Alex believes, to the overwhelming guilt and fear that he himself experiences in his response to life. Guilt and fear are terms that Portnoy constantly but ineffectively defies with all the reason he can summon. His earliest memories are of unreasonable punishments for the most insignificant of deeds: Alex is locked out of the house for some inscrutable wrong-doing ("Banishment? What can I possibly have done?"); for refusing to eat his bread, his mother threatens him with a knife ("Why a *knife*, why the threat of *murder*, why is such total and annihilating victory necessary . . ."); and always in the air are threats of catastrophic consequences for disregarding warnings about dressing properly, eating well, and acting dutifully. Alex concludes, "Doctor, these people are incredible! These people are unbelievable! These two are the outstanding producers and packagers of guilt in our time. They render it from me like fat from a chicken!"

The guilt-imposing admonitions thrust upon Portnoy by his parents and by his religion spring, he believes, from a fear of free-flowing involvement with life. Repressiveness becomes the index of timidity on both familial and religious levels. In fact, Jewishness itself is partially to blame for Portnoy's crippledness, he believes:

> What else, I ask you, were all those prohibitive dietary rules and regulations all about to begin with, what else but to give us little Jewish children practice in being repressed? Practice, darling, practice, practice, practice. Inhibition doesn't grow on trees, you know — takes patience, takes concentration, takes a dedicated and self-sacrificing parent and a hard-working attentive little child to create in only a few years' time a really constrained and tight-ass human being. Why else the two sets of dishes? Why else the kosher soap and salt? Why else, I ask you, but to remind us three times a day that life is boundaries and restrictions if it's anything. . . . Renunciation is all, cries the koshered and bloodless piece of steak my family and I sat down to eat at dinner time. Self-control, sobriety, sanctions — this is the key to a human life, saith all those endless dietary laws.
>
> (pp. 88-89)

Jake and Sophie, the dispensers of Judaic and family "law," are themselves, in Portnoy's eyes, the most victimized people he knows: "What in their world was not charged with danger, dripping with germs, fraught with peril? Oh, where was the gusto, where was the boldness and courage? Who filled these parents of mine with such a fearful sense of life?" For these questions Portnoy has no answers. He only knows that his own life has been circumscribed by rules and regulations that have become an ineluctable part of his outlook, and he bemoans "what my conscience, so-called, has done to my sexuality, my spontaneity, my courage!" In Portnoy's view, "that tyrant, my superego, he should be strung up, that son of a bitch. . . ."

Portnoy's battle with his tyrannical superego is at the center of virtually every incident that he drags up from "that inheritance of terror that I bring with me out of my ridiculous past." In adolescence masturbation is his guilt-ridden response to "being good." On the way to a bar mitzvah lesson, in the middle of class, after promising his mother not to eat hamburgers, the urge incessantly falls upon him to "grab that battered battering ram to freedom." As he explains to Spielvogel, "Doctor, do you understand what I was up against? My wang was all I really had that I could call my own." In later years his heterosexual experiences are no more satisfying, no less guilt-producing than his earlier practices. Kay Campbell, alias "The Pumkin," a prototype of the Midwestern *shikse*; Sarah Abbott Maulsby, the "Pilgrim," a product of New Canaan, Foxcroft and Vassar and an "ever-popular purveyor of the social amenities"; Mary Jane Reed, "The Monkey," a hyper-erotic fashion model from the impoverished hills of West Virginia; Naomi, "The Heroine," an Israeli soldier whose parents were Zionists from Philadelphia — all of these are recipients of Portnoy's loveless, revengeful advances. As Portnoy crudely but accurately says to Spielvogel, "What I'm saying, Doctor, is that I don't seem to stick my dick up these girls, as much as I stick it up their backgrounds" — a shrewd assessment of how far the insensitive Portnoy has gone in waging phallic war with the *goyim*, his parents, his religion, and his past. He pleads with Spielvogel, "If I could be somehow sprung from this obsession with fellatio and fornication, from romance and fantasy and revenge — from the settling of scores! the pursuit of dreams! from this hopeless, senseless loyalty to the long ago!"

It is evident that Portnoy's helpless loyalty to his past is a rejoinder to the pastless activist hero who effectively and easily divorces himself from pressures that, to Portnoy's (and Roth's) way of thinking, are actually inescapable. For Portnoy memories are "moments of history as crucial to my being as the moment of my conception," and in the very last scene of the novel we find Portnoy still "whimpering on the floor with MY MEMORIES! My endless childhood! Which I won't relinquish — or which won't relinquish me!" Like the activist heroes, Portnoy yearns for the unfettered life, perhaps best exemplified by his fond memories of the Turkish bath, "a place without *goyim* and women," and by Sunday morning softball games in Newark. The *shvitz* bath reminds Portnoy of a prehistoric time when family and social pressures did not exist. When Portnoy enters the bath, "I lose touch instantaneously with that ass-licking little boy who runs home after school with his A's in his hand, the little over-earnest innocent endlessly in search of the key to that unfathomable mystery, his mother's approbation, and am back in some sloppy watery time, before there were families such as we know them, before there were toilets and tragedies such as we know them. . . ." Equally in contrast to his home life is his beatific vision of center field on the softball diamond, a place where the self is fully in control:

Doctor, you can't imagine how truly glorious it is out there, so alone in all that space.... It is simply beyond the realm of possibility for any situation to arise in which I do not know how to move, or where to move, or what to say or leave unsaid.... And it's true, is it not? — incredible, but apparently true — there are people who feel in life the ease, the self-assurance, the simple and essential affiliation with what is going on, that I used to feel as the center fielder for the Seebees?   (pp. 76-79)

For Portnoy, however, these "craters of the spirit" (to use the phrase of Bellow's Joseph) are now inaccessible, a realization that throws Portnoy into despair.

As the child of Sophie and Jake, as the product of American society, and as the victim of irrational worldly schemes, Portnoy is unable to transcend the absurdities of his life in order to gain a guiltless encounter with his deepest desires for spiritual harmony, wholeness, and freedom. His affinities are not with Kafka's K. of *The Castle*, the spiritual activist hero who escapes the confusions of the absurd world, but rather with two of Kafka's victimized heroes, Joseph K., in *The Trial*, and Gregor Samsa in "The Metamorphosis." This is not to say that Roth has consciously modeled Portnoy after Kafka's victim-heroes; in fact, Roth denies any such conscious intention despite several explicit allusions to Kafka in his novel.[42] There are, nonetheless, some obvious similarities between the plight of Portnoy and the plight of Joseph K. in *The Trial*, as is made evident when we compare Weinberg's summary of Joseph K.'s victimization with Portnoy's victimization. After pointing out the similarities between *The Trial*, "The Metamorphosis" and "In the Penal Colony," Weinberg goes on to say that acceptance of reason as the governing force in the world is at the base of the guilty victim's situation. . . . Joseph K. sees the gap between the real and the ideal manifestations of the Law as part of an order which may be understood in a systematic way, and thus he tries only to get things right in reasonable, worldly terms, approaching the highest court through the gestures of a worldling: fawning, flattery, bribes, seduction. His case, therefore, is hopeless, and he enacts the prototypal absurd drama of our times. All his feverish activity is a kind of inactivity in the eyes of an ultimate, remote, probably indifferent, mysterious judge. . . . At the core of the absurdist novel is a vision of the absurd disjunction in the world, the disjunction between the probable and the wonderful, a disjunction seen through the eyes of a "probable" man, creating a situation that we may . . . call comic, in the broadest, or highest, sense of comedy. [43]

In his later years Portnoy brings to his battle with the mysterious laws of life his legal training (he graduated first in his class at the Columbia School of Law) and his highly developed reasoning powers (he has an I.Q. of 158), yet he finds himself, like Joseph K., unable to fathom the inexplicable disproportion between his hopes and his deserts, between his acts and his punishments. Even as a child — or so he recalls — his house was a "lunatic asylum" where "it was 'normal' for me to be in a state resembling torment." An hilarious example of Portnoy's "torment" occurs when he is five. Having bitten his mother and kicked her shins, Portnoy hears from her the ominous threat of eternal banishment from the house:

Is she *kidding*? Is she *serious*? Why doesn't she call the cops and get me shipped off to children's prison, if this

is how incorrigible I really am? "Alexander Portnoy,
aged five, you are hereby sentenced to hang by your
neck until you are dead for refusing to say you are sorry
to your mother." You'd think the child lapping up their
milk and taking baths with his duck and his boats in
their tub was the most wanted criminal in America. . . .
You simply cannot imagine how some people will
respond to having served fifteen- and twenty-year
sentences as some crazy bastard's idea of "good"! So if I
kicked you in the shins, Ma-má, if I sunk my teeth into
your wrist clear through to the *bone*, count your
blessings! For had I kept it *all* inside me, believe me,
you too might have arrived home to find a pimply
adolescent corpse swinging over the bath tub by his
father's belt.   (pp. 137-138, 141)

Portnoy's "sentence" is neither as mysterious nor as
cosmic as Joseph K.'s, but it is important to note that the
dynamics of *Portnoy's Complaint*, even down to the metaphors of judgment, sentencing, and execution, parallel those
of *The Trial*. What Portnoy cannot comprehend is the absurd
disparity between his so-called crimes and the resulting
"sentences" meted out by community, family, fate, and even
his own psyche. In order to enter the world of the *shikses*
("Who Will Do Anything"), Portnoy once donned ice skates,
and, taking on the *goyische* alias of Alton Christian Peterson,
glided after his heart's desire. Unfortunately, in his haste he
tripped and broke his leg. Conclusion: "For skating after
shikses, under an alias, I would be a cripple for the rest of my
days." When Portnoy discovers that two of his boyhood
friends have become successes in later life, he is appalled. "I
simply cannot believe in the survival, let alone the middle-
class success, of these two bad boys. Why, they're supposed
to be in jail — or the gutter. They didn't do their homework,
damn it!" In Portnoy's absurd world, such offenses against

"goodness" are punishable by death. At least he can understand the fate of Bubbles Girardi, a promiscuous girl recently shot to death in a bar. "Now there at least is a career that makes some sense," says Portnoy. "There's a case of cause and effect that confirms my ideas about human consequence! . . . That's the way the world is *supposed* to be run!" Most absurd of all, perhaps, is Portnoy's vision of the future, in which he becomes the Sisyphus of the bathroom — "poetic justice," says Portnoy, for the life he has lived: "Yes, yes, I see it all: for my abominations I awake one morning to find myself chained to a toilet in Hell. . . ." Confronted with the absurdities, Portnoy cries out at the end of the novel:

> Dreams? If only they had been! But I don't need dreams, Doctor, that's why I hardly have them — because I have this life instead. With me it all happens in broad daylight! The disproportionate and the melodramatic, this is my daily bread! The coincidences of dreams, the symbols, the terrifyingly laughable situations, the oddly ominous banalities, the accidents and humiliation, the bizarrely appropriate strokes of luck or misfortune that other people experience with their eyes shut, I get with mine open!   (p. 290)

One can carry the similarity between Roth's victim-hero and Kafka's victim-hero too far, but it is essential to note that Roth's treatment of Portnoy is indebted at least in spirit to the absurdist mode of fiction to which Kafka gave the clearest articulation. As in the novels of Bruce Jay Friedman, however, one finds in Roth's later fiction a sharper vision of social absurdity than is usually the case in Kafka's works. An untypically perceptive review in *Time* says, "Although sex, psychoanalysis, and Jewishness form the content of the novel, they are not its subject. The book is about absurdity — the absurdity of a man who knows all about the ethnic, sociological and Freudian hang-ups, yet is still racked by guilt because his ethical impulses conflict with the surge of his animal desires."[44]   Certainly a central concern of the novel is the absurd state of helplessness, crippledness and victimization in which Portnoy finds himself, but it is important to note that this condition is in large part due, in Portnoy's (and Roth's) view, to social, communal values that are hypocritical and duplicitous. One cannot help but suspect that Portnoy's impotent rage at the banalities of American public life is shared by Roth himself, which helps to explain the "jokelike" quality of the novel. We might recall that as early as 1961 Roth wondered why, if the world had grown so crooked and unreal, more fictional heroes did not end up in institutions like Holden Caulfield. Portnoy's speaking from a psychiatrist's couch is, one might suppose, Roth's way of dramatizing how insane American public life is and how adversely it affects its members. Roth says, "Portnoy's pains arise out of his refusal to be bound any longer by taboos which, rightly or wrongly, *he* experiences as diminishing and unmanning" — precisely the refusal we encounter in activist heroes who have the courage to forge a personal identity in the face of worldly schemes; but, Roth goes on to say, "the joke on Portnoy is that for him the breaking of the taboo turns out to be as unmanning in the end as the honoring of it. Some joke."[45] There is, Roth implies, no exit for the man who willingly confronts the recognizable social world in a quest for personal "wholeness"; the fault, however, is not in ourselves but in our social stars.

The strength — and the significance — of *Portnoy's Complaint* lies, as Tony Tanner says, in "the fact that at last Roth's interest in the social scene and his feeling for the obsessed self coalesced in the writing":

> All the doors on all the rooms of [Portnoy's] childhood are opened and while this permits us to see the comic-desperate strategies of the sexually maturing

child, it also enables us to hear the cacophony of conflicting imperatives which beset him, and to become aware of all the irrational rules and emotional bullyings which were visited on the bewildered child. It is in this way that self-obsession merges with social observation, for what Portnoy does is re-evoke scene after scene and situation after situation from his past so that environment and other characters appear vividly before us even while — and just because — he is conducting an inquiry into the determinants of his present sickness.[46]

What Tanner says is, I think, both appropriate and important. The baffled self so prominent in Roth's early fiction has at last, in *Portnoy's Complaint*, dragged the source of its bafflement and the cause of its victimization clearly into the open field, and if there are no palpable hits, at least Portnoy, unlike other of Roth's heroes, is able to get in some glancing blows at social inanity. Virtually nothing in the social landscape is invulnerable to the Portnoy attack.

One of the major areas of investigation in *Portnoy's Complaint* — an area that Roth had touched on in *Goodbye, Columbus*, "Novotny's Pain," *Letting Go*, and *When She Was Good* — is the complaisant normalcy of the *goyim*. The Protestant Midwest of Davenport, Iowa, with its promise of promiscuous *shikses* and familial security, is for Portnoy a mythic, inaccessible land of white-haired fathers, smiling, well-mannered mothers, football-playing sons and prom-going daughters — a land rendered to Portnoy through the stereotypical families of radio: Ozzie and Harriet, Ethel and Albert, Jack Armstrong, the All-American *Goy*. "To me," says Portnoy, "a child whose earliest movie memories are of Anne Rutherford and Alice Faye, America is a *shikse* nestling under your arm whispering love love love love love!" Portnoy receives the mass media stereotypes of public normalcy (which becomes the central subject of Roth's "On the Air") with a good deal of ambivalence, however; while he loathes the normalcy that informs the values of his female conquests, another part of him secretly desires the "brimming, hearty stew of family life."

Jewish family life, however, is as improbable in fact as Protestant family life is in fancy, in Portnoy's eyes. Selfishness and stupidity, shallowness and vanity are by no means the exclusive property of the gentiles. Despite Harry Golden's cozy portrayal of Jewish home life, Portnoy is of the opinion that Jews are no better off than the WASPS:

> Only in America, Rabbi Golden, do these peasants, our mothers, get their hair dyed platinum at the age of sixty, and walk up and down Collins Avenue in Florida in pedalpushers and mink stoles — and with opinions on every subject under the sun. It isn't their fault they were given a gift like speech — look, if cows could talk, they would say things just as idiotic. Yes, yes, maybe that's the solution then: think of them as cows, who have been given the twin miracles of speech and mah-jongg.
>
> (p. 110)

In Portnoy's world, inanity is everywhere: "The Jews I despise for their narrow-mindedness, their self-righteousness, the incredibly bizarre sense that these cave men who are my parents and relatives have somehow gotten of their superiority — but when it comes to tawdriness and cheapness, to beliefs that would shame even a gorilla, you simply cannot top the *goyim*." Portnoy concludes, "What a country! Is it any wonder we're all of us half nuts?"

All of this is by way of suggesting that Portnoy's victimization is not so much personal or cosmic as it is social. Roth is not dealing with an inscrutable, malevolent universe in the way that Kafka does in *The Trial* or Bellow does in *The Victim*; his interest is rather with "civilization and its discontents," and he has left no doubts that the banalities of a "crooked and unreal" American public life are at the heart of Portnoy's paralyzing guilt and fear: "Think of it," Portnoy says, "half the race is over, and I still stand here at the starting line . . . , still arguing with the authorities about the rules and regulations! disputing the course to be run! calling into question the legitimacy of the track commission!" Portnoy's complaint is, ultimately, directed at social and moral restrictions of the "track commission" of society rather than at Divine Injustice — a point that is underscored by the psychological disorder reported by Dr. Spielvogel in a preface to the novel as "Portnoy's Complaint," a disorder in which "strongly-felt ethical and altruistic impulses are perpetually warring with extreme sexual longings. . . . As a consequence of the patient's 'morality' . . . neither fantasy nor act issues in genuine sexual gratification, but rather in overriding feelings of shame and the dread of retribution. . . ."

Shame and fear of retribution are, of course, exactly those "social diseases" that have afflicted all of Roth's victim-heroes, but only Portnoy is able to articulate — in an overly-simplified and overly-dramatized fashion, to be sure — his helplessness, fear, and guilt in the face of an absurd society. If he is obscene, society is to blame; if he is self-pitying, society is to blame; if he is in desperate need of psychiatric help, society is to blame. Like other of Roth's victim-heroes, Portnoy's desires are simple, his punishment great, but unlike other of Roth's victim-heroes, Portnoy *sees* the discrepancy even though he is incapable of making sense of it. Although he declares that he "can't live any more in a world given its meaning and dimension by some vulgar nightclub clown" or by "some *black humorist*," Portnoy becomes increasingly aware that he has no other choice. The last scene that Portnoy evokes emphasizes clearly not only the essential themes and conflicts of the novel, but also Portnoy's awareness of how absurd is his condition and how limited is his ability to overcome it:

I mean, God forbid I should tear the tag from my
mattress that says, "Do Not Remove Under Penalty of
Law" — what would they give me for that, the chair? It
makes me want to *scream*, the ridiculous disproportion
of the guilt! May I? Will that shake them up too much
out in the waiting room? Because that's maybe what I
need most of all, to howl. A pure howl, without any
more words between me and it! "This is the police
speaking. You're surrounded, Portnoy. You better come
on out and pay your debt to society." "Up society's ass,
Copper!"   (p. 309)

Disproportionate guilt, absurd societal (not cosmic) law,
and the howl of outrage at forces surrounding the individual
are elements that are increasingly pervasive in Roth's fiction;
in *Portnoy's Complaint* these elements are given their most
emphatic expression. In Roth's "The Psychoanalytic
Special," another patient, Ella Wittig, had been trained by
Dr. Spielvogel to resist her promiscuous impulses, only to
conclude, "Truly, it was awful if this was what it was going
to be like, being better"; Portnoy, on the other hand, has
fought valiantly against the repressiveness inherent in his
family training, his religion, and his community, only to end
up, as Naomi says, as "the most unhappy person I have ever
known." Epstein, Paul and Libby Herz, Novotny, and Lucy
Nelson might well challenge Portnoy's claim to unhappiness,
for each has experienced the social victimization that results,
as Naomi says, from "acting as though justice, as though
human rights and human dignity could actually exist in that
[American] society — when obviously no such thing is
possible."

The impossibility — or at least the improbability — of a
fully-realized self-assertion in American public life is not, of
course, a happy theme, nor is it a theme that Roth embraces
as an incontrovertible truism. It is clear, however, that as
Roth works his way through the domestic, familial, social,

and cultural pressures depicted in his fiction, he, like his heroes, becomes increasingly "stupefied" and "repelled" by the reality he encounters. In *Portnoy's Complaint* this stupefaction and repulsion are given their most "absurd" and, as Tanner has rightly said, their most adequately fused expression, where at last Roth's interests in society and in the self coalesce. But as bitter and as hopeless as Portnoy's plight may seem, a glimmer of hope is held out by Dr. Spielvogel, who has the last line (albeit a punch line) in the novel: "Now vee may perhaps to begin. Yes?"

As early as 1963 Roth suggested that he had moved away from the American Jewish scene that had occupied his earlier fiction: "They were stories I had been carrying with me for a long time, and finally got around to writing. But then when I moved, as it were, not only geographically but moved in many ways, the subject of the fiction changed." (*SDI*, p. 37) In a real sense Roth's fiction has been more diverse, more "changing" than that of any other Jewish-American writer, with the possible exception of Norman Mailer. In his latest fiction Roth, it would seem, has followed Spielvogel's promise of a new beginning, for on the surface such works as "On the Air," *Our Gang, The Breast, The Great American Novel*, and *My Life As A Man* are radical departures from previous artistic attempts. How far has Roth "moved" as a writer of fiction, and to what degree is his most recent fiction "new"? How does his most recent fiction help define the essential aspects of his art? For the answers to such insistent questions we are obliged to turn to the latest works of Philip Roth.

IV

Post-Portnoy:
Roth's Most Recent Fiction

In his review of Roth's first work after *Portnoy's Complaint*, a political satire entitled *Our Gang*, Dwight MacDonald observed that "Philip Roth has become as hard to classify as Norman Mailer."[1] Given the wide variety of themes, characters, settings, and styles in Roth's fiction, MacDonald's predicament in classifying Roth is certainly an understandable one. The brittle and sharp-edged stories in *Goodbye, Columbus*, the ponderous, gloomy exploration of moral and psychological problems in *Letting Go*, the distinctive non-Jewish flavor of *When She Was Good*, and the comic first-person narration of *Portnoy's Complaint* suggest that Roth's talent as a writer of fiction has flowed into various channels that cut a wide path across artistic terrain. Roth himself, after having written *Portnoy's Complaint*, underscored the diversity of his fiction by saying, "Each book is a rebellion against the last one. When I begin a book I never know what it's going to be."[2]

Roth's unique presentation of the activist hero in his early fiction and the victim-hero in his later fiction provides valuable insights into the nature of his artistic vision. The movement of his fiction from the activist mode to the absurdist mode emphasizes the most prominent features of Roth's sensibility: his increasing pessimism over the possibilities for selfhood, his attention to the social landscape through which the hero wanders, and his continuing concern with moral and psychological crises experienced in and perpetuated by American public life. Roth's artistic concerns have divided between social observation and the obsessed self, two concerns that do not coalesce, as Tanner rightly maintains, until *Portnoy's Complaint.* For the most part, the early fiction focuses on "obsessed selves" struggling to get free of restrictive forces that are either grotesquely magnified and simplified or only hinted at; in *Portnoy's Complaint,* however, Roth's satiric talents raise the social world to the level of a recognizable antagonist, and we see at last, in painfully explicit detail, the nature of the antagonism leveled at the self. In his most recent fiction Roth has dramatized the division in his sensibility by producing three pieces of fiction that focus on social absurdity and two pieces of fiction that focus on the obsessed self. "On the Air," *Our Gang,* and *The Great American Novel* relentlessly explore the absurdities of the social and political landscape of American public life, whereas *The Breast* and *My Life As A Man* return to an exploration of the fettered self trying to break free of moral and psychological obsessions. One might say that in making the new beginning suggested by Dr. Spielvogel at the end of *Portnoy's Complaint,* Roth clarifies his most fundamental areas of concern.

In "On The Air" Roth picks up on social issues that he had treated in *Portnoy's Complaint.* The short story is clearly within the absurdist mode, and the central hero, Milton Lippman, is one of the most passive victims in Roth's fictional canon. Lippman, a small-time talent scout at the height of the popularity of radio, is at times a victim of the most insane cruelties and the most inane happenings imaginable; at other times, however, he is an observer of social absurdity who, like the author Roth describes in "Writing American Fiction," is repelled by what he sees in American public life. "A talent scout," says Lippman, "is only a person who happens to see what the other person doesn't — he doesn't make these things happen, *he only points them out!*" As a purveyor and surveyor of absurdities, Lippman gives savage testimony to Roth's belief that the actualities of American life continually out-do the talents of the author. At the same time, Lippman himself is in the grips of absurd values and attitudes that are logical extensions of "normalcy" as Roth conceives it.

In "On the Air" Roth explores the stupefying, sickening, infuriating reality of American public life as it is conveyed by radio shows of the 1940's. Roth had tapped much of this material in his presentation of Portnoy, but in "On the Air" the plight of the victim is subordinated to absurdities sent into the world on the air waves. As the radio dial turns, we cut from "The Answer Man" to "Duffy's Tavern" to "Kate Smith" to "Gang Busters" to "The Lone Ranger"; the catch, however, is that wild imagination becomes fact, the metaphorical becomes literal, the fantastic becomes historical: echoes of real violence, actual absurdities, and literal atrocities — Hitler, Mussolini, pogroms, mutilations, gunfights — are heard beneath the wildest hijinks. At one point Lippman observes, "The lesson he had learned as a talent scout was that what you could imagine could also be so. What was not could become!" At the height of the action, where he has been forced by a police chief to weigh his testicles on a bathroom scale (to affirm gentile sexual superiority), Lippman remarks,

> I am sleeping. It is just a matter of waking up, and then off to the office, to audition that blind xylophonist. Yes, I am in a trance, that's all. Somebody

has hypnotized me — by mistake. Maybe I went to some show where they called for a person to come up out of the audience and I was the one who let himself get hypnotized. No wonder I don't get what is happening. Probably I am walking around up on a stage somewhere, crowing like a rooster. I am under a spell —

"Kneel!" ordered the chief.   (p. 37)

Like Portnoy, Lippman perceives that he is living his life in the midst of a joke — "only it ain't no joke," after all.

Whereas the structure of "On the Air" is complex — with shifting points of view, role-changing characters, a potpourri of dialects, values, themes — the plot line is fairly simple. Milton Lippman takes it into his head to book Albert Einstein as Jewry's answer to "The Answer Man." He writes Einstein, explaining that he has a religious belief in the superiority of Jewish intelligence and in the power of radio. "I think sometimes that the Bible stories of God talking from above to the people down below is just what they had in those days instead of radio. People, whether then or now, like to hear 'the real thing.' Hearing is believing!" Einstein does not reply, so Lippman, his wife, and his five-year-old son begin a journey to Princeton to see him personally. On the journey he stops at a saloon for some ice cream; instead of experiencing the friendly confines of a Duffy's Tavern, however, he finds himself confronted with a foul-mouthed bartender by the name of Scully, a group of hostile, glassy-eyed women who look like Kate Smith, a garbage man, and a dartboard filled with ice picks, arrows, and a bayonet:

Oh, this puts little "Duffy's Tavern" to shame! This puts "Duffy's Tavern" right off the air! This is the real thing! That *nobody* could make up! . . .
Because this wasn't "Duffy's Tavern" with the familiar ding-a-ling start of each show, the phone ringing and

> Archie The Manager picking it off the hook. . . . No, this
> was no bullshit about good-natured *goyim* running a
> sweet and cozy little saloon. This was no bullshit tavern
> from the radio, *this was the real thing* — only more so!
> (p. 23)

In a continuing search for refreshment, Lippman and
family move on to a Howard Johnson's, where Lippman's
wife and son are apparently poisoned by eating ice cream
made from newspapers (an oblique comment, perhaps, on the
dangers of public consumption of that media), and Lippman
is subjected to idiocies perpetrated by a boy who has an ice
cream scoop where his right hand should be, a restaurant
manager who looks suspiciously like Scully, and a homosexual police chief (or a police chief pretending to be a
homosexual or a homosexual pretending to be a police chief).
While his wife and child lie in a comatose state, Lippman has
his sexuality, his Jewishness, and his very life threatened by
the gun-wielding, self-righteous, maniacal police chief, a
self-appointed judge who proposes to seek vengeance for
Lippman's crime of "Reckless Accusation Against Chris-
tians." Lippman ponders his predicament, aghast: "Yes,
himself murdered, his child poisoned, his wife attacked,
beaten, mutilated. . . . Why? *But why not?*" In the last scene,
one that is more violent and degrading than anything in
Burrough's *Naked Lunch* or Selby's *Last Exit to Brooklyn*,
the police chief fires a bullet that ricochets off Lippman's
nose and kills the chief, and we are left to ponder the voice
of the radio announcer: "For the startling conclusion to this
latest adventure in the life of Milton Lippman, Talent Scout!
tune in to this same wavelength tomorrow — till then, to all
those out there 'Beyond the Pale,' good night, brethren, and
sweet dreams!' "
"On the Air," like *Portnoy's Complaint,* is dedicated to
examining the social absurdities in public life, absurdities that

are so insane that they must be invented — only (and here is the punchline in the joke) they are not invented after all. The actualities of our culture exceed the most farfetched acts of imagination, as Lippman himself, a talent scout with an eye to the main chance, perceives:

> Oh, Jesus — the things you could make in this world! The things that were already *made*! The acts they were just *giving* away! For nothing! Gratus! Step right up, ladies and gentlemen, and pay *nothing*! of which ten per cent, Lippman's commission, was of course nothing too. Hitler, for instance — that little nut over in Germany thundering and howling at those millions of German people, and them saluting and cheering him back, goose-stepping for him all night long from one end of the country to the other, and all the time all this goose-stepping and *sieg-heil*ing is going on, all the time the torches are burning and the millions are on their feet roaring, all the time in the middle of that face *there is this little moustache*! Hitler! What an *idea*! Or that Mussolini character — with a neck on him like Two-Ton Tony Galento, with a collar on him made of his own thick flesh, and *he* is in charge of all of Italy! With *that neck*! Oh, just think about the big headliners and you could (in a way, in a way) die not to be handling them! "The Adolf Hitler Show." "The Benito Mussolini Comedy Hour." And how about that skinny Pope with the glasses. . . . Now if that is no hallucination, then what is? Only it is *not*! (pp. 17-18)

The metaphor of life as a stage is, of course, much older than Roth's "On the Air" — just as the metaphor of life as a courtroom is older than *Portnoy's Complaint*. Lippman, however, by turning the metaphor inside out, captures the desperate comedy that redeems the impossible absurdities of actual life; in Lippman's world, God becomes the "Greatest Talent Scout of Us All!" He explains to his tragic-minded wife:

> But what if the world is some kind of — of *show*! Don't you understand me? What *if*, is all I'm saying! What if we are only talent assembled by The Great Talent Scout Up Above. The Great Show of Life! Starring Everybody! Suppose entertainment is the Purpose of Life!
>
> (p. 20)

Lippman's strategy for survival — that is, his turning the literal into the metaphorical — is of some interest for our understanding of Roth's artistic vision. First, we see that Lippman's predicament is close to the predicament facing the writer as Roth describes it in "Writing American Fiction": In a world in which so much of ordinary life is absurd, like an insane, murderous joke, how do you recognize what is funny? The question is partially answered by "On the Air," where we are told, *via* a "Contest Announcement," that our own personal experiences will reveal many actual incidents so preposterous and so horrifying that they must be funny. Contest hint: "There is nothing funny about a person slipping on a banana peel — *unless he breaks his neck*." The announcer tells the listeners that to succeed in the contest all that is needed is a reasonable amount of reflection on things that have happened to mankind. "Are the glaciers really the funniest thing that ever happened? Or is Hitler? Or are the Jews?" The point that reality offers us grim humor enough is reinforced by a news bulletin interrupting the story of Lippman the Talent Scout — a bulletin that reports on the actions of Hitler, Goering, and the German war machine. The clear implication is that absurdist comedy is the most probable mode of fiction for the writer who wishes to write about the American scene in a realistic way.

A second implication embodied in the story is that survival — not only for the writer but for anyone who is sensitive to the onslaught of normalcy — may lie in the power of corrosive, redemptive laughter. One of the characters in the story asks, "... How are you going to begin to enjoy the times we live in, which just happen to be the richest comic era since the Ice Age — since the glaciers themselves!" The question cuts two ways (since we must contemplate the comedy of destructiveness), but the answer tentatively offered by the story is that survival itself may depend on an imaginative transformation of the literal into the figurative, thus nullifying actual horrors. This is the strategy not only of the author but of Lippman himself. "The real thing" stupefies and paralyzes the will, and hence Lippman, like Portnoy, is driven to reducing life to a play directed by a black humorist. The police chief, near the end of the story, stops playing his part: "You want literal, all right ... you Yankee son of a bitch, HERE IT IS." The chief's brand of "reality" is revealed in one of the most disgusting, revolting acts imaginable, one that drives the chief toward delirium and death. "With a swiftness that was awe-inspiring," the chief "jiujitsued the young soda jerk — pinned Scoop's shoulders beneath his knees, grabbed hold simultaneously of his forearm, and in one savage rising and falling motion, sent the ice cream scoop straight up his own rectum." "Kill the metaphor!" the chief cries; "I'm being driven literal, Scully — I'm going stark raving literal — at last!" Two pages later the chief dies, the lone casualty in the story; on the other hand, the imposed-upon, victimized, humiliated Lippman survives even a bullet between the eyes to continue uncertainly, as the announcer tells us, in his search for Einstein.

"On the Air" is certainly Roth's most vitriolic, vengeful attack on social realities. The essential vulgarity of the Patimkins in *Goodbye, Columbus,* the banality and emptiness of Jewish values in *Letting Go,* of Protestant values in *When*

She Was Good, of familial values in *Portnoy's Complaint* —
all of these pale beside the overwhelming inanities and
unspeakable absurdities confronting Lippman. As a social
realist Roth has always been tantalized by the social and
political phenomena of our time — precisely those phenomena that other writers, in Roth's view, have withdrawn from.
In "On the Air," however, Roth puts aside all restraint; in a
story that echoes the violence of West's *Miss Lonelyhearts*
and the black humor of Vonnegut's *Slaughterhouse Five*,
Roth explores the social landscape with relentless vigor. Like
Miss Lonelyhearts, Lippman is confronted with the grotesque
responses of individuals caught up in unrelieved misery, and
like Billy Pilgrim in *Slaughterhouse Five*, Lippman ventures
into the realm of fantasy to redeem otherwise inexplicable
and intolerable social absurdities.

Roth's interest in the political scene, an adjunct of his
social consciousness, has emerged most dramatically in his
Our Gang, but there is some evidence that this interest has
been an abiding one in Roth's thought. The satirical sting of
"On the Air" continues into Roth's less-than-kind handling
of Richard Nixon, but the impulse toward political satire can
be found in Roth as early as 1957, when he wrote an amusing
article directed at President Eisenhower. Norman Vincent
Peale had reported that, according to Mrs. Eisenhower, the
President addressed the Lord in prayer at night with the
words, "Lord, I want to thank You for helping me today.
You really stuck by me. I know, Lord, that I muffed a few
and I'm sorry about that. But both the ones we did all right
and the ones we muffed I am turning them all over to You."
Roth used these words (much as he uses Nixon's pronouncement about abortion) as a springboard into his satire, and he
concluded that the Lord is not so much Eisenhower's
shepherd as "his helper, his *aide-de-camp*."[3] In his "Writing
American Fiction" (1961), Roth had taken issue with several
political figures, and he was particularly appalled by Nixon's

political language in the Nixon-Kennedy debates. Roth concluded, "As a literary creation, as some novelist's image of a certain kind of human being, [Nixon] might have seemed believable, but I myself found that on the TV screen, as a real public image, a political fact, my mind balked at taking him in."[4] And in a 1970 article entitled "A Modest Proposal" Roth brings together his political interest, his attention to Nixon's speech mannerisms, and Swiftian satire. Roth's proposal is that American foodstuffs and commercial products be dropped on Southeast Asia instead of bombs:

> ... To those who would reject my proposal as one that would bring dishonor upon our nation and our flag, let me make one thing perfectly clear: I do not for one moment doubt the sincerity of those who for moral, religious, or patriotic reasons take such a position. I would assure them, however, that no less than they am I opposed to the crushing of an innocent Asian child under an American air conditioner. I would go even further and say that I am opposed to the crushing of any child anywhere under an air conditioner, even a *Communist child.*[5]

The important point to be made here is that *Our Gang* is not a radical and unanticipated departure from Roth's earlier works. From one point of view, *Our Gang* is a logical extension of Roth's artistic commitment to regarding the community as the proper subject for art; political satire, Roth implies, holds great possibilities for the writer who feels rebuffed when he turns to American public life for his material. Lippman in "On the Air" is a thinly-disguised Roth when he says, ". . . Every place you looked today (every place Lippman looked) there was entertainment material galore. Acts, acts, and more acts! He didn't pick up a newspaper that he didn't see another headliner passing himself off as a politician!" From another point of view, *Our Gang* is a product of Roth's growing pessimism, of his artistic shift from the activist to the absurdist mode, and of his developing comic talent for seizing upon gestures and mannerisms, turning them into indexes of a character's moral life.

Roth's method in *Our Gang* is that of the *reductio ad absurdum*, a device that he had utilized with some success in his previous fiction. The impetus for *Our Gang* was provided by Nixon's directive releasing William Calley from the stockade after his conviction for the My Lai massacre, a directive issued in the same week as the President's April 3 statement on abortion. The following excerpt from that statement serves as an epigram to Roth's satire.

> From personal and religious beliefs I consider abortions an unacceptable form of population control. Furthermore, unrestricted abortion policies, or abortion on demand, I cannot square with my personal belief in the sanctity of human life — including the life of the yet unborn. For, surely, the unborn have rights also, recognized in law, recognized even in principles expounded by the United Nations.

"The discrepancy," Roth said, "between [Nixon's] attitude toward Calley's crime and his attitude toward abortion was wholly revealing of the man's gross opportunism and moral stupidity. It seemed to me to merit special indignation."[6] By reducing the political stratagems of "Tricky Dixon" and his cohorts to absurdity, Roth turns, as he himself confesses, "my own indignation and disgust from raw, useless emotion into comic art."[7]

Indignation and disgust are not terms that are often linked openly with an artist's fiction. Who would venture the suggestion, for example, that Malamud and Bellow are so motivated? Yet Roth's personal rage at the way things are has been just beneath the surface of most of his novels and short stories; and especially in recent works like *Portnoy's Complaint*, "On the Air," and *Our Gang*, the esthetic distance between the author and his fiction is short indeed. It would seem that Roth's latest fiction is in part an answer to the problem that he raised in 1963 at the symposium held in Tel Aviv. At that symposium Roth suggested that the problem for the American Jew and the American gentile, beset as each is with affronts to human dignity in American society, "is, to discover a mode of action through which he can express perhaps his anger and his frustration at this horrible situation." (*SDI*, p. 29) Portnoy's final howl, Lippman's humiliation, and Tricky Dixon's grotesque assassination certainly register Roth's anger and frustration with American public life, and no one can miss the indignation and disgust motivating these three works. Consider, for example, the words of Tricky Dixon, who at the end of *Our Gang* is in Hell, where he is running a campaign against Satan for the rule of the nether regions:

> And now let me say a word to those who point to my own record as President of the United States and contend that it is less than it could have been, as regards suffering and anguish for all people, regardless of race, creed or color.... Despite my brief tenure in the "White" House, I firmly believe that I was able to maintain and perpetuate all that was evil in American life when I came to power. Furthermore I think I can safely say that I was able to lay the groundwork for new oppressions and injustices and to sow seeds of bitterness and hatred between the races, the generations, and the social classes that hopefully will plague the American people for years to come. Surely I did nothing whatsoever to decrease the eventuality of a nuclear holocaust, but rather continued to make progress in that direction by

maintaining policies of belligerence, aggression and subversion around the globe. I think I might point with particular pride to Southeast Asia, where I was able to achieve considerable growth in just the sort of human misery that the vengeful and vindictive souls here in our great inferno would wish upon the whole of mankind.

(pp. 197-198)

In *The Great American Novel* Roth turns the audience addressed by David Kepesh in *The Breast* — the "morons and madmen" and all "strangers, distracted and unblessed" — into the unheroic heroes of a tale at once bitter and funny, rambling and pointed, realistic and absurd. Like *Vanity Fair*, with which *The Great American Novel*, curiously enough, shares some common themes, Roth's literary adventure might be subtitled a novel without a hero. The "real" subject of the novel is America itself, its literature, its morals, its most pervasive myths. And again, as in "On the Air" and *Our Gang*, Roth explores the incredible and stupefying reality of American public life, the bizarre relation between social convention and personal motivation characterizing, in Roth's view, the cultural predicament facing our country and its citizens.

The narrator of the story, an eighty-seven-year-old sportswriter named Word Smith (a folksy, alliterating prose polisher modeled after Colonel John R. Stingo of the old New York *Evening Inquirer*), is attempting to write the Great American Novel, which, he believes, can best be accomplished by telling the "truth" about the 1943 Ruppert Mundys, a homeless war-time major league baseball team in the now-defunct Patriot League. The Mundys are an accumulation of freaks, misfits, and displaced persons: Nickname Damur, a fourteen-year-old second baseman; John Baal, a gambling, drinking, home-run hitting ex-convict and product of the Nicaraguan leagues; O.K. Ockatur, a midget relief pitcher with a "fierce hatred of all men taller than himself"; Hot Ptah, a hotheaded catcher with a wooden leg; Bud Parusha, a one-armed outfielder who uses his mouth to remove the ball from his glove; Roland Agni, an all-American Adonis who is forced by his father, as a lesson in humility, to bat eighth on the worst team of all time; Ulysses S. Fairsmith, the evangelical and morally stern manager who is literally driven to his death by the inept Mundys; Gil Gamesh, one-time star who returns from exile to manage the last-place Mundys. It is the baleful fate of the Mundys, exiled from their home in Port Ruppert, New Jersey, and forced to wander across the face of the country, that contains the key, the narrator believes, to understanding "the enemy within," the forces that produce perpetual pain and homelessness not simply for the Mundys, but for most Americans. As Smith tells us, "the fortunate reader who has never felt himself a stranger in his own land may pick up some idea of what it is like."

What most outrages Smith is that those in authority and power have waged a concerted and successful battle to surpress the truth about the Mundys, the Patriot League, and even the very origins of the game of baseball:

> My quarrel with Cooperstown, however, is over nothing so inconsequential as who invented the game and where. I only draw attention to the longevity of this lie to reveal how without conscience even the highest authorities are when it comes to perpetuating a comforting, mindless myth everyone has grown used to, and how reluctant the ordinary believer, or fan, is to surrender one. When both the rulers and the subjects of the Holy Baseball Empire can sanctify a blatant falsehood with something supposedly so hallowed as a "Hall of Fame," there is no reason to be astonished (I try to tell myself) at the colossal crime against the truth that has been

perpetrated by America's powers-that-be ever since 1946. I am speaking of what no one in this country dares ever to mention any longer. I am speaking of a chapter of our past that has been torn from the record books without so much as a peep of protest, *except by me.* I am speaking of a rewriting of our history as heinous as any ordered by a tyrant dictator abroad. Not thousand-year-old history either, but something that only came to an end *twenty-odd years ago.* Yes, I am speaking of the annihilation of the Patriot League. Not merely wiped out of business, *but willfully erased from the national memory.* (p. 16)

Again and again Smith asserts his belief that an important part of America's past has been blotted out by the powers-that-be because "the truth to them has no meaning! The real human past has no importance! They distort and falsify to suit themselves! They feed the American public fairy tales and lies! Out of arrogance! Out of shame! Out of their terrible guilty conscience!" And why should the authorities lie? The "profit motive," to "fleece the public!"

Economic opportunism is to *The Great American Novel* what political opportunism is to *Our Gang.* Consider, for example, the exploits of Frank Mazuma, owner of the Kakoola Reapers and a man who "could out-bizarre you any day of the week." It is Mazuma who thinks of recruiting Bob Yamm, the first midget ever to play the major leagues, reasoning that if the fans "wanted to make a hero out of somebody who was only forty inches high, that was their business — especially as it was good for business." Yamm and his wife Judy capture the hearts of the country and, after Yamm's retirement from baseball, the Democrats and Republicans agree that the time is ripe to send a midget to Congress, while three major film companies bid for the movie rights to the Bob Yamm story. Meanwhile, Mazuma, having purchased the one-armed Bud Parusha from the Mundys, proceeds to capitalize on his acquisition by holding a bizarre and tasteless pre-game ceremony to demonstrate to the public that Parusha does indeed have only one arm. As Mazuma explains to the press, "Do you think I want you boys leaving here half-believing that you've been had? . . . Do you think I want our brave allies to harbor the slightest suspicion that this is a country run by con-men and crooks?"

Of course, one of the main points of *The Great American Novel* is that the Patriot League is indeed run by con-men and crooks. Roth leaves little doubt that the Patriot League represents America, just as the homeless Ruppert Mundys represent the ordinary citizens who have been victimized by the insatiable greed and insane thirst for power of those at the top of the socio-economic structure. "The fate of the Mundys and of the republic were inextricably bound together," says Smith, and the "R" that once stood for Ruppert "must henceforth be considered to stand for nothing less than this great Republic." But just as Hester Prynne's scarlet letter takes on different meanings, so does the scarlet "R" at various times stand for "rootless," "ridiculous," "refugee." The embattled Gil Gamesh (who, like his counterpart in the Babylonian epic *Gilgamesh*, is forced to wander through the world for his sin of thinking himself superior to his fellow man) returns from exile in Russia to tell his fellow Ruppert Mundys a hard and hate-filled truth:

> *You* are the true Mundys, boys, and not because it was the name of your robber-baron father, either! No, because it is short for Mundane! Meaning *common*, meaning *ordinary* — meaning the man in the street who's fed up to here with the Muny [*sic*!] brothers and their ilk dancing the rhumba down in Rio while the ordinary Joe toils without honor and without reward! . . . What the hell good is a country to you

anyway, if there is no place in it you can call your own?
(pp. 346-347)

In commenting on his *Our Gang,* Roth had said that he hoped to shock the reader "for the purpose of challenging habitual beliefs and values; for the purpose of dislocating the reader, getting him to view a familiar subject in a way he may be unwilling to, or unaccustomed to. . . ."[8] Clearly, Roth wrote *The Great American Novel* to convey a similar shock. Roth has endured in believing that American reality repels and stupefies the artist, and "for a writer of fiction to feel that he does not really live in the country in which he lives . . . must certainly seem a serious occupational impediment." (*WAF*, p. 225) Yet from the ponderous treatment of "homelessness" in *Letting Go* through the increasingly bitter and "shocking" treatment of the same theme in *Portnoy's Complaint,* "On the Air," and *The Great American Novel,* Roth has continued to hold on to the American landscape as subject matter for his fiction, exploring the traditional Jewish themes of persecution and exile from a distinctly American point of view. Norman Podhoretz recently suggested, no doubt because of the negativism of Roth's viewpoint, that Roth was anti-American, but, as Wilfred Sheed says, this is as absurd as calling Dickens anti-British: "There is no other frame of reference for Roth, no world outside America. It is his Universe, his Good and Evil."[9]

In *The Great American Novel* — written, interestingly enough, at a time when critics are again proclaiming loudly that the novel is dead — Roth reaffirms his belief that American public life provides both the audience and the subject for the writer of fiction. What Roth has attempted to do in *The Great American Novel* is essentially what he attempted to do in *Our Gang* — to attack the "unreality" of some of the grander social and political phenomena of our times rather than withdraw from the field. In speaking of *Our*

Gang, Roth says that he had attempted "to demonstrate that there is a world of feeling and ideas and values that remains un-impressed by the Official Version of Reality. Frustrated as we are in the face of governmental treachery and stupidity and heartlessness, we still have the right to hate our governors for the deeds they perpetrate in our name and at our expense...."[10] It is precisely this stance that Roth takes in *The Great American Novel.* At the end of the novel Word Smith asserts that truth is indeed stranger than fiction, "but stranger still are lies." He compares himself and his novel to the work of the "traitor" Solzhenitsyn, for he knows that *The Great American Novel* "is at variance with the U.S. Government Officially Authorized Version of Reality." Of course we cannot overlook the fact that Smith, too, is offering only a "version" of reality, one that is wildly inventive and fantastic; nevertheless, like his "precursors and kinsmen" Hawthorne and Melville, Smith is, as Roth has recently said, "in search of some encapsulating fiction, or legend, that would, in its own oblique, charged, and cryptic way, constitute 'the truth' about the national disease."[11]

Roth does not claim that *The Great American Novel* is by any means great; rather, he views this novel as the fulfillment of "the task of *not* writing a great book."[12] He prefers to see the novel as an adventure into comic "recklessness," an attempt at demythologizing some of his earlier pretensions about the high seriousness of art. But although it departs from the high seriousness of Roth's earlier novels, *The Great American Novel* reflects, like earlier works, Roth's perception of the ongoing struggle between the individual and his culture, a culture that is becoming, in Roth's view, increasingly "unreal." In fact, Roth says, he is not at all sure what America is really like, and "*not* knowing, or no longer knowing for sure, is just what perplexes many of the people who live and work here and consider this country home. That, if I may say so, is precisely why I invented that para-noid fantasist Word Smith...."[13]

Despite its "reckless" and unrealistic aspects — and despite Roth's assertion that the novel is dedicated only to "playful" comic invention — we can see in *The Great American Novel* Roth's continuing attempt to reflect the changing face of American public life. Given Roth's conviction that a "fierce, oftentimes wild and pathological assault [was] launched in the sixties against venerable American institutions and beliefs,"[14] Roth's depiction of a paranoid fantasist attacking the institution of baseball takes on clear social implications indeed. As Roth says, it was the sixties decade and its "social phenomena that furnished me with a handle by which to take hold of baseball, of all things, and place it at the center of a novel. It was not a matter of demythologizing baseball — there was nothing in that to get fired up about — but of discovering in baseball the means to dramatize *the struggle* between the benign national myth of itself that a great power prefers to perpetuate, and the relentlessly insidious, very nearly demonic reality (like the kind we had known in the sixties) that simply will not give an inch in behalf of that idealized mythology."[15] Certainly Word Smith's "struggle" is marked by high flights into the comic and fantastic, but Roth emphasizes the serious — and realistic — undertones of that struggle when he insists that Smith's "version of history has its origins in something that we all recognize as *having taken place*" and that Smith's fantasies are "not so unlike the sort of fantasies with which the national imagination began to be plagued during this last demythologizing decade of disorder, upheaval, assassination, and war."[16]

If, as Roth contends, the decade of the sixties was the demythologizing decade, characterized by paranoia, fantasy, and the fall of mythologies, *The Great American Novel* reflects that decade and its demonic reality with a fiercely comic accuracy that testifies to Roth's persistence in examining the absurdities in the grander social and political phenomena of American life — satirically, "absurdly," without giving an inch to the "incredible credible" of benign myth and demonic fact.

In turning to satire and absurdity, Roth finds a viable mode for expressing his discontent with American public life, while at the same time he exploits one of the richest veins of his own talent. In 1963 Roth said, "I think what one feels in America is that there are still the ignorant, the stupid and the cruel" (*SDI*, p. 72) — exactly those qualities that Roth attacks with increasing openness and directness in *Portnoy's Complaint*, "On the Air," *Our Gang*, and *The Great American Novel*. In assessing this shift in Roth's artistic technique, Dwight MacDonald goes so far as to assert that in *Portnoy's Complaint* Roth found his "true voice" (a conclusion with which many critics agree) and that he "discovered his congenial mode, satire, and his natural style, the vernacular, which he used with an unerring ear to get humorous effects that are most serious when they are funniest."[17] This shift to the vernacular and the satirical is, certainly, the most observable and most predominant characteristic in Roth's development as a writer, and "On the Air," *Our Gang* and *The Great American Novel* add weight to MacDonald's assessment of Roth's direction of development. However, Roth's *The Breast* (1972) is clearly neither satirical nor vernacular, even though the novella is laced with absurdist and "fantastic" elements (Roth says of *The Breast*, "If I had intended to write a satire, even of the most muted kind, I would have flashed an entirely different set of signals from the coach's box to the reader"[18]). And Roth's latest novel, *My Life As A Man*, clearly represents Roth's return to his earlier realistic treatments of obsessed selves trying to break free of moral and psychological obsessions. It seems, then, that some qualification of MacDonald's over-simplified thesis is needed.

The Breast is Roth's most innovative and, in some respects, his most complex literary effort. At the same time, however, this short, brilliant novel is a logical, if extreme, extension of Roth's most essential artistic concerns. The central character, Professor David Alan Kepesh, is cut from the same cloth as

Neil Klugman, Gabe Wallach, and Paul Herz. By his own admission "a serious and intelligent person" and "a citadel of sanity," Kepesh has for several years lived the quiet, sensible life of a lecturer in comparative literature. With a broken marriage and five years of psychoanalysis behind him, Kepesh finds contentment and comfort with "the even-tempered and the predictable," which in his case means a gratifying affair with Claire Ovington, a fourth-grade teacher and former Cornell Phi Beta Kappa whose "dependable sobriety" contributes to Kepesh's orderly and stable life. It is, then, with surprise and dismay that Kepesh awakes on the morning of February 18, 1971, to find himself metamorphosed into a six-foot female breast "such as could only appear, one would have thought, in a dream or a Dali painting." His predicament is, of course, absurd, but it is neither imagined or imaginary. Like Portnoy and Lippman, Kepesh grudgingly comes to the perception that his absurd situation is the real thing, no joking matter:

> Alas, what has happened to me is like nothing anyone has ever known: beyond understanding, beyond compassion, beyond comedy, though there are those, I know, who claim to be on the brink of some conclusive scientific explanation; and those, my faithful visitors, whose compassion is deeply felt, sorrowful and kind; and there are still others — there would have to be — out in the world who cannot help but laugh. And I, at times, am one with them: I understand, I have compassion, I see the joke. If only I could sustain the laughter for more than a few seconds, however — if only it wasn't so brief and so bitter. (p.11)

The Breast is clearly indebted to Kafka's "The Metamorphosis" for both its tone and its subject matter. Like Kafka, Roth utilizes the metamorphosis of his central character to probe the vexations, frustrations, and absurdities suffered by the individual in society; and, like Kafka, Roth asks the reader "to accept the fantastic situation as taking place in the recognizable world"[19] — a request that emphasizes Roth's realistic creed. Despite Kepesh's unusual metamorphosis, the story departs from the "vernacular" style of *Portnoy's Complaint* and "On the Air" and returns to the more serious style of *Letting Go*. As Roth says, "it has the formal design of a rebuttal or a rejoinder, rather than a hallucination or a nightmare. Above all I magined that it would be in the story's best interest to try to be straightforward and direct about this bizarre circumstance...."[20] If we were to imagine Gabe Wallach telling the story of Lippman's plight we would come close to the tone of *The Breast*. As Roth explains, "...It seemed to me that if I was going to come up with anything new (in terms of my own work), it would only be by taking [a] potentially hilarious situation and treating it perfectly seriously."[21]

The startling metamorphosis through which Kepesh goes is handled matter-of-factly with scientific explanations of "massive hormonal influx," an "endocrinopathic catastrophe," and "a hermaphroditic explosion of chromosomes." From his hammock in a private room on the seventh floor of Lenox Hill hospital, Kepesh does valiant battle with his situation, refusing to believe that he has indeed been victimized by his glands. He wryly observes, "The shock of it all had been so enormous that it had taken me nearly six months to question the reality of it." To his psychiatrist, Dr. Klinger, he pours out his disbelief in a complaint that Lippman and Portnoy would understand: "But, look, this isn't happening — it can't!" Unwilling to accept scientific explanations, Kepesh turns to alternative possibilities. Perhaps he has been having a nightmarish dream: "Stop torturing me! *Let me get up*! I howled and cursed at my captors, though of course if it was a dream I was only cursing captors of my own invention." Or if he is not dreaming, surely he has gone insane:

. . .I understood for the first time that I had gone mad. I was not dreaming, I was crazy. There was to be no magical "waking up," no throwing off this nightmare to get up out of bed, to brush my teeth, to drive out on the expressway to Long Island to teach; if there was to be anything (and I prayed that there was and that I was not *so* far gone), it was the long road back, getting better, becoming sane again. And of course the first big step toward recovering my sanity was this realization that my sense of myself as a breast, my life as a breast, was the delusion of a lunatic.   (p. 51)

Or perhaps he has read too much fiction, with the result that life, as Oscar Wilde once observed, has become an imitation of art. With his recollection of Kafka's "The Metamorphosis" and Gogol's "The Nose" in mind, Kepesh confronts Dr. Klinger with yet another possible explanation: "I explained to him that whatever the traumatic event itself had been, it appeared that in order to escape it I had grabbed hold of the handiest preposterous idea, which was the Kafkaesque, Gogolian fantasy of physical transformation that I had been talking about in my classroom only the week preceding the catastrophe."

All of these possibilities are, his psychiatrist insists, merely evasions. As Roth himself says, Kepesh learns by the end of the story that "whatever else it is, it is the real thing: he *is* a breast, and he must act accordingly." [22] Dr. Klinger, who clings to reality with the same tenacity that Kepesh clings to him, refutes each of Kepesh's attempts to deny what has happened: "I can understand the temptation, even the necessity at some point, to give in to the appealing idea that this is all just a dream, a hallucination, a delusion, or what have you — perhaps a drug-induced state," says Dr. Klinger. "But it is none of these things. It is something that has happened to you. And the way *to* madness, Mr. Kepesh, do you hear me? — *the way into madness*, is to pretend otherwise."

It is clear enough that Kepesh is in several ways the culmination of a long line of heroes in Roth's fiction. Like the activist heroes in Roth's early fiction, Kepesh is determined to fathom the mysteries of selfhood so that he can "live by my own lights." But so grotesque is his predicament, so absurdly limited are his possibilities, that he surpasses even Lippman's hopeless victimization. Nevertheless, Kepesh, who, as Theodore Solotaroff conjectures, "might be Portnoy five years later,"[23] turns to every avenue in order to understand the cause and consequence of his victimization. In his immobile hammock he groans, reasons, rationalizes, and celebrates, in an attempt to make some sense of the larger hook he is on (to use the image Gabe Wallach evokes less literally at the end of *Letting Go*). "How I strain to be sane and whole!" cries the desperate Kepesh — the familiar cry of virtually all of Roth's heroes. "I will not be defeated *if only I do not quit*!" But strength of character and the will to live (or "S. of C. and W. to L.," as Kepesh calls them in his discussions with Klinger) are not enough to save Kepesh or to change his predicament. "These banal phrases are the therapeutic equivalent of my lame jokes," explains Kepesh; and then, as if to conclude an argument against the central premise of activist fiction, Kepesh continues, "In these, my preposterous times, we must keep to what is ordinary and familiar."

Despite the grotesque and fabulistic elements, *The Breast* is most interesting in its continuing attack on the ordinary and the familiar. Roth does not allow the reader to forget that Kepesh, like Portnoy, Lucy Nelson, Paul Herz, Novotny and others, has come from a socially "normal" environment, which has placed upon him the same restrictions that have contributed to the inadequate self-definitions of earlier heroes. As Kepesh explains to Dr. Klinger, his upbringing has in no way equipped him to understand, let alone overcome, his absurd predicament:

I was never "strong." Only determined. One foot in
front of the other. Punctuality. Honesty. Courtesy.
Good grades in all subjects. It goes back to handing my
homework in on time and carrying off the prizes. Dr.
Klinger, *it's hideous in here.* I want to quit, I want to go
crazy, to go spinning off, ranting and wild, *but I can't.* I
sob. I scream. I touch bottom. I lay there on that
bottom! But then I come around. I make jokes, a little
bitter and quite lame. I listen to the radio. I listen to the
phonograph. . . . I restrain my rage and restrain my rage
and I wait for you to come again. But this is madness,
this coming around. To be putting one foot in front of
the other is madness *in that I have no feet!* A ghastly
catastrophe has befallen me and I listen to the six
o'clock news! I listen to the weather!   (pp. 22-23)

Early in the story Kepesh believes that his unique
condition provides him with a new perspective on his
heretofore ordinary life: "In the midst of the incredible, the
irredeemably ordinary appears to remind me of the level at
which most of one's life is usually lived. Really it is the
silliness, the triviality, the *meaninglessness* of experience that
one misses most in a state like this." What he comes to discover,
however, is that even his metamorphosis does not lift him
above the triviality, nor does his changed state bring with it
special privileges. His father, Abe, his mistress, Claire, and his
colleague at Stony Brook, Arthur Schonbrunn, serve as
reminders of the banality that insistently impinges on
Kepesh's life. Abe regales his son with "incredible" stories of
mixed marriages and local news. Claire continues to lavish
sexual favors with "imperturbability" on the metamorphosed
Kepesh, and the stodgy, pedantic Schonbrunn, after giggling
hysterically on first seeing him, sends Kepesh, by way of
apology, an LP recording of the Laurence Olivier version of
Hamlet. Most forceful of all, however, is Dr. Klinger, who

insists that Kepesh's only salvation is to accommodate himself to the reality of his situation — to the meaningless-ness and triviality and silliness, *not* of being a breast, but of being human. Kepesh's initial response is understandable outrage, but in that outrage is the central theme of the novel: "This is no longer ordinary life and I am not going to pretend that it is! *You* want me to be *ordinary* — *you* expect me to be *ordinary* in this condition! I'm supposed to be a sensible man — when I am like this! . . . There's the madness, Doctor, *being sensible*!"

Certainly John Gardner is correct in saying that *The Breast* gives Roth a chance "to reconsider (lightly and slyly, of course) the whole theory of the non-realistic novel." [24] One can go further, however, by saying that *The Breast* is a devastating, if somewhat oblique, examination of the stupe-fying, incredible, frustrating experience of living in America — "the Land of Opportunity in the Age of Self-Fulfillment," as Kepesh says with no little irony. Roth, after suggesting that "perhaps a man who turns into a breast is the first truly heroic character I've ever been able to portray," points out his intentions in *The Breast*: "I want the reader to accept the fantastic situation as taking place in what we call the real world at the same time that I hope to make the reality of the horror one of the issues of the story." [25] What needs to be added, however, is that Kepesh's problem as a breast is, paradoxically, to be understood as a human problem. As Kepesh says near the end of the story, "This is not tragedy anymore than it is farce. It is only life, and, like it or not, I am only human." In attempting to accommodate himself to American society, Kepesh reasons — and here the comment on economic opportunism and the social theme are obvious — that if the Beatles can fill Shea Stadium, so can he. If Charles Manson and the Rolling Stones can attract twelve-year-old girls, so can he. If his father, his mother, and his mistress can heroically endure the absurdity of their normal lives, so can he. Kepesh need not turn to fantasy or theories of wish-fulfillment to explain his predicament, for, as he himself realizes, "Reality is grander than that. Reality has more style."

When Roth gives his view of Kepesh, there is no mention of the fantastic metamorphosis. Rather, he insists that Kepesh's problem is one that has an "epistemological dimension," connected as it is with the difficulties of self-definition in America: "Kepesh is *lost* — somewhat in the way that Descartes claims to be lost at the beginning of the *Meditations*: 'I am certain that I am, but what am I? What is there that can be esteemed true?' " [26] The human-ness of Kepesh's predicament is underscored by Klinger, who throughout the novel represents attitudes of an objective, rational realist who has (as Roth says in the June, 1974 *Literary Guild*) a "homely, anti-apocalyptic, de-mystifying view of things":

> There is no disease in the psychic realm. That is to say there has been none thus far. There has been shock, panic, fury, despair, disorientation, profound feelings of helplessness and isolation, deep depression, but through it all, quite miraculously, nothing I would call disease.
> (p. 57)

What Kepesh suffers is, in the final analysis, the debilitating helplessness, fury, and despair afflicting most of Roth's heroes. Kepesh decides to tell the world his story in his own words, for society would otherwise surely misunderstand: "Better famous by way of the truth than by way of sadistic gossip and crazy tabloid fantasy. Better from me, surely, than from the madmen and morons out there." The question that *The Breast* raises is, then, the question asked by Roth's earlier "Eli, the Fanatic." Who in American society is crazy and who is sane? The scope of Kepesh's last words is revealing, for his address is to "morons and madmen, tough guys and skeptics, friends, students, relatives, colleagues, and all you strangers, distracted and unblessed" — all of whom are "my fellow mammalians," the final joke.

If Kepesh is most human when he is a breast, his readers "out there" are most breast-like when they are human, the last irony and certainly the most important one in the story. Yet education *is* possible, misfortune *can* instruct, metamorphosis *may* happen even for Kepesh's "fellow mammalians" — a hope that Kepesh conveys by citing, at the end of his tale, Rilke's "Archaic Torso of Apollo." His own misfortune allows him to instruct his fellow victims ("Yes, let us proceed with our education, one and all"), and his bizarre predicament allows him, as resident expert in metamorphosis, to call upon Rilke, "particularly his concluding admonition, which is not necessarily as elevated a sentiment as we all might once have liked to believe," to express a warning that is at once abrasive and poignant, radical and desperate: "there is no place/that does not see you. You must change your life."

Unlike *Our Gang* and *The Great American Novel*, *The Breast* has a clear focus on human character — in this case, not surprisingly, on the character of a sensible and sensitive artist-teacher confronted (radically and comically, to be sure) with the mysteries of his own being. In light of the ironic presentation of Kepesh, we might say confidently that Roth has put some distance between himself and the somber sensibility reflected in such works as *Letting Go* and *When She Was Good*; nevertheless, Roth has been quick to point out that the moral and psychological problems treated in *The Breast* may be seen as a continuation of his treatment of such problems in his earlier fiction, and he reminds us that his concern in *The Breast* is with the hero himself, rather than with social satire or social absurdity:

> The question of moral sovereignty, as it is examined in *Letting Go*, *Portnoy's Complaint*, and *The Breast*, is

really a question of the kind of commandment the hero of each book will issue to himself; here the skepticism is directed inwards, upon the hero's ambiguous sense of personal imperatives and taboos. I can think of these characters — Gabe Wallach, Alexander Portnoy, and David Kepesh — as three stages of a single explosive projectile that is fired into the barrier that forms one boundary of the individual's identity and experience: that barrier of personal inhibition, ethical restraint, and plain old conformism and fear, beyond which lies the moral and psychological unknown. Gabe Wallach crashes up against the wall and collapses; Portnoy proceeds on through the fractured mortar, only to become lodged there, half in, half out; it remains for Kepesh to pass right on through the bloodied hole, and out the other end, into no-man's-land. [27]

In his latest work, *My Life As A Man*, Roth — again, in realistic, non-satirical fiction — continues to focus on human character, but he does so as if he were now on the "other side" in no-man's-land. The central character, a serious young Jewish writer-teacher named Peter Tarnopol, looks back through the "bloodied hole" through which he has passed and attempts to explain its presence *there*, his presence *here* on the other side. Having undergone experiences quite as dislocating and painful to him as those suffered by David Kepesh, Tarnopol reconstructs his life as a man by writing fiction and autobiography at Quahsay Colony, an isolated rural Vermont retreat for writers and artists. Through "his" two short stories, "Salad Days" and "Courting Disaster" (which constitute Part I of *My Life As A Man*) and through his long autobiographical narrative, "My True Story" (which constitutes Part II of *My Life As A Man*), Tarnopol makes a retrospective attempt, as he says, to "demystify the past and mitigate his admittedly uncommendable sense of defeat" — an attempt that tantalizes the reader with the complicated yet tenuous relationships existing among author, narrator, fiction, autobiography and actual experience. Demonstrating how complex these relationships are is, in fact, one of the major achievements of *My Life As A Man*. Consider, for example, that to "demystify the past" Roth tells us a story about a Jewish writer, Tarnopol, who is telling us his "true story" in a "nonfictional narrative"; but Tarnopol begins by presenting two short stories in Part I, stories that he has supposedly written about *another* Jewish writer and teacher, Nathan Zuckerman — who in "Courting Disaster" is supposedly telling us *his* true story. Despite these complexities, however, Parts I and II of *My Life As A Man*, when taken together, give a mosaic of the hero's ambiguous sense of personal imperatives — an ambiguity that results when the hero passes, as Tarnopol says, "out of Eden into the real unreal world."

The Peter Tarnopol of Part II and the Nathan Zuckerman of Part I of *My Life As A Man* are in most ways counterparts, which is not surprising in light of Tarnopol's contention that Zuckerman is a fictionalized version of himself. Both are young Jewish writers who, like Kepesh, are in anguished quest of explanations for the strange turns of events that have radically altered the expected course of their lives. Additionally, both are characterized, during their twenties, as intensely "moral" young writers aspiring to high seriousness in their lives and in their creative work. Although Tarnopol, like Roth, considers moving away from such seriousness (Tarnopol says toward the end of his narrative that he will not continue to be "such an Olympian writer as it was my ambition to be back in the days when nothing called personal experience stood between me and aesthetic detachment"), both Tarnopol and Zuckerman are self-admittedly the products — and victims — of values imbedded, mysteriously, in their cultures and their psyches. Roth's assessment of his own early career goes far toward helping us understand the misfortunes suffered by Tarnopol and Zuckerman, men who are, in Tarnopol's words, "sensitive to nothing in all the world as I am to my moral reputation." Roth himself confesses a similar sensitivity when he says of his initial encounter with criticism:

> At that time, still in my twenties, I imagined fiction writing to be something like a religious calling, and literature a kind of sacrament — a sense of things I have had reason to modify since. Such elevated notions aren't uncommon in vain young writers; in my case they dovetailed nicely with ideas of ethical striving that I had absorbed as a Jewish child, and with the salvationist literary ethos in which I had been introduced to high art in the fifties, a decade when cultural, rather than political loyalties, divided the young into the armies of the damned and the cadre of the blessed. I might turn out to be a bad artist, or no artist at all, but having declared myself *for* art — the art of Tolstoy, James, Flaubert, and Mann, whose appeal was as much in their heroic literary integrity as in their works — I imagined I had sealed myself off from being a morally unacceptable person, in others' eyes as well as my own. The last thing I expected, having chosen this vocation — *the* vocation — was to be charged with heartlessness, vengeance, malice, and treachery. Yet that was to be one of the first experiences of importance to befall me out in the world. Ambitious and meticulous (if not wholly enlightened) in conscience, I had gravitated to the genre that constituted the most thoroughgoing investigation of conscience that I knew of — only to be told by more than a few Jews that I was a conscienceless young man holding attitudes uncomfortably close to those of the Nazis. As I saw it then, at twenty-seven, I had to argue in public and in print that I was not at all what they said I was; the characterization was ill-founded, I explained,

and untrue, and yes, I maintained that Conscience and Righteousness were the very words emblazoned upon the banner I believed myself to be marching under, as a writer *and* as a Jew.[28]

The fictionalized genesis and development of an ambitious and meticulous (if not wholly enlightened) Nathan Zuckerman is the subject of "Salad Days" (a third-person narration of Zuckerman's adolescent and college years) and "Courting Disaster" (a first-person narration of Zuckerman's disastrous encounter with matrimony). The supposed author of the Zuckerman tales, Tarnopol, suggests that from a psychological point of view "Salad Days" is "something like a comic idyll honoring a Pannish (and as yet unpunished) id," while "Courting Disaster" may be read as "a legend composed at the behest and under the influence of the superego, my adventures as seen through its eyes." Of the two stories in Part I, which Tarnopol calls "useful fictions," the more useful in illuminating Peter Tarnopol is "Courting Disaster." Tarnopol, a man attached to two inimical realms of experience, suggests himself that the entirety of the nonfiction narrative of Part II of *My Life As A Man* might be thought of as the ego's answer to the superego's questions and imperatives as conveyed by "Courting Disaster" — "the 'I' owning up to its role as ringleader of the plot," says Tarnopol, with self-deprecating irony. However far we may trust Tarnopol's assessment of the psychological implications in the structure of *My Life As A Man*, there is no denying that in "Courting Disaster" Roth returns — even though motivated, perhaps, by an impulse toward self-parody — to both the style and subject matter of his earlier fiction.

Perhaps the most obvious feature of "Courting Disaster" is its avowed intention to explore the milieu of the fifties as experienced by the narrator, Nathan Zuckerman. The subtitle of the story, "Serious in the Fifties," indicates the tone, the theme, and the subject matter of the story; but lest the reader miss the significance of the subtitle, the narrator of the tale digresses from his narration to underscore the point:

> In the story at hand, it would seem to me that from the perspective of this decade particularly, there is much that could be ridiculed having to do with the worship of ordeal and forbearance and the suppression of the sexual man. . . . To some, the funniest thing of all, or perhaps the strangest, may not be how I conducted myself back then, but the literary mode in which I have chosen to narrate my story today: the decorousness, the orderliness, the underlying sobriety, that "responsible" manner that I continue to affect. For not only have literary manners changed drastically since all this happened ten years ago, back in the middle fifties, but I myself am hardly who I was or wanted to be.   (p. 81)

Here we see that Roth (obliquely, of course, through the Zuckerman and Tarnopol personas) is returning to the style and subject matter of his earlier fiction. The narrator is, like Gabe Wallach and David Kepesh, a young Jewish professor of English literature. At the time of narration he, like Gabe, is living in exile in Europe where he ponders the puzzling forces, both personal and social, that have caused him to act in ways that seem diametrically opposed to his earliest ideals and his own best interests. But as if Zuckerman himself were rejecting the author of *Portnoy's Complaint,* "On the Air," and *Our Gang,* he declares that he intends to complete his story "in a traditional narrative mode": "I leave it to those writers who live in the flamboyant American present, and whose extravagant fictions I sample from afar, to treat the implausible, the preposterous, and the bizarre in something other than a straightforward and recognizable manner." The conscious intention of Zuckerman to return to a decorous, orderly, traditional narrative mode is further suggested by Zuckerman's confession that he is quite aware that his "subject" *could* be treated in a comic mode:

> To the reader who "believes" in Zuckerman's predica-
> ment as I describe it, but is unwilling to take such a
> person as seriously as I do, let me say that I am tempted
> to make fun of him myself. To treat this story as a
> species of comedy would not require more than a slight
> alteration in tone and attitude. In graduate school, for a
> course titled "Advanced Shakespeare," I once wrote a
> paper on *Othello* proposing just such a shift in emphasis.
> (p. 80)

At this point the similarities between Zuckerman and Roth become evident. In a recent interview Roth said that after *When She Was Good* he was aching to turn his themes of suffering and guilt into "something extravagant and funny." Interestingly, *Othello* played a part in his next fictional work, the extravagant and funny *Portnoy's Complaint*: "It was all so *funny*, this morbid preoccupation with punishment and guilt. . . . Hadn't I recently sat smirking through a perfor-mance of 'Othello'? And not just because it was badly done either, but because something in that bad performance revealed how *dumb* Othello is."[29] In "Courting Disaster," however, Roth is clearly returning to the narrative mode of *Letting Go* and *When She Was Good*. Roth concluded "Salad Days," his third-person narration of Zuckerman's early life, the teenage years, by declaring:

> The story of Zuckerman's suffering calls for an ap-
> proach far more *serious* than that which seems appro-
> priate to the tale of his easeful salad days. To narrate
> with fidelity the misfortunes of Zuckerman's twenties
> would require deeper dredging, a darker sense of irony,

a grave and pensive voice to replace the amused,
Olympian point of view . . . or maybe what that story requires is neither gravity nor complexity, but just another
author, someone who would see it too for the simple five-
thousand-word comedy that it very well may have been.
Unfortunately, the author of this story, having himself
experienced a similar misfortune at about the same age,
does not have it in him, even yet, midway through his
thirties, to tell it briefly or to find it funny.   (p. 31)

Roth does "discover" another author for the tale of
Zuckerman's twenties, Zuckerman himself — and yet *another*
author, Tarnopol — but Zuckerman as author-narrator of
"Courting Disaster" is like Tarnopol in that he finds it
impossible to regard a personal collapse as either simple or
funny.

Rejecting the comic tone and attitude of *Portnoy's
Complaint* and "On the Air" and returning to a more serious
and traditional narrative mode, Roth explores the atmosphere of the fifties to which the characters in "Courting
Disaster" pay tribute. The narrator, Zuckerman, is in some
senses the composite Rothian hero, the sensitive man of
feeling who longs for self-fulfillment and purity (at one point
Zuckerman cries, "Oh, how I wanted a soul that was pure
and spotless!"), but who finds himself entrapped by attitudes
and values embedded in his environment. Like Portnoy, Gabe
Wallach, and Paul Herz, Nathan discovers in himself a division
between duty and passion, between obedience to social
mores and a commitment to personal yearnings; like
Novotny, he is beset with inexplicable pains (in Nathan's
case, migraine headaches) that begin with army life; like Neil
Klugman, he has a desire to see beneath the surface of his
pretensions, and for both Neil and Nathan the library is a
symbol of the ordered, tranquil, paradisiacal life; and, again
like Portnoy, Nathan is both attracted to and repelled by gen-

tile women who cast him into the role of savior — a role that gives him limited access into the treacherous, barbaric, but nonetheless enticing world of *goyim*. The costs of acting "morally," the difficulties of behaving responsibly, the pressures of living conventionally in America of the fifties — all these are concerns that have dominated Roth's fiction. In "Courting Disaster" Roth gives these concerns his most concentrated and coherent expression.

"Courting Disaster" traces the rise, fall and exile of Nathan Zuckerman, a bright young teacher and writer who finds himself perversely attracted to Lydia Ketterer, an unattractive, sexless divorcee whose life has been marked by one disaster after another. At the age of twelve, Lydia had been seduced by her own father; subsequently, she had married the sadistic Eugene Ketterer, a savage, gross, ugly man whose favorite pastime had been to hurl Lydia against the wall of their small apartment. The only results produced by the short-lived marriage are a doltish daughter, Monica, and a nervous breakdown for Lydia. At this point in Lydia's tragic life Zuckerman appears. The question that, in retrospect, obsesses Nathan is why a conventional, sober young man like himself should be so implausibly drawn to such a victimized woman. Is it perhaps *because* Lydia had been so victimized? At one point in his reflections, Zuckerman believes that this must be the case:

> I was drawn to Lydia, not out of a passion for Monica — not yet — but because she had suffered so and because she was so brave. Not only that she had survived, but *what* she had survived, gave her enormous moral stature, or glamor, in my eyes: on the one hand, the puritan austerity, the prudery, the blandness, the xenophobia of the women of her clan; on the other, the criminality of the men. Of course, I did not equate being raped by one's father with being raised on the wisdom of the

Chicago Tribune; what made her seem to me so valiant
was that she had been subjected to every brand of
barbarity, from the banal to the wicked, had been
exploited, beaten, and betrayed by every last one of her
keepers, had finally been driven crazy — and in the end
had proved indestructible. . . .   (p. 70)

Against every conscious instinct, Nathan finds himself
perversely drawn to Lydia even though he "loathed making
love to her" and "wished to be rid of her." Just as his
"missionary spirit" leads him in his teaching to wage "a kind
of guerrilla war against the army of slobs, philistines, and
barbarians who seemed to me to control the national mind,
either through the media or the government," so does he
explain his love-making to Lydia as an act of salvation, *"as
though that would redeem us both."* Although intellectually
appealing, such a notion hardly does justice, Nathan perceives, to the destructive attraction he has for such misery —
an attraction that leads to his marrying Lydia, to her suicide
four years later, and to his subsequent flight to Italy with the
imbecilic Monica, who has become his mistress. Late in the
story the narrator pauses to reflect on the inadequacy of his
attempts to explain his attraction for a "uniformly dismal
situation":

To the reader who has not just "gotten the drift," but
begun to balk at the uniformly dismal situation that I
have presented here, to the reader who finds himself
unable to suspend his disbelief in a protagonist who
voluntarily sustains an affair with a woman sexless to
him and so disaster-ridden, I should say that in
retrospect I find him nearly impossible to believe in
myself. Why should a young man otherwise reasonable,
farsighted, watchful, judicious, and self-concerned, a
man meticulously precise in the bread-and-butter

concerns of life, and the model of husbandry with his endowment, why should he pursue, in this obviously weighty encounter, a course so *defiantly* not in his interest? For the sake of defiance? Does that convince *you*?. . . I look in vain for anything resembling a genuine sense of religious mission — that which sends mission- aries off to convert the savages or to minister to lepers — or for the psychological abnormality pronounced enough to account for this preposterous behavior. To make *some* sort of accounting, the writer emphasizes Lydia's "moral glamor" and develops, probably with more thoroughness than is engrossing, the idea of Zuckerman's "seriousness," even going so far, in the subtitle, as to describe that seriousness as something of a social phenomenon; but to be frank, it does not seem, even to the author, that he has, suggestive subtitle and all, answered the objection of implausibility, any more than the young man Zuckerman's own prestigious interpretations of his migraines seemed to him con- sonant with the pain itself. And to bring words like "enigmatic" and "mysterious" into the discussion not only goes against my grain, but hardly seems to make things any less inconceivable.   (pp. 79-80)

As is readily evident, "Courting Disaster," like Malamud's *The Tenants,* is a story that deals in part with the problems of writing a story, of rendering a believable picture of the "mystery of personality" as it unfolds in the impenetrable climate of a cultural milieu. What Zuckerman discovers is what virtually every hero, activist or victim, in Roth's fiction discovers: "I was supposed to be elsewhere and otherwise. This is not the life I worked and planned for! Was made for!" The problems confronting Zuckerman the character are in part the same problems that confront Zuckerman (Roth) the author: how can one explain the incredible turns of personality in a credible way? How can one turn the actually unbelievable into the fictionally believable? How can one realistically account for the sense of shame and humiliation deriving from the American experience, an experience that drives one, like the fictional heroes of Dostoevski and Ellison, to withdrawal and retreat? Zuckerman, who stands for both the author and the hero, flees to Europe, where he feels "the panic of the escaped convict who imagines the authorities have picked up his scent — only I am the authority as well as the escapee. *For I do want to go home.*" But home, for the sensitive Zuckerman, means returning to a classroom "as perplexing as a Kafka courtroom" and to a domestic scene where "there was murder in the air." Even the great European writers — Mann, Tolstoy, Gogol, Proust — offer him no enduring moral strength, and he concludes, "I can't imagine that I shall ever have the courage to return to live in Chicago, or anywhere in America":

> The country may have changed, I have not. I did not know such depths of humiliation were possible, even for me. A reader of Conrad's *Lord Jim* and Mauriac's *Thérèse* and Kafka's "Letter to His Father," of Hawthorne and Strindberg and Sophocles — of Freud! — and still I did not know that humiliation could do such a job on a man. It seems either that literature too strongly influences my ideas about life, or that I am able to make no connection at all between its wisdom and my existence. For I cannot fully believe in the hopelessness of my predicament, and yet the line that concludes *The Trial* is as familiar to me as my own face: "It was as if the shame of it must outlive him"! Only I am not a character in a book, certainly not *that* book. I am real. And my humiliation is equally *real. . . .* How I wanted a dignified life! And how confident I was!   (pp. 86-87)

"Courting Disaster" is of interest for a study of Roth primarily because the story brings to the surface both the subject matter and the technique that Roth had utilized in his early fiction, particularly *Letting Go*. Certain that Roth was following in the tracks of Bellow, critics as different as Helen Weinberg, Arthur Mizener, Alfred Kazin, and Baruch Hochman complained that *Letting Go* was unaccountably gloomy and that its hero, Gabe Wallach, was childish, whining, and ineffectual. Theodore Solotaroff was the only critic to perceive that Roth was attempting to capture the particular mood of the fifties, a backdrop against which the moral life of the hero was to be examined:

> It was a time when the deferred gratifications of graduate school and the climb to tenure ... seemed the warranty of "seriousness" and "responsibility": those solemn passwords of a generation that practiced a Freudian/Jamesian concern about motives, pondered E.M. Forster's "only connect," and subscribed to Lionel Trilling's "moral realism" and "tragic sense of life."[30]

In "Courting Disaster" Roth returns to precisely this area of interest. Through Nathan Zuckerman he explores the difficulties not only of heroic self-assertion but also of articulating, in fiction that is both "moral" and "realistic," the motives behind the actions taken by the hero. At the end of "Courting Disaster" Zuckerman recognizes that Lydia had accepted him "as her means of salvation," but he is incapable — as Augie March and Henderson are not — of understanding his own motives: "She saw the way out of her life's misery, and I, in the service of Perversity or Chivalry or Morality or Misogyny or Saintliness or Folly or Pent-up Rage or Psychic Illness or Sheer Lunacy or Innocence or Ignorance or Experience or Heroism or Judaism or Masochism or Self-Hatred or Defiance or Soap Opera or Romantic Opera or the

Art of Fiction perhaps, or none of the above, or maybe all of
the above and more — I found the way into mine." Roth had
asserted in "Writing American Fiction" that the mystery of
personality is the writer's ultimate concern, but that activist
writers attempted to assert the self rather than understand it.
As Zuckerman's last words suggest, human action is far more
complex than writers of activist fiction make it out to be, far
more complex, in fact, than even Roth's own Gabe Wallach,
Lucy Nelson, and Alexander Portnoy perceive.

In Part II of *My Life As A Man*, entitled "My True Story,"
Roth continues to investigate the complexities of marriage as
they impinge, painfully, on the consciousness of the thirty-
four-year-old narrator, Peter Tarnopol. Tarnopol is able to
bring more perception to these complexities than Zuckerman, in part because, as the supposed author of the
Zuckerman stories in Part I, he is able to comment on the
limitations of any one fictionalized stance and "voice" to
convey the whole truth of the mystery of personality. Of
course the complicated wrinkle of a double-narrator allows
Roth to put some additional esthetic distance between
himself and the quasi-autobiographical material explored in
My Life As A Man (Tarnopol is keenly aware of legal and
ethical problems that could result from his "nonfictional"
memoirs, but he is convinced that "it's in the nature of being
a novelist to make private life public — that's a part of what a
novelist is up to"); more importantly, however, the double-
narrator device allows Roth to explore, through Tarnopol,
complexities that the straightlaced Zuckerman cannot
fathom. Indeed, Tarnopol, as supposed author of the
Zuckerman stories, goes so far as to send copies of "Salad
Days" and "Courting Disaster" to his "real life" family,
friends, and associates, recording both "actual" and imagined
responses. Through a narrator such as Tarnopol, Roth is able
to give depth and perspective to his depiction of the
psychological obsession at the center of *My Life As A Man*.

At the same time, author-narrator-central character Tarnopol serves as a highly effective medium through which Roth can articulate, with both the ironic detachment of a Zuckerman and the passionate intensity of a Kepesh, some of the more puzzling and intractable ambiguities confronting the contemporary Jew, writer, and man. Tarnopol emphasizes both his detachment and his intense involvement in his attempts to penetrate the psychological "conspiracy-to-abscond-with-my-life" when he says of himself:

> Tarnopol, as he is called, is beginning to seem as imaginary as my Zuckermans anyway, or at least as detached from the memoirist — his revelations coming to seem like still another "useful fiction," and not because I am telling lies. I am trying to keep to the facts. Maybe all I'm saying is that words, being words, only approximate the real thing, and so no matter how close I come, I only come *close*. Or maybe I mean that as far as I can see there is no conquering or exorcising the past with words — words born either of imagination or forthrightness — as there seems to be (for me) no forgetting it. Maybe I am just learning what a past is. At any rate, all I can do with my story is tell it. And tell it. And tell it. And *that's* the truth.   (p. 231)

In light of Tarnopol's stance toward the difficulties of telling the "truth" in words, Roth's own comments about his narrator in the June, 1974 *Literary Guild* are illuminating indeed: "To my mind, Tarnopol's attempt to realize himself with the right words — as earlier in life he attempted realizing himself through the right deeds — is what's at the heart of the book, and is what accounts, clearly, for my joining his fictions about his life with his autobiography.... I would hope that when the novel is considered in its entirety, it will be understood as Peter Tarnopol's struggle to achieve a description."

At his isolated Vermont retreat Tarnopol pieces together the true history of his past, "the real thing," in five related stories. The third and central story, "Marriage à la Mode," is, however, the most significant, for it not only joins Tarnopol most clearly to Zuckerman but it also describes the crucial event that colors and controls all subsequent action in "My True Story": Tarnopol's disastrous marriage to his nemesis and victimizer, Maureen Johnson. It is a marriage that sends him reeling into unfulfilling affairs with women and equally unfulfilling psychoanalytic sessions with Dr. Otto Spielvogel and that forces him finally to confront the ultimate of mysteries: himself.

The action of "Marriage à la Mode" takes place principally between 1958 and 1960, a period during which Tarnopol had settled in a Lower East Side apartment to carve out a career as a writer of fiction. In 1958, the twenty-four-year-old Tarnopol envisions himself as a "nice Jewish boy from Westchester who cared only about Success," but not the conventional success of his friends and colleagues:

> I did not think of myself as an ordinary or conventional university graduate of those times. My college acquaintances were all off becoming lawyers and doctors; a few who had been friends on the Brown literary magazine were working on advanced degrees in literature — prior to my induction into the army, I had myself served a year and a half in the Ph.D. program at the University of Chicago, before falling by the wayside, a casualty of "Bibliography" and "Anglo-Saxon"; the rest — the fraternity boys, the athletes, the business majors, those with whom I'd had little association at school — were by now already married and holding down nine-to-five jobs. Of course I dressed in blue button-down oxford shirts and wore my hair clipped short, but what else was I to wear, a serape? long curls? This was 1958. Besides, there were other ways in which it seemed to me I was

> distinguishable from the mass of my contemporaries: I
> read books and I wanted to write them. My master was
> not Mammon or Fun or Propriety, but Art, and Art of
> the earnest moral variety.   (p. 174)

Having published several short stores in literary magazines
and having begun writing *A Jewish Father,* his first "serious
novel dense with moral ambiguity," Tarnopol is in no way
prepared for the catastrophic shaking of his ordered world
when there appears in his life "that temptingly unknown
creature of a young man's eroto-heroic imaginings, *an older
woman.*"

   Tarnopol's attraction to the older woman, twenty-nine-
year-old Maureen Johnson, is, like Zuckerman's attraction to
Lydia Ketterer, an inexplicable phenomenon. Tarnopol
admits that he liked "something taxing in my love affairs,
something problematical and puzzling," and that Maureen's
"chaotic, daredevil background had a decidedly exotic and
romantic appeal." Her divorces from Mezik, "a heavy drinker
with a strong right hook," and from Walker, a homosexual
actor, make the tough-minded, embattled Maureen enticing
to Tarnopol, perhaps because she was "the first person of her
sex I had ever known intimately to be so completely adrift
and on her own." What Tarnopol discovers, however, is what
other Roth heroes discovered before him: the apparently
victimized Maureen becomes victimizer, leeching onto
Tarnopol's life with the viciousness of a vampire. "Imagine
the meaning she must have found," says Tarnopol, "in
one whose youthful earnestness and single-minded de-
votion to a high artistic calling might magically become
her own if only she could partake forever of his flesh and
blood."

   It is precisely this highminded earnestness that makes
Tarnopol so ill-equipped to deal with the conniving Maureen.
When he finally summons the courage to expel her from his

apartment, Maureen immediately — and successfully — deceives Tarnopol by claiming to be pregnant, a claim that she substantiates with the trumped-up results of a pregnancy test. What can Tarnopol do except make the "morally responsible" and "manly" decision to marry Maureen? In accents that Gabe Wallach, Paul Herz, David Kepesh, and Nathan Zuckerman would certainly understand, an older and wiser Tarnopol looks back in time through the "bloodied hole" to evaluate his early crisis:

> It seemed then that I was making one of those moral decisions that I had heard so much about in college literature courses. But how different it all had been up in the Ivy League, when it was happening to Lord Jim and Kate Croy and Ivan Karamazov instead of to me. Oh, what an authority on dilemmas I had been in the senior honors seminar! Perhaps if I had not fallen so in love with these complicated fictions of moral anguish, I never would have taken that long anguished walk to the Upper West Side and back, and arrived at what seemed to me the only "honorable" decision for a young man as morally "serious" as myself. But then I do not mean to attribute my ignorance to my teachers, or my delusions to books. Teachers and books are still the best things that ever happened to me, and probably had I not been so grandiose about my honor, my integrity, and my manly duty, about "morality itself," I would never have been so susceptible to a literary education and its attendant pleasures to begin with. Nor would I have embarked upon a literary career. And it's too late now to say that I shouldn't have, that by becoming a writer I only exacerbated my debilitating obsession. Literature got me into this and literature is gonna have to get me out. My writing is all I've got now, and though it happens not to have made life easy for me either in the

years since my auspicious debut, it is really all I trust.

My trouble in my middle twenties was that rich with confidence and success, I was not about to settle for complexity and depth in books alone. Stuffed to the gills with great fiction — entranced not by cheap romances, like Madame Bovary, but by *Madame Bovary* — I now expected to find in everyday experience that same sense of the difficult and the deadly earnest that informed the novels I admired most. My model of reality, deduced from reading the masters, had at its heart *intractability*. And here it was, a reality as obdurate and recalcitrant and (in addition) as awful as any I could have wished for in my most bookish dreams.
(pp. 193-194)

As the story closes, Tarnopol talks to his father on the phone, explaining that he is marrying Maureen because "I'm doing what I want." Unspoken are the words that convey his true feeling: *"Take me home. This isn't what I want to do. You're right, there's something wrong with her: the woman is mad. Only I gave my word!"* Finally Tarnopol hangs up the phone before he loses control, before he can beg his father to "take back to his home his twenty-six-year-old baby boy."

The remaining stories in the second part of *My Life As A Man* trace Tarnopol's subsequent attempts to live with Maureen — and then to live without her. Although he gains a legal separation from Maureen in 1962, he finds that her threatening presence cannot be shaken, despite the aid of a love affair with the rich and complying Susan McCall, the support of his brother Morris, and the counsel of Dr. Spielvogel. Even after having been separated from Maureen for four years, Tarnopol desperately cries, "I have got to get her fangs out of my neck! Before I drown in this rage!" Although he tries every avenue to "get myself to feel like something other than a foreigner being held against his will in a hostile and alien country," the rage that accompanies his sense of victimization remains to choke all his efforts to assert his independence and manhood. His growing sense of persecution colors his every perception, and, in retrospect, he must admit that "I could never make a dent in my feeling of foreignness or alter my sense of myself as someone who had been *detained* here by the authorities, stopped in transit like that great paranoid victim and avenger of injustice in the Kleist novella that I taught with such passion out at Hofstra." Only with the accidental death of Maureen in 1967 can Tarnopol tell Spielvogel that he feels "free" — to which Spielvogel ominously replies, "That I don't know about." In his final joy he seems willing enough to forget the one answer to his problem posed by the timid, sensitive Susan McCall; when Tarnopol complained that it was impossible to escape the trap he had been in since his marriage to Maureen, Susan's answer was clear enough for all, except Tarnopol, to hear: "But the trap is *you.*"

Certainly there are social implications in *My Life As A Man*, as there are in *The Breast*. At the beginning of "Marriage à la Mode," for example, the narrator admits he is "looking around to see how much of my experience with women has been special to me and — if you must have it that way — my pathology, and how much is symptomatic of a more extensive social malaise." Both Tarnopol and Zuckerman suggest that the "serious fifties," with (in Tarnopol's words) its "myth of male inviolability, of male dominance and potency," and its "conventional assumptions about the strong and the weak," was perhaps responsible for the self-deceptions and for the ultimate sense of "homelessness" experienced by the two heroes. Additionally, Tarnopol, as he nears the end of his "true" story, points to the connection between his personal struggles and the political and cultural struggles of the sixties — even though at the time he was not able to see the connection:

As I begin to approach the conclusion of my story, I should point out that all the while Maureen and I were locked in this bruising, painful combat — indeed, almost from the moment of our first separation hearing in January 1963, some six months after my arrival in New York — the newspapers and the nightly television news began to depict an increasingly chaotic America and to bring news of bitter struggles for freedom and power which made my personal difficulties with alimony payments and inflexible divorce laws appear by comparison to be inconsequential. Unfortunately, these highly visible dramas of social disorder and human misery did nothing whatsoever to mitigate my obsession; to the contrary, that the most vivid and momentous history since World War Two was being made in the streets around me, day by day, *hour by hour*, only caused me to feel even more isolated by my troubles from the world at large, more embittered by the narrow and guarded life I now felt called upon to live — or able to live — because of my brief, misguided foray into matrimony. For all that I may have been attuned to the consequences of this new social and political volatility, and like so many Americans moved to pity and fear by the images of violence flashing nightly across the television screen, and by the stories of brutality and lawlessness appearing each morning on page one of the *New York Times*, I simply could not stop thinking about Maureen and her hold over me, though, to be sure, my thinking about her hold over me was, as I well knew, the very means by which she continued to hold me. Yet I couldn't stop — no scene of turbulence or act of terror that I read about in the papers could get me to feel myself any less embattled or entrapped.

(pp. 268-269)

Despite the social implications, however, *My Life As A Man*, like *The Breast*, focuses fundamentally on the hero himself, not on society in general. As Tarnopol says, "I do not contend — to make the point yet again — that my story furnishes anything like an explanation or a paradigm; it is only an instance, a postchivalric instance to be sure, of what might be described as the Prince Charming phenomenon. In this version of the fairy tale the part of the maiden locked in the tower is played consecutively by Maureen Johnson Tarnopol and Susan Seabury McCall. I of course play the prince."[31] The hero's struggle is to free himself of social and personal myths and misconceptions associated with the fifties and sixties generations but dramatized concretely in *human* characters anguishing through ordeals of consciousness — the ordeal, as Tarnopol says, of being "humanish: manly, a man."

In *My Life As A Man* Roth clearly returns to the obsessed self facing moral and psychological problems inherent in familial and personal situations. Unlike "On the Air," *Our Gang*, and *The Great American Novel*, the focus in this work is on character rather than on the social and political absurdities in American life. The narrator and central character, Tarnopol, has a refined sensibility and an analytical bent, and his quest for self-fulfillment is rendered in the realistic, "nonvernacular" fiction of *Letting Go* — a novel that one critic has significantly called "Jamesian."[32] I will return to the implications of the term *Jamesian* shortly; for the present, it is sufficient to say that the term is a convenient one for specifying the fiction of Roth that is non-satirical, that focuses on a character's moral and psychological problems rather than on social and political absurdities, and that (as T.S. Eliot once said of James's fiction) focuses on "a situation, a relation, an atmosphere, to which the characters pay tribute."[33] Although "On the Air," *Our*

Gang, and *The Great American Novel* are clear departures from the Jamesian quality of *Letting Go,* the tales of Nathan Zuckerman and Peter Tarnopol suggest that Roth has by no means abandoned the self in order to satirize the social and political aspects of American life. In fact, the concurrence of the Jamesian and the non-Jamesian strains in Roth's sensibility is emphasized by the fact that Roth interrupted his story of Nathan Zuckerman to write *Our Gang.*

In Roth's most recent fiction, then, we discover concurrent concerns with social absurdity and satirical techniques, on the one hand, and, on the other hand, with more traditionally "serious" renditions of human characters finding themselves in unknown waters, "beyond the last rope." In all of Roth's recent fiction, however, we observe a tenacious, increasingly inventive attempt to "demystify" the mystery of personality, both the personality of the individual and of the American culture. And in all of Roth's recent fiction we perceive the hard core of realism beneath a variety of fictional worlds — a variety that underscores Roth's willingness to follow out the impulses that literary realism suggests. As Saul Bellow contends, "The realistic tendency is to challenge the human significance of things. The more realistic you are the more you threaten the grounds of your own art. Realism has always both accepted and rejected the circumstances of ordinary life."[34] In quite different ways, "On the Air," *Our Gang, The Great American Novel, The Breast* and *My Life As A Man* bear out the truth of Bellow's contention. Each story is in part a response to the challenge placed on art by life itself.

V

Distinctive Features of Roth's Artistic Vision

In examining the "circumstances of ordinary life," Roth has employed a wide range of artistic techniques resulting in a fictional canon notable for its variety. In fact, the diversity of Roth's fiction has generated evident difficulty in assessing Roth's intention and achievement as a writer of fiction. Certainly most critics acknowledge Philip Roth as a major talent, as one who has been keenly responsive to the human condition as it is revealed in contemporary American experience. Richard Locke, in a recent review of Updike's *Rabbit Redux*, makes this point succinctly:

> Who are the novelists who have tried to keep a grip on our experience as we've wobbled along in the past decade or two, the writers to whom we turn to find out something of where we are and what we're feeling, the writers who give the secular news report? I'd suggest that there are five: Saul Bellow Norman Mailer, Bernard Malamud, Philip Roth — and John Updike himself.[1]

Despite such acknowledgment, however, the critical community has been divided in its response to Roth as a significant contemporary author. Critics have taken stances toward his achievement that are as diverse as the fiction itself: he has been called an anti-semitic and a Jewish moralist, a romantic writer and a realistic writer, a polemicist, a satirist, a mannerist, a sentimentalist, and a liar; he has been praised for having "a clear and critical social vision,"[2] condemned for having a "distorted" view of society,[3] and accused of entertaining an "exclusively personal" vision of life that does not include society at all.[4] Whereas Alfred Kazin recently spoke so confidently of what he calls Saul Bellow's "signature,"[5] it seems that from the collective viewpoint of the critical community Roth's mark has been something of an indecipherable scrawl.

Some attempts have been made to place Roth in relation to other contemporary American writers, but such attempts have often been accompanied by a distortion of clearly observable facts emerging from Roth's fiction and artistic creed; too, such attempts have resulted in a blurring of Roth's most distinctive characteristics as a writer of fiction. For example, Theodore Solotaroff joins Roth with Bellow and Malamud under the banner of Jewish moralists — writers who "feel and think with their Jewishness and [who] use the thick concreteness of Jewish moral experience to get at the dilemmas and decisions of the heart generally."[6] The difficulty with Solotaroff's assessment, however, is that it was made on the basis of only one collection of Roth's fiction, *Goodbye, Columbus*; furthermore, Solotaroff's assertion is vitiated by Roth's subsequent "non-Jewish" fiction and his expressed uncertainty about Jewish values, Jewish morality, and his indebtedness to the Jewish heritage.[7] Moving away from a Jewish point of reference, Helen Weinberg, David L. Stevenson, and Albert J. Guerard suggest that Roth can be viewed, along with Mailer, Malamud, Salinger, and Gold, as a disciple of Saul Bellow, or at least as one who writes in the activist mode initiated in America by Bellow. Although this assessment is helpful in point out a shared concern for the plight of the self in the American experience, such a view does not account for Roth's strong commitment to social and political concerns, nor does it account for the shift in Roth's fiction *toward* the victim-hero and *away* from the activist hero — a shift that is the reverse of the stages of development through which Bellow, Malamud, Gold, and Salinger have gone. Certainly Irving and Harriet Deer are correct in saying, "If Roth had to make a choice, he would side with Ralph Ellison as opposed to Salinger, Malamud, Bellow Gold. . . ."[8]

Despite general affinities among Roth, Salinger, Malamud, Bellow and Gold, one can approach Roth's "signature" most effectively by contrasting him to these contemporaries. Such an approach is suggested by the perceptible shift toward victimization, absurdity, and satire in Roth's presentation of character. Weinberg has argued persuasively that the pattern of development in the fiction of Bellow, Malamud, Mailer, and Gold is from the closed-structure tale to the open-structure tale and from the victim-hero to the activist hero. "The turning is away from the cognitive victim-hero in a world unavailable to reasonable minds, toward the activist hero, the seeker open to all life-mysteries."[9] But to suggest, as Weinberg, Stevenson, and Guerard do, that Roth's fiction has taken such a turn or that he is under the influence of Bellow's activist hero is to fly in the teeth of Roth's own statements and of his emphatic if not total shift toward victimization and absurdity in his fiction. Roth has indeed responded favorably to some of Bellow's fiction, but on the basis of Roth's public statements about Bellow's work, we might well assume that the early, realistic presentations in *Dangling Man* and *The Victim*, not the activist stance that Bellow takes in *The Adventures of Augie March* and *Henderson the Rain King*, most appeal to Roth. Although Roth has disparaged the latter two activist works, he goes so far as to say that "*The Victim* is a book which isn't as well-known as it should be, but I think it's perhaps one of the great books written in America in the 20th century." (*SDI*, p. 73) M. Gilbert

Porter has recently said, "Saul Bellow's *Herzog* seems to speak for the representative new hero in American fiction when he exclaims to the lawyer handling his divorce case, 'I'm not going to be a victim. I hate the victim bit.' " If, as Porter says, "The movement away from the 'victim bit' seems clearly the direction of the recent American novel,"[10] one might conclude that Roth has been swimming upstream, against the main current of contemporary American fiction. Such a conclusion at least has the advantage of clarifying the outlines of Roth's fiction, outlines that have been unfortunately blurred by a facile inclusion of Roth in the coterie of Jewish-American writers led by Bellow, Malamud, Salinger, Mailer and Gold.

The uniqueness of Roth's "signature" is intimately associated with his commitment to social realism, to a willingness to confront the community — its manners and its mores — as subject for his art. The confrontation between the hero (activist or victim) and world, between private and public realms, between "un-isolated" individuals and the shaping forces of general life, is the confrontation that is central to the realistic mode — and the fiction of Philip Roth. Certainly many critics have detected in Roth's fiction a noticeable attention to manners, to moral issues, and to literary realism; too often, however, Roth's most characteristic mode has been dismissed in the cavalier manner of Irving Malin, who complained that Roth's "loyalty to social realism is unfortunate," and that, "unlike Malamud, Roth is also comfortable, too comfortable, with . . . realism."[11] It is my contention that we can best assess Roth's artistry by viewing him, rather broadly, as a writer whose artistic intentions are "moral," whose method is realistic, and whose subject is the self in society.

Given Solotaroff's contention that Roth's sensibility is embedded in a Jamesian concern for motives and for what Trilling calls "moral realism," it is altogether possible to think that Roth writes, in part, to fill a void that Trilling pointed out in 1948:

Perhaps at no other time has the enterprise of moral realism ever been so much needed, for at no other time have so many people committed themselves to moral righteousness. We have the books that point out the bad conditions, that praise us for taking progressive attitudes. We have no books that raise questions in our minds not only about conditions but about ourselves, that lead us to refine our motives and ask what might lie behind our good impulses.[12]

As our examination of Roth's fiction has shown, the question of what lies behind "good impulses" is one that virtually every major character in his fiction asks. The crises depicted in Roth's fiction are not so much ontological as they are moral, for although the character may begin with the question of identity and selfhood, he is likely to conclude with the questions of Neil Klugman, Gabe Wallach, and Peter Tarnopol: what do I owe to my fellow man, and how do I explain my actions toward him? What is my relation to society, and what are the dangers of the moral life? To what extent have I been victimized by false ideals and self-deceptions grounded in the society of which I am an ineluctable part?

Inevitably, when we hear such questions we think immediately of Tolstoy, Conrad, Dostoevski, Gogol — the great European novelists — and Henry James, America's most prominent novelist of manners and moral realism; nor is it surprising that allusions to these novelists and their works appear frequently in Roth's fiction. For example, Henry James plays an important role in *Letting Go*. Gabe Wallach spends a good part of his graduate school life writing a dissertation on James — so much so that when the novel opens, Gabe declares that his "one connection with the world of feeling was not the world itself but Henry James." In fact, James's *The Portrait of a Lady* serves as a link between Gabe and the Herzes (Gabe meets Libby as a consequence of loaning the novel to the Herzes, and the affinities between Libby Herz and Isabel Archer lead Gabe into a long discussion of the realistic technique and moral concern of James's work). Certainly Murray Kempton is correct in seeing a Jamesian essence brooding over *Letting Go*, but one might go even further to say that the novel presents characters who are engaged in a Jamesian "ordeal of consciousness" (to use Dorothea Krook's phrase for James's fiction), and that Roth is clearly interested in the working out of moral and psychological problems involved in such an ordeal. The burdens of responsibility, the clash between the actual world and the "invented reality" that grows out of what one "sees and feels,"[13] the moral difficulties of "letting go" (a phrase that Roth borrowed from Mrs. Gereth in *The Spoils of Poynton*, who tells Fleda Vetch, "Only let yourself go, darling — only let yourself go!") — all these are concerns that Roth has in common not only with James but with other European novelists of manners and moral realism as well. Roth underscores this point when he declares,

> As for a moral concern, that I feel is certainly central to the novel I wrote and I care most about — *Letting Go*. Is that Jewish? I do not know. I feel that two writers whom I care a good deal about, and who have influenced me considerably, although it may not be apparent, are Tolstoy and Henry James. The center of both seems to me to be a very strong moral concern. Neither is a Jew. So whether the moral concern in my work comes from the fact that it is fiction, or the fact that I am Jewish, I simply do not know. It is very difficult for a writer to speak about his own sources, and one winds up either being wrong or sounding terribly pretentious. I do know that there are certain writers, like Gogol and Dostoievski, to whom I respond with a lot of feeling. . . .   (*SDI*, p. 75)

The moral concerns in Roth's fiction, its attempts to get at the truths of the heart generally, have been pointed out by several critics.[14] I should only like to add that Roth gives the basis of the central moral problem that recurs in his fiction when he says that the condition of men is that they are strangers to one another, and "because *that* is our condition . . . it is incumbent upon us not to love one another — which is to deny the truth about ourselves — but to practice no violence and no treachery upon one another, which is to struggle with the darkest forces within ourselves."[15] Here is a touchstone with which we can evaluate the moral condition of virtually every character in Roth's fiction — from the "soul-battered" Ozzie Freedman to the treacherous Tricky Dixon.

Perhaps the most significant aspect of Roth's moral interests is that they extend clearly into his conception of art (and here the affinity between Roth and such writers as Henry James is at its strongest). In Roth's view, "It is the job of fiction to redeem [the] stereotype and give it its proper weight and balance in the world." He goes on to assert:

> I do not think that literature, certainly not in my country and in my time, has direct social and political consequences. I think that it alters consciousness and I think that its goal is to alter consciousness, not to alter the housing problem or Jewish-Gentile relations and so on. Its task and its purpose is to create shifts in what one thinks is reality and what the reader does. When the reader then goes on to act differently in his life, as a result of reading your story, I do not know how responsible you are for his actions. I think that what you are responsible for is the honesty of the portrayal, for the authenticity of your vision. If that is distorted you are a bad artist. To sum up, I do not think that literature is a call to action; it speaks for the consciousness.   (*SDI*, pp. 75-76)

Roth clearly embraces James's belief that fictional experience "is our apprehension and our measure of what happens to us as social creatures."[16] Furthermore, Roth ventures the hope that "literary investigation may even be a way to redeem the facts, to give them the weight and value that they should have in the world, rather than the disproportionate significance they probably have for some misguided or vicious people"(*WAJ*, p. 449) — an observation that illuminates not only the stereotypic attitudes Roth attacks in his early fiction but also the satiric thrusts in his later fiction. In speaking of the satire in *Portnoy's Complaint*, "On the Air" and *Our Gang*, Roth insisted that "writing satire is essentially a literary, not a political, act," for, in his thinking, "satire is moral rage transformed into comic art." After all, asks Roth, isn't "challenging moral certainties a good part of what literature aspires to do?"[17]

Literature as a call to consciousness is, of course, precisely the note struck by James and Conrad. Roth has brought a similar notion to bear when critics from the Jewish community state that he is doing the Jews a disservice or when other critics recoil from the pointed social and political satire in his fiction:

> ... At this point in human history, when power seems the ultimate end of government, and "success" the goal of individual lives; when the value of humility is in doubt, and the nerve to fail hardly to be seen at all; when a willful blindness to man's condition can only precipitate further anguishes and miseries — at this point, with the murder of six million people fixed forever in our imaginations, I cannot help but believe that there is a higher moral purpose for the Jewish writer ... than the improvement of public relations.[18]

For Roth, as for James, fiction not only treats moral issues, but has the purpose of elevating and liberating the reader's social and moral consciousness through realistic examination of "man's condition." Just as "those of us who are willing to be taught, and who needed to be, have been made by *Invisible Man* less stupid than we were about Negro lives," so can the stereotypes of Jewish malingerers, Jewish mothers, Jewish family life, and Protestant Midwestern fathers, mothers, sons and daughters be put into new perspectives — for "the stereotype as often arises from ignorance as from malice." (*WAJ*, pp. 451-452)

A strong social and moral consciousness, coupled with a readily evident persuasion toward a realistic portrayal of man in society, points toward Roth's distinctiveness as a contemporary American author, for it is the prevailing opinion that such concerns have never been central to the American literary tradition. In 1948 Lionel Trilling asserted, "The fact is that American writers of genius have not turned their minds to society.... In America in the nineteenth century, Henry James was alone in knowing that to scale the moral and aesthetic heights in the novel one had to use the ladder of social observation."[19] Trilling's contention that "Americans have a kind of resistance to looking closely at society"[20] is not a startling observation, most critics of the American novel would agree. Walter Allen maintains that "The classic American novels have dealt not so much with the lives of men in society as with the life of solitary man, man alone and wrestling with himself."[21] R. W. B. Lewis sees in writers like Bellow, Salinger, and Mailer a continuation of what Walt Whitman called the "principle of individuality, the pride and centripetal isolation of a human being in himself — identity — personalism."[22] Mark Schorer speaks of the representative American novel as the "evocative novel," one that, in opposition to the social novel, demonstrates that the "gap between the individual human being and the social circumstances in which he exists has become hazardously wide."[23] The point to be made here is that the American novelistic tradition, unlike the European tradition, has not sustained a concern for man in society, and, as Jonathan Baumbach says, "The novel of manners has always been, with the notable exception of Henry James, a secondary and somewhat artificial tradition in American literature. . . ."[24] Certainly Roth is not a proponent of the documentary social novel or a novel of manners in the European sense of the term (for, as Trilling persuasively argues in "Art and Fortune," such a novel is not possible in America); nonetheless, Roth's relation to his contemporaries is more sharply defined if we consider him as a social realist — as a writer, that is, who does not yield to the romantic impulse as defined by Chase, Allen, Lewis, and others. Roth has been characteristically associated with such Jewish-American writers as Mailer, Salinger, Bellow, Malamud, and Gold, when in fact his closest associates among American authors are Sinclair Lewis, F. Scott Fitzgerald, John O'Hara, John P. Marquand — writers who, as James Tuttleton demonstrates, are primarily "concerned with social conventions as they impinge upon character."[25]

Although Roth has been tantalized by the figure of the essentially romantic activist hero — as is suggested by his presentation of Neil Klugman and Gabe Wallach — he ultimately cannot accept the hero who quests for selfhood outside the boundaries of society and its manifold pressures. If this is so, we might suspect that Roth rejects the typical heroes of contemporary literature — heroes that Joseph Waldmeir describes in his essay "Quest Without Faith":

> Whether by force or by choice (since a too great concern with the problems of existence in an age of conformity can push one willy-nilly outside the pale) the heroes of the new American novel are disaffiliates. Saul Bellow's Augie March and Henderson are both irrevocably separated from society. So too are Norman Mailer's Sergius O'Shaugnessy and Mikey Lovett, Nelson

Algren's Frankie Machine and Dove Linkhorn, Bernard Malamud's Frank Alpine, J. D. Salinger's Holden Caulfield, William Styron's Cass Kinsolving and Peyton and Milton Loftis, Herbert Gold's Bud Williams. . . .[26]

When we look at Roth's criticisms of his contemporaries, what we discover is that it is precisely this disaffiliated hero who earns Roth's displeasure. Bellow is right in stating that a writer reads the fiction of his contemporaries "with a special attitude,"[27] but in Roth's case the attitude itself is of interest, for it emphasizes the most salient features of his artistic creed. In "Writing American Fiction," Roth undertakes a casual but nonetheless illuminating examination of Bellow, Malamud, Salinger, Mailer, Gold and Styron, and in so doing he places his own distinctive artistic concerns in bold relief.

Of these six writers, Roth feels the greatest affinity with Salinger, primarily because Salinger's fictional world, "in all its endless and marvelous detail, is decidedly credible." (*WAF*, p. 228) Roth is often touched by the lovingness that is attributed to Seymour Glass, and he feels that the note of despair in Salinger's fiction, dramatized by Seymour's committing suicide and Holden's being institutionalized, is an understandable one. Ultimately, however, Roth is at odds with Salinger's fictional heroes and with his fictional strategy. His major complaint against Salinger is that he avoids confronting the recognizable social world. Salinger's conception of mysticism — which, in Roth's view, is based on the premise that the deeper one goes into the world the further one gets away from it — is symptomatic of Salinger's turning away from the community: "For all the loving handling of the world's objects, for all the reverence of life and feeling, there seems to me, in the Glass family stories as in *The Catcher*, a spurning of life as it is lived in this world, in this reality. . . ." (*WAF*, p. 228) This spurning of life, in Roth's view, is conveyed by Salinger's fictional heroes, who have learned to live in this world by not living in it. Roth concludes, "Since madness is undesirable and sainthood, for most of us, out of the question, the problem of how to live *in* this world is by no means answered; unless the answer is that one cannot." (*WAF*, p. 228)

Roth feels that the spurning of life as it is actually lived in society is evident, too, in the fiction of Bernard Malamud. *The Natural* is a book about baseball, but "it is not baseball as it is played in Yankee Stadium," just as the Jews of *The Magic Barrel* and *The Assistant* "are not the Jews of New York City or Chicago." (*WAF*, p. 228) Roth discovers in Malamud's fiction a world "which has a kind of historical relationship to our own, but is by no means a replica of it." To clarify his point, Roth goes on to say that the Jews in Malamud's fiction

> are a kind of invention, a metaphor to stand for certain human possibilities and certain human promises, and I find myself further inclined to believe this when I read of a statement attributed to Malamud which goes, "All men are Jews." In fact we know this is not so; even the men who are Jews aren't sure they're Jews. But Malamud, as a writer of fiction, has not shown specific interest in the anxieties and dilemmas and corruptions of the modern American Jew, the Jew we think of as characteristic of our times; rather, his people live in a timeless depression and a placeless Lower East Side; their society is not affluent, their predicament not cultural.
>
> (*WAF*, pp. 228-229)

Roth does not mean to say that Malamud has avoided moral issues or turned away from the problems of being human; in fact, the contrary is true. But Roth insists that Malamud has not engaged the recognizable social life that the realistic writer thrives on, for Malamud "does not — or has not yet —

found the contemporary scene a proper or sufficient backdrop for his tales of heartlessness and heartache, of suffering and regeneration." (*WAF*, p. 229)

In Roth's view, Salinger and Malamud are two of America's best authors, yet their works seem to be curiously out of touch with the actual world. Neither writer "has managed to put his finger on what is most significant in the struggle going on today between the self (all selves, not just the writer's) and the culture." (*WAF*, p. 227) In the fiction of Saul Bellow and William Styron Roth finds a similar inability or unwillingness to confront the social world in all of its recognizable aspects. In Roth's opinion, the fiction of Bellow and Styron, peopled by heroes who affirm life in foreign and unrealistic climes, is further evidence that our best writers have avoided examining American public life. The end of *Henderson the Rain King* (where Henderson is pictured galloping around a Newfoundland airfield) makes a deep impression on Roth, for here he sees "a man who finds energy and joy in an imagined Africa, and celebrates it on an unpeopled, icebound vastness." (*WAF*, p. 232) Roth complains of a similar, if somewhat more muted ending in Styron's *Set This House on Fire*. ". . . At the end of the book, for all his disgust with what the American public life does to a man's private life, Kinsolving, like Henderson, has come back to America, having opted for existence." But, Roth goes on to say, "the America that we find him in seems to me to be the America of his childhood, and, if only in a metaphoric way, of all our childhoods." (*WAF*, p. 233) Roth is right in saying that "using a writer for one's own purposes is of course to be unfair to him" (*WAF*, p. 230); nevertheless, Roth's objection to the novelistic strategies of Bellow and Styron certainly places his own attitudes clearly in front of us: the author must confront the social world squarely if he is to describe human character faithfully, and affirmation achieved through geographic displacement or metaphoric evasion is, finally, no affirmation at all.

Herbert Gold and Norman Mailer demonstrate a quite different "spurning of life" in their fiction, for what one discovers, Roth argues, is that both writers adopt a pose — with the result that elation and affirmation, on the one hand, and anger and disgust, on the other, arise from the personality of the artist rather than from the fiction itself. In Gold Roth perceives a writer whose concern is with his own individuality rather than with the individuality of his fictional characters, and there is "a good deal of delight in the work of his own hand. And, I think, with the hand itself." Hence, in works like Gold's *Therefore Be Bold* and *Love and Like* the reader is confronted with "a writer in competition with his own fiction," with the result that "reality" is replaced by personality — "and not the personality of the character described, but of the writer who is doing the describing." (*WAF*, p. 230) Roth detects in Salinger's novelistic strategy a similar inclination to place the writer's persona (Buddy Glass) in the reader's line of vision — but in Gold's fiction the technique is employed not as an act of desperation but rather as an act of willful and mannered euphoria that has little to do with the reality of Gold's fictional realm. In his recent work, Norman Mailer, like Gold, has employed "life as a substitute for fiction" — particularly in *Advertisements for Myself*, "an infuriating, self-indulgent, boisterous, mean book." (*WAF*, p. 226) Roth maintains that the novelistic strategy adopted by Mailer is indicative of the contemporary author's plight, for just as Salinger, Malamud, Styron and Gold have in various ways spurned life as it is actually lived, so does Mailer give up on making an imaginative assault on the American experience.

Roth's remarks about his contemporaries are quite revealing and, in light of his artistic creed, certainly understandable. In "Writing American Fiction" Roth is ostensibly pressing home the thesis that the present social world is not as manageable or suitable as it once may have been, a thesis that underscores Roth's awareness of social and political absurdity. Equally revealing, however, is Roth's charge that some of our best American writers have rejected the moral, social, and realistic requirements of art that he himself is committed to — a point that, perhaps ironically, Bellow also makes: "American novelists are not ungenerous, far from it, but as their view of society is fairly shallow, their moral indignation is non-specific. What seems to be lacking is a firm sense of a common world, a coherent community. . . ."[28] Despite this concern for a lack of moral and social commitment by American artists, however, Bellow, in a 1968 response to "Writing American Fiction," suggests where the writers of activist fiction and Roth part company:

> The modern writer specialises in grotesque facts, and he cannot compete with the news, with "life itself." Perhaps he should begin to think of interesting himself in something other than the grotesque. There is good reason to think that absurdities are traveling in two directions, from art into life and from life into art. We cannot continue to ignore Oscar Wilde's law. "Nature imitates art." Roth is right if — and only if — fiction cannot leave current events without withering away.[29]

In contending that modern writers cannot compete with current events, with "life itself," Bellow dramatizes the very real differences between the sensibility of writers of activist fiction and the sensibility of Philip Roth. Following the major American (romantic) tradition, Bellow, Mailer, Salinger, and Gold have explored the human condition through characters who have cut themselves off from the grotesque facts of the recognizable American public life; Roth, on the other hand, following the tenets of social realism, has explored the human condition through characters who have descended into the midst of the absurdities of the American experience. Roth is under no delusion, however, that social realism is either a prevailing or an easily manageable literary mode, nor does he regard the moral function of art as a light burden, easily cast aside:

> Fiction is not written to affirm the principles and beliefs that everybody seems to hold, nor does it seek to guarantee us of the appropriateness of our feelings. The world of fiction, in fact, frees us from the circumscriptions that the society places upon feeling; one of the greatnesses of the art is that it allows both the writer and the reader to respond to experience in ways not always available in day-to-day conduct. . . . We may not even know that we have such a range of feelings and responses *until* we have come into contact with the work of fiction. . . . Ceasing for a while to be upright citizens, we drop into another layer of consciousness. And this dropping, this expansion of moral consciousness, this exploration of moral fantasy, is of considerable value to a man and to society.   (*WAJ*, pp. 446-47)

Roth's assault on the American experience — his exploration of moral fantasy, his concern for moral consciousness, his willingness to confront the grander social and political phenomena of our time — is, I think, the most significant aspect of his art. Despite the diversity of Roth's fiction, despite the variety of themes, values, and characters that emerge from his novels and short stories, we see an abiding faith beneath Roth's pessimism, a faith that leads him to answer one of his critics by saying, "I find that Mr. Liptzin's view of the universe is negative; I think of my own as positive." (*SDI*, p. 60) Roth has demonstrated a willingness to explore the limits of his artistic creed with a deeply felt concern for man and society, a concern that is detectable beneath his ponderous realistic novels and his most vitriolic satire. It is that concern,

I think, that leads Roth, in his most recent fiction, to employ some of the same artistic strategies that he has criticized in his fellow writers. *Our Gang*, for example, comes perilously close to substituting "life for art," a point that is emphasized by Roth's preface to the May, 1973 "Watergate Edition" of the novel; too, works such as "On the Air," *The Breast*, and *The Great American Novel* utilize fantasy and metaphor, often at the expense of credibility (how seriously can we take a character who turns into a breast, it might be asked — and how realistic is *that*?). That much is frighteningly recognizable even in Roth's most recent fiction is, however, Roth's best defense against charges of inconsistency, and certainly Roth has remained hell-bent (*Our Gang* makes the term an irresistible one to use) on putting his finger on our cultural predicament, on sending us a secular news report, however grotesque the facts of "life itself" may be.

Writing in 1959, the year that *Goodbye, Columbus* was published, Alfred Kazin posed a challenge to which Roth has responded more sensitively than perhaps any other writer of the past decade:

> What many writers feel today is that reality is not much more than what *they* say it is. This is a happy discovery only for genius. . . . There has probably never been a time when the social nature of the novel was so much at odds with the felt lack of order in the world about us. In the absence of what used to be *given*, the novelist must create a wholly imaginary world — or else he must have the courage, in an age when personal willfulness rules in every sphere, to say that we are *not* alone, that the individual does not have to invent human values but only to rediscover them. The novel as a form will always demand a commonsense respect for life and interest in society. [30]

The shape of Roth's future fiction is as indeterminate and unpredictable as the shape of our future society, but one can say, with assurance, that in the past decade Roth has maintained an abiding respect for life and an unyielding interest in society. Above all, he has had the courage, in an age of personal willfulness, to say that we are not alone.

Notes

CHAPTER I

1. *The American Novel and Its Tradition* (Garden City, N.Y.: Doubleday and Company, Inc., 1957), p.ix.

2. Foreword to *The Politics of Twentieth Century Novelists*, ed. George A. Panichas (New York: Hawthorn Books, Inc., 1971), p. xv.

3. "Looking for Intelligence in Washington," *Hells and Benefits* (New York: Basic Books, 1962), p. 96 (DeMott's italics).

4. *Beyond the Wasteland: A Study of the American Novel in the Nineteen-Sixties* (New Haven: Yale Univ. Press, 1972), p. 1.

5. *Radical Innocence: Studies in the Contemporary American Novel* (Princeton: Princeton Univ. Press, 1961), p. 15.

6. "Philip Roth Reconsidered," *Commentary*, 54 (Dec. 1972), 69.

7. "Laureate of the New Class," *Commentary*, 54 (Dec. 1972), 4.

8. *The Liberal Imagination* (Garden City, N.Y.: Doubleday and Company, 1953), p. 176.

9. *The Modern Novel in Britian and the United States* (New York: E.P. Dutton and Company, 1964), p. xv.

10. John Enck, "John Barth: An Interview," *Wisconsin Studies in Contemporary Literature*, 6 (Winter-Spring 1965), p. 4.

11. "Realism and Contemporary Novel," *Partisan Review*, 26 (Spring 1959), 201.

12. "The Novel Alive or Dead," *A Gathering of Fugitives* (Boston: Beacon Press, 1956), p. 125.

13. John Enck, p. 11.

14. "Reading Myself," *Partisan Review*, 40, No. 3 (1973), 417.

15. Theodore Solotaroff, a friend of Roth, argues persuasively that Roth drew extensively on personal experiences at the University of Chicago for materials for his *Letting Go* ("The Journey of Philip Roth," *Atlantic Monthly*, April 1969, pp. 64-72). In "Recollections From Beyond the Last Rope" we discover that Roth's father, like Portnoy's, is an insurance salesman whose main problem is collecting premiums from impoverished blacks. Roth's dismay at Midwestern morality — which is at the center of *When She Was Good* — is associated with his two years of teaching at the University of Iowa (in this regard, see Roth's non-fictional essay "Iowa: A Very Far Country Indeed," *Esquire*, December 1962, pp. 132ff). Peter Tarnopol in *My Life As A Man* is a serious young Jewish writer whose novel *The Merchant of Yonkers* carries the same epigraph as Roth's *Letting Go;* he, like Roth, has gone through a divorce, and his age is the same as Roth's. These parallels merely invite us to consider certain *proximities*, however, and I am not suggesting that Roth's fiction is to be read as thinly-disguised autobiography.

16. "From the First 18 Years of My Life," *New York Times*, 24 Oct. 1971, Dec. 2, p. 1D.

17. "Reading Myself," p. 405, p. 409.

18. "Recollections From Beyond the Last Rope," *Harper's Magazine*, July 1959, pp. 45-46.

19. "On *The Breast:* An Interview," *New York Review of Books*, 19 Oct. 1972, p. 26.

20. "Reading Myself," p. 412.

21. "Rabbi to Rabbi," *To Our Colleagues*, No. 8 (1964), 9.

22. An interesting consequence of these charges is reported in Joseph C. Landis, "The Sadness of Philip Roth: An Interim Report," *Massachusetts Review*, 3 (Winter 1962),

259. Landis says that in 1960 Roth's *Goodbye, Columbus* had been awarded the Daroff Memorial Award of the Jewish Book Council of America; so great was the outcry from the Jewish community, however, that the Jewish Book Council announced in February of 1961 that in the future it would consider only fiction "characterized by an affirmative expression of Jewish values."

23. Howe, "The Suburbs of Babylon," 15 June 1959, p. 18.

24. "Philip Roth and the Jewish Moralists," in *Breakthrough: A Treasury of Contemporary American-Jewish Fiction*, ed. Irving Malin and Irwin Stark (New York: McGraw-Hill Book Company, 1964), p. 356.

25. *Philip Roth and Bernard Malamud* (Grand Rapids: William B. Eerdmans Publishing Company, 1968), p. 6.

26. "In Defense of Philip Roth," *Chicago Review*, 17, Nos. 2 and 3 (1964), 96.

27. "Escape and Confrontation in the Short Stories of Philip Roth," *Christian Scholar*, 49 (Summer 1966), 133.

28. *Ibid.*

29. "Philip Roth and the Test of Dialogic Life," *Four Spiritual Crises in Mid-Century American Fiction* (Gainesville: Univ. of Florida Press, 1964), pp. 25-35.

30. "Jewish Fiction and the Affluent Society," *Northwest Review*, 4 (Spring 1961), 95.

31. Landis, p. 267.

32. "Roth, Updike, and the High Expense of Spirit," *Univ. of Windsor Review*, 5, No. 1 (1969), 120.

33. *The Jewish Writer in America: Assimilation and the Crisis of Identity* (New York: Oxford Univ. Press, 1971), p. 87.

34. "On the Road, or the Adventures of Karl Shapiro," *Poetry*, 96 (June 1960), 171.

35. "Three Generations: An Account of American Jewish Fiction (1896-1969)," *Jewish Social Studies*, 34 (January 1972), 37.

36. *Jews and Americans* (Carbondale: Southern Illinois Univ. Press, 1965), p. 5.

37. *Ibid.*, pp. 10-11.

38. *Ibid.*, pp. 9-10.

39. *Ibid.*, p. 9.

40. "Saul Bellow," *Prairie Schooner*, 31 (1957), 105.

41. *Waiting for the End* (New York: Stein and Day, 1964), p. 93. See also his essay "The Breakthrough: The American Jewish Novelist and the Fictional Image of the Jew," *Midstream*, 4 (Winter 1958), 15-35.

42. *Radical Sophistication: Studies in Contemporary Jewish-American Novelists* (Athens: Ohio Univ. Press, 1969), pp. viii-ix.

43. "American Jewish Fiction: So What's the Big Deal?" *Chicago Review* 19, No. 1 (1966), 92.

44. *Ibid.*, p. 95.

45. "Jewishness and the Younger Intellectuals," *Commentary* 31 (April 1961), 350-351.

46. Roth re-emphasized this point recently by saying, ". . .I myself have always been far more pleased by my good fortune in being born a Jew than any of my critics may begin to imagine. It's a çomplicated, interesting, morally demanding and very singular experience, and I like that. There is no question but that it has enriched my life, but when I say 'enriched' I don't know that I mean the same things that my rabbinical critics may mean when they use that word. What I do mean is that I find myself in the historic predicament of being Jewish, with all its implications. Who could ask for more?" ("Philip Roth's Exact Intent," interview with George Plimpton, *New York Times Book Review*, 23 Feb. 1969, p. 24).

47. "The New Jewish Stereotypes," *American Judaism*, II (Winter 1961), 51.

48. Saul Bellow, "Sealed Treasure," *Times Literary Supplement*, 1 July 1960, p. 414.

49. "Child and Man in Philip Roth," *Midstream*, 13 (Dec. 1967), 74.

50. In his contribution to the symposium entitled "Jewishness and the Younger Intellectuals," Roth says, "Where the Jewish past has informed my spirit and imagination, so too has the political and cultural past of America, and the literary past of England." (p. 351) Freedman, Malin, and others seem to minimize the possibility of literary influence or concern outside the Jewish tradition. Roth does believe, however, that early criticism from the Jewish community "was instructive," for "I became aware of enormous differences of *sensibility* between my Jewish critics and myself." Such criticism "made me begin to understand that admira-

tion for me and my mission on earth was, somewhat to my surprise, going to be less than unanimous, and probably hardest to win closest to hearth and homeland" ("Reading Myself," p. 407).

CHAPTER II

1. "Jewish Writers in America: A Place in the Establishment," *Commentary*, 31 (Feb. 1961), 133.

2. Quoted in Haskel Frankel, "Bernard Malamud," *Saturday Review*, 10 Sept. 1966, p. 40.

3. For discussion of the existential hero in contemporary American fiction see Howard M. Harper, *Desperate Faith: A Study of Bellow, Salinger, Mailer, Baldwin and Updike* (Chapel Hill: The Univ. of North Carolina Press, 1967); Richard Lehan, "Existentialism in Recent American Fiction: The Demonic Quest," *Texas Studies in Literature and Language*, 1 (Summer 1959), 181-202; David Galloway, *The Absurd Hero in American Fiction* (Austin: Univ. of Texas Press, 1966); Ihab Hassan, *Radical Innocence: Studies in the Contemporary American Novel* (Princeton: Princeton Univ. Press, 1961), and his "The Existential Novel," *Massachusetts Review*, 3 (Summer 1962), 795-97; James E. Miller, *Quests Surd and Absurd: Essays in American Literature* (Chicago: Univ. of Chicago Press, 1967); Richard Boyd Hauck, *A Cheerful Nihilism: Confidence and "The Absurd" in American Humorous Fiction* (Bloomington: Indiana Univ. Press, 1971); and Helen Weinberg, *The New Novel in America: The Kafkan Mode in Contemporary Fiction* (Ithaca: Cornell Univ. Press, 1970).

4. "Dogmatic Innocence: Self-Assertion in Moden American Literature," *Texas Quarterly*, 6, No. 2 (1963), 159.

5. For an elaboration on this point, see Maurice Kramer, "The Secular Mode of Jewishness," *Works*, 1 (Autumn 1967), 97-116; and Wolfgang Fleischmann, "The Contemporary 'Jewish Novel' in America," *Jahrbuch Fuer Amerikastudien*, 12 (1967), 159-166.

6. Many of our best critics have used the quality of heroic response as an index of contemporary fiction, primarily because the pattern of contemporary fiction so obviously demands such an approach. According to Lionel

Trilling, "There is scarcely a great writer of our own day who has not addressed himself to the ontological crisis. . ." (*The Opposing Self* [New York: The Viking Press, 1955], p. 140). Ihab Hassan says that "the pattern of experience in contemporary fiction is largely existential," and therefore the character of the hero "emerges with some clarity in this pattern" (*Radical Innocence*, p. 115). Frederick J. Hoffman says, "Much of the literature since 1945 describes a self entirely cut off from a heroic center; he is a hero without a cause, a man without meaningful relation, a truly marginal figure" (*The Mortal No: Death and the Modern Imagination* [Princeton: Princeton Univ. Press, 1964], p. 484).

7. "The Activists, *Daedalus*, 92 (Spring 1963), 238-240.

8. Weinberg, p. xi.

9. Introduction to Saul Bellow's *The Adventures of Augie March* (Greenwich, Conn.: Fawcett Publications, Inc., 1967), p. xv.

10. "The Nature of the Novel," *Hudson Review*, 10 (Spring 1957), 32-33.

11. "Dogmatic Innocence: Self-Assertion in Modern American Literature," p. 152.

12. *The Literature of America: Nineteenth Century* (New York: McGraw-Hill Book Company, 1970), p. 22.

13. Schulz, p. 22.

14. Saul Bellow, *Dangling Man* (New York: The American Library, 1965), p. 102.

15. Saul Bellow, *The Adventures of Augie March* (New York: Viking Press, 1960), p. 454.

16. Guerard, p. vii.

17. Weinberg, p. 165.

18. "Some Notes on Recent American Fiction," *Encounter*, 21 (Nov. 1963), 23.

19. *Advertisements for Myself* (New York: G.P. Putnam's Sons, 1959), p. 339.

20. Stevenson, p. 238.

21. Weinberg, p. 126.

22. "Tough-Minded Mr. Roth," in *Contemporaries* (Boston: Little, Brown, 1962), p. 259.

23. Glenn Meeter rightly concludes that "the real conversion, one that occurs in Ozzie if in no one else, is the conversion wrought by comedy, a conversion from a world of arbitrary

law and ritual bondage ... to one of spiritual freedom" (*Philip Roth and Bernard Malamud*, p. 20).

24. Siegel, p. 96.

25. "Philip Roth and the Crisis in American Fiction," *Minnesota Review*, 6 (Winter 1966), 357. Roth himself has said of this story, "Ultimately, the central fantasy of Christianity is, to me, highly comic; I particularly find the Virgin Birth hysterical." (*SDI*, p. 61) Clearly the story is concerned with Ozzie's attempt to become a "freed man" in a personal sense. It is equally clear that neither Roth nor Ozzie is concerned with a *religious* conversion of Jews.

26. *Fear and Trembling*, trans. Walter Lowrie (Princeton: Princeton Univ. Press, 1941), p. 175.

27. *Ibid.*, p. 115.

28. "Eli Agonistes: Philip Roth's Knight of Faith," in *The Process of Fiction*, ed. Barbara McKenzie (New York: Harcourt, Brace and World, Inc., 1969), p. 245.

29. *Fear and Trembling*, p. 157.

30. Stevenson, p. 241.

31. Siegel, p. 91.

32. Isaac, p. 89.

33. Landis, pp. 261-262.

34. The social theme in *Goodbye, Columbus* is emphasized by almost every critic of the novel. For example, Alfred Kazin sees the theme as "romantic and credulous youth defeated in love by a brutally materialistic society, like Fitzgerald's Gatsby" ("Tough-Minded Mr. Roth," p. 259); Bernard Sherman says that "Philip Roth uses the education novel plot to examine the dream of success as it is envisioned by the suburban generation at mid-century" (*The Invention of the Jew* [New York: Thomas Yoseloff, 1969], p. 167); Saul Bellow says that in this novel Roth "has a greater interest in society and in manners and is aware of a great change in the condition of the Jews" ("The Swamp of Prosperity," *Commentary*, 28 [July 1959], 78).

35. Stevenson, p. 238.

36. Weinberg, pp. 27-28.

37. Hochman, p. 70.

38. "Bumblers in a World of Their Own," *New York Times Book Review*, 17 June 1962, p. 1.

39. Weinberg, p. 182.

40. *Ibid.*, p. 185.

41. In his "Some Notes on Recent American Fiction," Bellow distinguishes his conception of the self from Roth's conception of the self. In Roth's fiction, says Bellow, "The public realm, as it encroaches on the private, steadily reduces the powers of the individual." In Bellow's view, Gabe's inner life "is a rather feeble thing of few watts. Conceivably it may guide him to a more satisfactory adjustment, but it makes me think of the usher's flashlight in the dark theater guiding the single ticket-holder to his reserved seat" (p. 27). Bellow, on the other hand, is less convinced that the "jig of the Self is up," and he suggests the need to examine the spiritual richness of the private and inner life unencumbered by social pressures (p. 29).

42. "Manners, Morals, and the Novel," in *The Liberal Imagination*, p. 213.

43. Irving and Harriet Deer, p. 353.

44. Detweiler, p. 32. Detweiler goes on to say, "It is no accident, I think, that Roth relates Paul's crisis to the story of Abraham and Isaac, the same example that Kierkegaard employed to explain existential faith. . . . [Paul] is forced by the pressure of life to reflect upon himself; he enters a critical period of extreme doubt and anguish; he is moved by the awareness of death to ponder the meaning of life; he is brought through a kind of grace to a moment of decision, and in that decision he loosens himself from the hindrances of the past and achieves freedom" (*Ibid.*).

CHAPTER III

1. "Mass Society and Post-Modern Fiction," *Partisan Review*, 26 (Summer 1959), 433.

2. Weinberg, p. 12.

3. Galloway, p. 6.

4. Weinberg, p. ix.

5. Although Joseph in *Dangling Man* articulates a creed of spiritual activism, he ultimately bows to the wishes of "worldly schemes." In accepting his draft notice, Joseph admits, ". . . Things were now out of my hands. The next move was the world's. I could not bring myself to regret it."

Joseph's last words underscore his capitulation: "I am no longer to be held accountable for myself; I am grateful for that. I am in other hands, relieved of self-determination, freedom canceled.... Long live regimentation!" In Bellow's *The Victim*, Asa Leventhal is victimized by the mysterious Kirby Allbee (whose last name suggests all existence) and by his own feelings of guilt and persecution. As Baumbach says in *The Landscape of Nightmare*, "What Albee and Leventhal share most is the feeling that the dark forces that control civilization are for one reason or another persecuting them." (p. 51).

6. *Radical Innocence*, pp. 69-70.

7. The texts cited in my footnote three, chapter two give extensive treatment to the phenomenon of the victim in modern literature. See also Northrup Frye, *Anatomy of Criticism* (Princeton: Princeton Univ. Press, 1957), especially his first essay on "Theory of Modes." Frye traces the shift in hero types in Western literature down through the ages from the mythic to the ironic mode. Also of some interest in this respect is Mario Praz, *The Hero in Eclipse in Victorian Fiction* (New York: Oxford Univ. Press, 1956) and Raymond G. Giraud, *The Unheroic Hero* (New York: Octagon Books, 1969). These two texts examine nineteenth century influences that have curtailed the possibilities for heroism. Perhaps the fullest treatment of victimization in modern fiction is given by Frederick J. Hoffman in *The Mortal No.* After asserting that "the full range of modern violence may be comprehended in terms of the metaphor of the assailant and victim," Hoffman goes on to trace the assailant-victim relationship through five levels of confrontation, concluding with "violence as landscape" as the most extreme metaphor of victimization in modern literature (see his chapter three entitled "The Assailant and the Victim: Some Definitions of Modern Violence").

8. *Radical Innocence*, p. 21.

9. Frye, p. 41.

10. *Loss of Self* (New York: Random House, 1962), p. 14.

11. Chase, p. 19.

12. Interview with Saul Bellow in "The Act of Fiction, XXXVII," *The Paris Review*, 9 (Winter 1966), 61.

13. "Some Notes on Recent American Fiction," pp. 26, 29.

14. "Where Do We Go From Here: The Future of Fiction," in Shiv K. Kumar and Keith McKean, editors, *Critical Approaches to Fiction* (New York: McGraw-Hill Book Company, 1968), p. 11.

15. "Some Notes on Recent American Fiction," p. 23.

16. Weinberg, p. x.

17. *Ibid.*, pp. 9-10. According to Weinberg, absurdist novels having at their center a "passive, rationalistic, or hopelessly ineffectual victim-hero" include the following: Bellow's *The Victim* and *Dangling Man*, Friedman's *Stern*, Malamud's *The Assistant*, Mailer's *Barbary Shore*, Pynchon's *V*, Hawkes's *The Cannibal* and *Second Skin*, Barth's *The End of the Road*, and, with some qualification, Heller's *Catch-22* and Salinger's *The Catcher in the Rye* (p. 11).

18. *Ibid.*, p. 11.

19. *Radical Innocence*, p. 22.

20. *The Myth of Sisyphus and Other Essays*, trans. Justin O'Brien (New York: Alfred A. Knopf, 1958), p. 50.

21. Irving and Harriet Deer, pp. 357-358.

22. "American Fiction," *Commentary*, 32 (Sept. 1961), 250-251.

23. "Philip Roth: An Interview," *Mademoiselle*, Aug. 1961, p. 255.

24. *The Myth of Sisyphus and Other Essays*, p. 29.

25. "Philip Roth: An Interview," p. 255.

26. *Advertisements for Myself*, p. 23.

27. "Philip Roth and the Jewish Moralists," p. 362.

28. There is no justification for Glenn Meeter's assertion that "this conversion, though portrayed comically, is both genuine and 'ecumenical'" (*Philip Roth and Bernard Malamud*, p. 40). Robert Detweiler is closer to the truth when he says of Libby, "Her experiences are the least profound, and Roth uses her and her situation to satirize the traditional positions. . . . Libby has become religious, but religion has done nothing for her" (*Four Spiritual Crises in Mid-Century American Fiction*, pp. 31-32).

29. It seems at this point that Paul has come to the hopeful stance of what Camus calls the absurd man. Camus says that the absurd man is he who, with help of courage and

reason, learns to "live *without appeal* and to get along with what he has. . . . Assured of his temporarily limited freedom . . . and of his mortal consciousness, he lives out his adventure within the span of his lifetime" (*The Myth of Sisyphus and Other Essays*, p. 66).

30. Theodore Solotaroff correctly assesses the thrust of *Goodbye, Columbus* when he says, "In story after story, there was an individual trying to work free of the ties and claims of the community" ("The Journey of Philip Roth," p. 66).

31. Quoted in Granville Hicks, "A Bad Little Good Girl," *Saturday Review*, 17 June 1967, p. 25.

32. Robert Alter, "When He is Bad," *Commentary*, 44 (Nov. 1967), 86.

33. "Let's Lynch Lucy," *New Republic*, 24 June 1967, p. 19.

34. *The Myth of Sisyphus and Other Essays*, p. 28. I am not, of course, suggesting a direct influence; however, Camus' philosophy of the absurd does illuminate the central pattern of *When She Was Good.* Lucy's life takes place at what Camus calls "the very meeting-point of that efficacious but limited reason with the ever resurgent irrational" (p. 36). Lucy does not have the insight of the absurd man, however, who "admits the irrational" (p. 37); rather, Lucy is at the mercy of her own limited reason, which wants, as Camus says, "to make everything clear," and in so doing negates awareness of the absurd (p. 36). With the exception of Paul Herz, Portnoy, and David Kepesh, Roth's heroes do not demonstrate an awareness of the absurd, even though they find themselves in absurd situations.

35. Quoted in Granville Hicks, "A Bad Little Good Girl," pp. 25-26.

36. Baruch Hochman correctly says that in *Letting Go* and *When She Was Good* one finds the "legitimate pathos" of "an entire middle-class generation or generation-and-a-half whose culture is organized in such a way as to make it impossible for them to find an adequate perspective in which to view their lives and feelings. This is not merely a matter of a few individual psyches. It is the experience of a whole class today . . . who, like Lucy and her husband, are trapped prematurely in familial or professional situations which they do not begin to

understand and with which they cannot possibly cope" ("Child and Man in Philip Roth," p. 72).

37. "Philip Roth's Exact Intent," p. 25.
38. "The Journey of Philip Roth," p. 67.
39. "Philip Roth's Exact Intent," pp. 24-25.
40. *Ibid.*, p. 25.
41. *Ibid.*, p. 23.
42. Roth himself admits that he was "strongly influenced in this book by a sit-down comic named Franz Kafka and a very funny bit he does called 'The Metamorphosis.' " Roth qualifies the remark, however, by saying, "I don't mean I modeled my book after any work of his, or aspired to write a Kafka-*like* novel" ("Philip Roth's Exact Intent," p. 24). It is interesting to note that Portnoy makes passing mention of Joseph K. and Kafka, and in recounting an adolescent memory he makes a reference to Gregor Samsa. It seems that young Alexander has refused to apologize for some inexcusable but unknowable wrong, and has taken to hiding under the bed. Sophie "is after me with a broom, trying to sweep my rotten carcass into the open. Why, shades of Gregor Samsa! Hello Alex, goodbye Franz!" (p. 135) Shortly thereafter he calls himself a "metamorphosed child" and, like Gregor Samsa, is at a loss to explain the inexplicable punishment visited upon so dutiful a son.
43. Weinberg, p. 10.
44. *Time*, 21 Feb. 1969, p. 82.
45. "Philip Roth's Exact Intent," pp. 23-24.
46. Tanner, p. 313.

CHAPTER IV

1. "Our Gang," *New York Times Book Review*, 7 Nov. 1971, p. 31.
2. Quoted in Raymond A. Sokolov, "Alexander the Great," *Newsweek*, 14 Feb. 1969, p. 92. Roth emphasized this point more recently in speaking of the "self-conscious and deliberate zig-zag that my own career has taken, each book veering sharply away from the one before" ("Reading Myself," pp. 410-411).

3. "Positive Thinking On Pennsylvania Avenue," *New Republic*, 3 June 1957, p. 11.

4. "Writing American Fiction," p. 225. Roth goes on to say that the absurdity of Nixon during the debates produced in him "a type of professional envy," for the entire debate "was so beside the point, so fantastic, so weird and astonishing, that I found myself beginning to wish I had invented it. That may not, of course, be a literary fact at all, but a simple psychological one — for finally I began to wish that *someone* had invented it, and that it was not real and with us" (p. 225). That Roth was to explore the redeeming power of art in "On the Air" and that he turned the "psychological fact" of his dismay into the literary fact of *Our Gang* are two points of great interest. We see that for Roth art offers a way to utilize and neutralize the horrors and absurdities in American public life.

5. "A Modest Proposal," *Look*, 6 Oct. 1970, p. 100.

6. Quoted in *Newsweek*, 8 Nov. 1971, p. 110.

7. *Ibid.*, p. 112.

8. "On Satirizing Presidents: An Interview with Philip Roth," *Atlantic*, Dec. 1971, p. 83.

9. "The Good Word: Howe's Complaint," *New York Times Book Review*, 6 May 1973, p. 2.

10. "On Satirizing Presidents: An Interview with Philip Roth," p. 88.

11. "Reading Myself," p. 417.

12. *Ibid.*, p. 413.

13. *Ibid.*, p. 416.

14. *Ibid.*, p. 415.

15. *Ibid.*, p. 416.

16. *Ibid.*, p. 417.

17. MacDonald, p. 30.

18. "On *The Breast*: An Interview," p. 28.

19. "On *The Breast*: An Interview," p. 26.

20. *Ibid.*

21. *Ibid.*, p. 28.

22. *Ibid.*

23. "Fiction," *Esquire*, Oct. 1972, p. 84.

24. "The Breast," *New York Times Book Review*, 17 Sept. 1972, p. 10.

25. "On *The Breast*: An Interview," p. 26.

26. *Ibid.*, p. 28.

27. "Reading Myself," p. 411-412.

28. *Ibid.*, p. 406.

29. "Philip Roth's Exact Intent," p. 25. In this same interview Roth says that when he looked back on the literature course he was teaching at the University of Pennsylvania he realized "that the course might have been called 'Studies in Guilt and Persecution' — 'Metamorphosis,' 'The Castle,' 'In the Penal Colony,' 'Crime and Punishment,' 'Notes From Underground,' 'Death in Venice,' 'Anna Karenina' " (pp. 24-25). *Portnoy's Complaint* was, as Roth says, his attempt to move away from such somber preoccupations. Peter Tarnopol makes a similar attempt in Part II of *My Life As A Man*. As he says of his literature course at Hofstra, "At the outset I had thought I was just assigning great works of fiction that I admired and wanted my fifteen senior literature students to read and admire too — only in time did I realize that a course whose core had come to be *The Brothers Karamazov*, *The Scarlet Letter*, *The Trial*, *Death in Venice*, *Anna Karenina*, and Kleist's *Michael Kohlhaas* derived of course from the professor's steadily expanding extracurricular interest in the subject of transgression and punishment" (p. 233). My only point here is that Roth does not hesitate to explore personal artistic concerns through his narrators in *My Life As A Man*.

30. "The Journey of Philip Roth," p. 67.

31. Interestingly enough, the third-person narrator of the original version of "Salad Days" (published in *American Review*) says of the young Nathan Zuckerman, ". . . The price would begin to be paid, for the conceit, for the ignorance, but above all for the contradictions, the confusion in him of spiritual pretension and lewd desire, of soft boyish need and manly, *princely* ambition — and what a surprise that pin would be" (p. 46). These words suggest that Zuckerman, like Tarnopol, mistakenly sees himself as a "prince" and that he, like Tarnopol, finds himself attached to two seemingly inimical realms of experience — precisely those two realms that in "Reading Myself" Roth confesses himself to be attached to.

32. Murray Kempton, "Nixon Wins," *New York Review of Books*, 27 Jan. 1972, p. 22. Kempton goes on to say that

Letting Go is Jamesian "in an essence that broods over the inescapable responsibility for the suffering of others" (p. 22).

33. Quoted in Warner Berthoff, *The Ferment of Realism: American Literature, 1884-1919* (New York: The Free Press, 1965), p. 104.

34. "The Act of Fiction, XXXVII," p. 63.

CHAPTER V

1. "Rabbit Redux," *New York Times Book Review*, 14 Nov. 1971, p. 1.

2. Isaac, p. 96.

3. Jeremy Larner, "Conversion of the Jews," *Partisan Review*, 27 (Fall 1960), p. 761.

4. Mizener, p. 1.

5. "Bellow's Purgatory," *New York Review of Books*, 28 March 1968, p. 32.

6. "Philip Roth and the Jewish Moralists," p. 357.

7. Several other critics have made similar questionable comparisons, based on Roth's early fiction. For example, Ben Siegel declares that "Roth — as well as such 'older' contemporaries as Saul Bellow, Bernard Malamud, J.D. Salinger, Herbert Gold, and the underrated Peter Martin — has replaced [a] rejection of religious concern with a deeply felt commitment to Judaic values" ("Jewish Fiction and the Affluent Society," p. 95). In this regard see also Glenn Meeter's comparison between Roth and Malamud as Jewish romantics in *Philip Roth and Bernard Malamud*, Marvin Mudrick's treatment of Roth, Bellow and Malamud in "Who Killed Herzog? Or Three American Novelists," *Denver Quarterly*, I (Spring 1966), 61-97, and Irving Malin's assessment of Roth in *Jews and Americans*.

8. Irving and Harriet Deer, p. 353.

9. Weinberg, p. 205. Weinberg also says, "The structural pattern and spiritual commitments of the contemporary activist novel are most obviously embodied in the fiction of Saul Bellow and Norman Mailer (and, softened and sentimentalized, in the work of J.D. Salinger). . . . Bernard Malamud, Herbert Gold, and Philip Roth . . . have certainly moved toward the activist mode. Malamud in his third novel, *A New Life*, falls into this category, seemingly through a

process of novelistic realization on his own part rather than through imitation. Herbert Gold and Philip Roth, younger men, seem more imitative in their adaptions of the activist mode to their own writings; they seem influenced by Bellow, and perhaps by Mailer or Malamud also" (p. 165).

10. "Review Essay: 'Spiritual Activism' and 'Radical Sophistication' in the Contemporary American Novel," *Studies in the Novel*, 3 (Fall 1971), 332.

11. *Jews and Americans*, pp. 156, 173. Writers who have touched upon these areas in Roth's fiction include Theodore Solotaroff, Baruch Hochman, Irving Howe, Glenn Meeter, and Max Schulz. Solotaroff finds in *Goodbye, Columbus* a "tough-minded realism" ("Philip Roth and the Jewish Moralists," p. 362); Hochman says of the same collection, "The technique, to be sure, remains 'realistic,' and there continues to be an interest in manners. . . ." ("Child and Man in Philip Roth," p. 69); Irving Howe believes that the best parts of *Goodbye, Columbus* "are those in which Mr. Roth sketches the manners and morals of the Patimkins," even though the work as a whole is too "ferociously exact" ("The Suburbs of Babylon," p. 17); Glenn Meeter compares Roth's technique in *Goodbye, Columbus, Letting Go,* and *When She Was Good* with the realistic technique of Wordsworth; most significant of all, perhaps, is Max Schulz's assertion that Roth's "stringent realism" and his preoccupation with "Jewish manners" exclude him from the "radically sophisticated" Jewish-American writers such as Bellow, Salinger, Mailer, and Malamud (*Radical Sophistication*, pp. viii-ix).

12. "Manners, Morals and the Novel," p. 213.

13. Roth, *SDI*, p. 75. See Raymond Williams' assertion that in the realistic mode "the reality of personal feeling, growing into phantasy, interacts at the necessary tension with the world in which the feelings must be lived out" ("Realism and the Contemporary Novel," p. 209).

14. The critics who give extended treatment to the moral issues in Roth's fiction are Ben Siegel, Glenn Meeter, and Theodore Solotaroff. Although all three unfortunately stress the Jewishness of the moral issues, there is general agreement that, in Siegel's words, Roth "wishes to capture and describe as compellingly as possible the deep yet paradoxical moral

and social factors shaping each character's . . . awareness"
("Jewish Fiction and the Affluent Society," pp. 95-96).

15. "The New Jewish Stereotypes," p. 51.

16. *The Art of the Novel* (New York: Charles Scribner's
Sons, 1950), pp. 64-65.

17. "On Satirizing Presidents," pp. 86, 88.

18. "The New Jewish Stereotypes," p. 51.

19. "Manners, Morals, and the Novel," p. 206. Trilling
maintains that the novel "is a perpetual quest for reality, the
field of its research being always the social world, the
material of its analysis being always manners as the indication
of the direction of man's soul." Trilling admits, however,
that "the novel as I have described it has never really
established itself in America" (pp. 205-206).

20. *Ibid.*, p. 207.

21. *The Modern Novel in Britain and the United States*,
pp. xiv-xv.

22. "Recent Fiction: Picaro and Pilgrim," in *A Time of
Harvest*, ed. Robert Spiller (New York: Hill and Wang, 1962),
p. 146.

23. *Society and Self in the Novel* (New York: Columbia
Univ. Press, 1956), p. x. Raymond Williams makes the same
charge in almost the same terms when he warns that in recent
fiction "the gap between our feelings and our social
observation is dangerously wide" ("Realism and the Contemporary Novel," p. 208).

24. *The Landscape of Nightmare*, p. 4. For additional
information on the social novel in American literature, see
Richard Chase's "Three Novels of Manners," in *The Ameri-
can Novel and Its Tradition*; Ihab Hassan, *Radical Innocence*,
chapter four; John W. Aldridge, *In Search of Heresy* (New
York: McGraw-Hill Book Company, 1956), especially chapter three, entitled "The Heresy of Literary Manners"; Lionel
Trilling, "Art and Fortune," in *The Liberal Imagination*;
Arthur Mizener, "The Novel of Manners in America,"
Kenyon Review, 12 (Winter 1950), 1-19; and Louis Auchin-
closs, *Reflections of a Jacobite* (Boston: Houghton Mifflin
Company, 1961), especially the chapters entitled "The Novel
of Manners Today: Marquand and O'Hara" and "James and
the Russian Novelists."

25. *The Novel of Manners in America* (Chapel Hill: The Univ. of North Carolina Press, 1972), p. 12.

26. In *Recent American Fiction: Some Critical Views*, ed. Joseph Waldmeir (Boston: Houghton Mifflin Company, 1963), p. 54.

27. "Some Notes on Recent American Fiction," p. 159.

28. Quoted in Tony Tanner, *City of Words*, p. 298.

29. *Ibid.*

30. "The Alone Generation," in *The American Novel Since World War II*, ed. Marcus Klein (Greenwich, Conn.: Fawcett Publications, Inc., 1969), p. 122-123.

Philip Roth: A Bibliography

The following bibliography has been divided into two major parts. In the first part I have attempted to include all of Roth's writings, fiction and nonfiction. Paperback editions of novels are given in parenthesis. I have also included novel excerpts that were printed in magazines before the completed novels were published. The second part of the checklist includes major book reviews, critical articles, and book chapters that give Roth specific and pronounced attention; excluded are minor book reviews readily available in *Book Review Digest*.

By Philip Roth

A. *Novels and collected short stories*

Goodbye, Columbus and Five Short Stories. Boston: Houghton Mifflin Company, 1959. (New York: Bantam Books, Inc., 1963.)

Letting Go. New York: Random House, Inc., 1962. (New York: Bantam Books, Inc., 1963.)

When She Was Good. New York: Random House, Inc., 1967. (New York: Bantam Books, Inc., 1968.)

Portnoy's Complaint. New York: Random House, Inc., 1969. (New York: Bantam Books, Inc., 1970.)

Our Gang. New York: Random House, 1971. (New York: Bantam Books, Inc., 1972. Reissued in June, 1973 with new preface by Roth; includes Roth's interview with Alan Lelchuk which originally appeared in the *Atlantic Monthly* of December, 1971.)

The Breast. New York: Holt, Rinehart and Winston, Inc., 1972.

The Great American Novel. New York: Holt, Rinehart and Winston, Inc., 1973.

My Life As A Man. New York: Holt, Rinehart and Winston, Inc., 1974.

B. *Uncollected short stories, novel excerpts, and satirical pieces*

"The Day It Snowed." *Chicago Review*, 8 (Fall 1954), 34-44.

"The Contest For Aaron Gold." *Epoch*, 7 (Fall 1955), 37-51.

"Heard Melodies are Sweeter." *Esquire*, August 1958, p. 58.

"Good Girl." *Cosmopolitan*, May 1960, pp. 98-103. Excerpt from *Letting Go.*

"Very Happy Poems." *Esquire*, January 1962, pp. 79-86. Excerpt from *Letting Go.*

"Separations." *Mademoiselle*, May 1962, pp. 142-143, 200, 202-206. Excerpt from *Letting Go.*

"Paul Loves Libby." *Harper's Magazine*, June 1962, pp. 58-73. Excerpt from *Letting Go.*

"Novotny's Pain." *The New Yorker*, 27 October 1962, pp. 46-56.

"The Psychoanalytic Special." *Esquire*, November 1963, pp. 106-109, 172-176.

"An Actor's Life for Me." *Playboy*, January 1964, pp. 84-86, 228-235.

"In Trouble." *Atlantic*, November 1966, pp. 72-79. Excerpt from *When She Was Good.*

"O Beautiful For Spacious Skies." *Harper's Magazine*, November 1966, pp. 66-78. Excerpt from *When She Was Good.*

"A New Man." *Saturday Evening Post*, 11 February 1967, pp. 50-59. Excerpt from *When She Was Good.*

"Jewish Patient Begins His Analysis." *Esquire*, April 1967, pp. 104-107, 191-193. Excerpt from *Portnoy's Complaint*.

"Whacking Off." *Partisan Review*, 34 (Summer 1967), 385-399. Excerpt from *Portnoy's Complaint*.

"The Jewish Blues." *New American Review*, No. 1 (September 1967), pp. 136-164. Excerpt from *Portnoy's Complaint*.

"Nature Boy." *Cosmopolitan*, September 1967, pp. 130-134. Excerpt from *When She Was Good*.

"The Mistaken." *The American Judaism Reader*. Edited by Paul Kresh. New York: Abelard-Schuman, 1967.

"Civilization and Its Discontents." *New American Review*, No. 3 (April 1968), pp. 7-81. Excerpt from *Portnoy's Complaint*.

"On the Air." *New American Review*, No. 10 (August 1970), pp. 7-49.

"A Modest Proposal." *Look*, 6 October 1970, pp. 98-100.

"Salad Days." *Modern Occasions*, 1 (Fall 1970), 26-46. Excerpt from *My Life As A Man*.

"Imaginary Conversation with Our Leader." *New York Review of Books*, 6 May 1971, p. 12. Excerpt from *Our Gang*.

"Courting Disaster." *Esquire*, May 1971, pp. 93-101, 158-168. Excerpt from *My Life As A Man*.

"Imaginary Press Conference with Our Leader." *New York Review of Books*, 3 June 1971, pp. 15-17. Excerpt from *Our Gang*.

"Tricky Has Another Crisis." *Modern Occasions*, 1 (Fall 1971), 469-500. Excerpt from *Our Gang*.

"The Great American Rookie." *Sports Illustrated*, 12 March 1973, pp. 36, 38, 41-44, 47-50, 55. Excerpt from *The Great American Novel*.

" 'I Always Wanted You To Admire My Fasting'; Or, Looking at Kafka." *American Review*, No. 17 (May 1973), pp. 103-126.

"Every Inch A Man." *Esquire*, May 1973, pp. 128-130, 208, 210, 212, 214. Excerpt from *The Great American Novel*.

"The President Addresses the Nation." *New York Review of Books*, 14 June 1973, p. 11.

"Marriage à la Mode." *American Review*, No. 18 (September 1973), 211-244. Excerpt from *My Life As A Man*.

"Susan." *Esquire*, June 1974, p. 104. Excerpt from *My Life As A Man*.

C. *Articles, symposia, and interviews*

"Positive Thinking on Pennsylvania Avenue." *New Republic*, 3 June 1957, pp. 10-11.

"Mr. Lindbergh, Mr. Ciardi, and the Teeth and Claws of the Civilized World." *Chicago Review*, 11 (Summer 1957), 72-76.

"The Kind of Person I Am." *The New Yorker*, 29 November 1958, pp. 173-178.

"Recollections From Beyond the Last Rope." *Harper's Magazine*, July 1959, pp. 42-48.

"Writing American Fiction." *Commentary*, 31 (March 1961), 223-233.

"Jewishness and the Younger Intellectuals." *Commentary*, 31 (April 1961), 350-351. (Roth's contribution to a symposium.)

√ "Philip Roth: An Interview." *Mademoiselle*, August 1961, pp. 254-255.

"American Fiction." *Commentary*, 32 (September 1961), 248-252.

"The New Jewish Stereotypes." *American Judaism*, 11 (Winter 1961), 10-11, 49-51.

"Iowa: A Very Far Country Indeed." *Esquire*, December 1962, pp. 132, 240, 242-244, 247-248, 250-251.

"Novelist Advises Teenagers That Novels Are Bad For You." Library Journal, 88 (15 April 1963), 1738.

"Second Dialogue in Israel." *Congress Bi-Weekly*, 30 (16 September 1963), 4-85. Symposium.

"Writing About Jews." *Commentary*, 36 (December 1963), 446-452.

"Philip Roth's Exact Intent." Interview with George Plimpton. *New York Times Book Review*, 23 February 1969, pp. 2, 23-25.

"Reflections On the Death of a Library." *Wilson Library Bulletin*, 43 (April 1969), 746-747.

"From the First 18 Years of My Life." *New York Times*, 24 October 1971, sec. 2, pp. 1D, 3D.

Newsweek, 8 November 1971, pp. 110, 112. Interview with Philip Roth.

"On Satirizing Presidents: An Interview With Philip Roth." With Alan Lelchuk. *Atlantic*, 228 (December 1971), 81-88. Reprinted in the "Watergate Edition" of *Our Gang*, June 1973.

"On *The Breast*: An Interview." With Alan Lelchuk. *New York Review of Books*, 19 October 1972, pp. 26-28.

"Which Writer Under Thirty-five Has Your Attention And What Has He Done To Get It?" *Esquire*, October 1972, pp. 133, 198. (Roth's contribution to a symposium.)

"Reading Myself." *Partisan Review*, 40, No. 3 (1973), 404-417.

"Milan Kundera, The Joker," *Esquire*, April 1974, pp. 85, 178, 182, 184.

About Philip Roth

Alter, Robert. "When He Is Bad." Review of *When She Was Good. Commentary*, 44 (November 1967), 86-87.

Amis, Kingsley. "Waxing Wroth." *Harper's Magazine*, April 1969, pp. 104, 106-107.

Bellow, Saul. "Some Notes on Recent American Fiction." *Encounter*, 21 (November 1963), 22-29.

———. "The Swamp of Prosperity." *Commentary*, 28 (July 1959), 77-79.

Bettelheim, Bruno. "Portnoy Psychoanalyzed." *Midstream*, 15 (June-July 1969), 3-10.

Brewer, Joseph E. "The Anti-Hero in Contemporary Literature." *Iowa English Year Book*, 12 (1967), 55-60.

Broyard, Anatole. "A Sort of Moby Dick." Review of *Portnoy's Complaint. New Republic*, 1 March 1969, pp. 21-22.

Buchen, Irving H. "*Portnoy's Complaint* of the Rooster's Kvetch." *Studies in the Twentieth Century*, No. 6 (Fall 1970), pp. 97-107.

Cheuse, Alan. "A World Without Realists." *Studies on the Left*, 4, No. 2 (1964), 68-82.

Chyet, Stanley F. "Three Generations: An Account of American Jewish Fiction." *Jewish Social Studies*, 34 (January 1972), 31-41.

Cohen, Richard. " 'Best Novel' — Worst Award." *Congress Bi-Weekly*, 27 (19 December 1960), 12-14.

Cooperman, Stanley. "Philip Roth: 'Old Jacob's Eye' With A Squint." *Twentieth Century Literature*, 19 (July 1973), 203-216.

Cowley, Malcolm. "The Literary Situation, 1965." *University of Mississippi Studies in English*, 6 (1965), 91-98.

Crews, Frederick. "Uplift." Review of *The Breast. New York Review of Books*, 16 November 1972, pp. 18-19.

Davenport, Guy. "Magic Realism in Prose." Review of *Letting Go. National Review* 28 August 1962, pp. 153-154.

Deer, Irving, and Deer, Harriet. "Philip Roth and the Crisis in American Fiction." *Minnesota Review*, 6 (Winter 1966), 353-360.

DeMott, Benjamin. "Jewish Writers in America: A Place in the Establishment." *Commentary*, 31 (February 1961), 127-134.

Detweiler, Robert. "Philip Roth and the Test of Dialogic Life." *Four Spiritual Crises in Mid-Century American Fiction*. Gainesville: University of Florida Press, 1964.

Ditsky, John. "Roth, Updike, and the High Expense of Spirit." *University of Windsor Review*, 5, No. 1 (1969), 111-120.

Donaldson, Scott. "Family Crises in the Popular Novel of Nixon's Administration." *Journal of Popular Culture*, 7 (Fall 1972), 374-382.

———. "Philip Roth: The Meanings of *Letting Go*." *Contemporary Literature*, 11 (Winter 1970), 21-35.

Dupree, Robert. "And the Mom Roth Outgrabe Or, What Hath Got Roth?" *Arlington Quarterly*, 2 (Autumn 1970), 175-189.

Edwards, Thomas R. "The Great American Novel." *New York Times Book Review*, 6 May 1973, pp. 27-28.

Fiedler, Leslie. "The Image of Newark and the Indignities of Love." *The Collected Essays of Leslie Fiedler*, 2, New York: Stein and Day, 1971.

Fleischmann, Wolfgang Bernard. "The Contemporary 'Jewish Novel' in America." *Jahrbuch Fuer Amerikastudien*, 12 (1967), 159-166.

Freedman, William. "American Jewish Fiction: So What's the Big Deal?" *Chicago Review*, 19, No. 1 (1966), 90-107.

Friedman, Alan Warren. "The Jew's Complaint in Recent American Fiction: Beyond Exodus and Still in the Wilderness." *Southern Review*, 8 (1972), 41-59.

Gardner, John. "The Breast." *New York Times Book Review*, 17 September 1972, pp. 3, 10.

Gass, William H. "The Sporting News." Review of *The Great American Novel. New York Review of Books*, 31 May 1973, pp. 7-8.

Geismar, Maxwell. "The American Short Story Today." *Studies on the Left*, 4 (Spring 1964), 21-27.

Gilman, Richard. "Let's Lynch Lucy." Review of *When She Was Good. New Republic*, 24 June 1967, pp. 19-21.

Goldman, Albert, "Wild Blue Shocker." Review of *Portnoy's Complaint. Life*, 7 February 1969, 58B-D, 58F, 61-64.

Gordon, Lois G. " 'Portnoy's Complaint': Coming of Age in Jersey City." *Literature and Psychology*, 19, Nos. 3-4 (1969), 57-60.

Gross, John. "Marjorie Morningstar, Ph.D." Review of *Letting Go. New Statesman*, 30 November 1962, p. 784.

Guttmann, Allen. "The Conversion of the Jews." *Wisconsin Studies in Contemporary Literature*, 5 (1965), 161-176.

———. *The Jewish Writer in America; Assimilation and the Crisis of Identity*. New York: Oxford University Press, 1971.

Harper, Howard M., Jr. "Trends in Recent American Fiction." *Contemporary Literature*, 12 (1971), 204-229.

Hicks, Granville. "A Bad Little Good Girl." Review of *When She Was Good. Saturday Review*, 17 June 1967, pp. 25-26.

Hochman, Baruch. "Child and Man in Philip Roth." *Midstream*, 13 (December 1967), 68-76.

Hollis, James R. "Eli Agonistes: Philip Roth's Knight of Faith." *The Process of Fiction*. Ed. Barbara McKenzie. New York: Harcourt, Brace and World, Inc., 1969.

Howe, Irving. "The Suburbs of Babylon." Review of *Goodbye, Columbus. New Republic*, 15 June 1959, pp. 17-18.

———. "Philip Roth Reconsidered." *Commentary*, 54 (December 1972), 69-77.

Hyman, Stanley Edgar. "A Novelist of Great Promise." *On Contemporary Literature*. Ed. Richard Kostelanetz. New York: Avon Books, 1964.

Isaac, Dan. "In Defense of Philip Roth." *Chicago Review*, 17, Nos. 2 and 3 (1964), 84-96.

Kazin, Alfred. "Tough-Minded Mr. Roth." *Contemporaries.* Boston: Little, Brown, 1962.

Kempton, Murray. "Nixon Wins." Review of *Our Gang. New York Review of Books*, 27 January 1972, pp. 20-22.

Kliman, Bernice W. "Names in *Portnoy's Complaint.*" *Critique*, 14, No. 3 (1973), 16-24.

Kramer, Maurice. "The Secular Mode of Jewishness." *Works*, 1 (Autumn 1967), 97-116.

Landis, Joseph C. "The Sadness of Philip Roth: An Interim Report." *Massachusetts Review*, 3 (Winter 1962), 259-268.

Larner, Jeremy. "Conversion of the Jews." Review of *Goodbye, Columbus. Partisan Review*, 27 (Fall 1960), 760-768.

Leer, Norman. "Escape and Confrontation in the Short Stories of Philip Roth." *Christian Scholar*, 49 (Summer 1966), 132-146.

Lehan, Richard. "Fiction 1967." *Contemporary Literature*, 9 (1968), 538-553.

Leonard, John. "Cheever to Roth to Malamud." *Atlantic Monthly*, June 1973, pp. 112-116.

Levine, Mordecai H. "Philip Roth and American Judaism." *CLA Journal*, 14 (December 1970), 163-170.

Ludwig, Jack. "Sons and Lovers." Review of *Portnoy's Complaint. Partisan Review*, 36, No. 3 (1969), 524-526, 528-534.

MacDonald, Dwight. "Our Gang." *New York Times Book Review*, 7 November 1971, pp. 31-32.

Malin, Irving. *Jews and Americans.* Carbondale: Southern Illinois University Press, 1965.

Mizener, Arthur. "Bumblers in a World of Their Own." Review of *Letting Go. New York Times Book Review*, 17 June 1962, pp. 1, 28-29.

Mudrick, Marvin. "Who Killed Herzog? Or, Three American Novelists." *Denver Quarterly*, 1 (Spring 1966), 61-97.

Nelson, Gerald B. "Neil Klugman." *Ten Versions of America.* New York: Alfred A. Knopf, 1972.

Pétillon, Pierre-Yves. "Philip Roth N'est Pas Mort." *Critique*, 26 (October 1970), 821-838.

Podhoretz, Norman. "The Gloom of Philip Roth." *Doings and Undoings.* New York: Farrar, Straus, and Giroux, 1964.

———. "Laureate of the New Class." *Commentary*, 54 (December 1972), pp. 4, 7.

Shaw, Peter. "Portnoy and His Creator." *Commentary*, 47 (May 1969), 77-79.

Sheed, Wilfrid. "Pity the Poor Wasps." Review of *When She Was Good*. *New York Times Book Review*, 11 June 1967, pp. 5, 50.

———. "The Good Word: Howe's Complaint." *New York Times Book Review* 6 May 1973, p. 2.

Siegel, Ben. "Jewish Fiction and the Affluent Society." *Northwest Review*, 4 (Spring 1961), 89-96.

Sokolov, Raymond A. "Alexander the Great." *Newsweek*, 24 February 1969, pp. 91-92.

Solotaroff, Theodore. "Philip Roth and the Jewish Moralists." *Chicago Review*, 13 (Winter 1959), 87-99. Reprinted in *Breakthrough: A Treasury of Contemporary American-Jewish Fiction*. Edited by Irving Malin and Irwin Stark. New York: McGraw-Hill Book Company, 1964.

———. "The Journey of Philip Roth." *Atlantic Monthly*, April 1969, pp. 64-72.

———. "Fiction." Review of *The Breast*. *Esquire*, October 1972, pp. 82, 84, 178.

Spacks, Patricia Meyer. "About Portnoy." *Yale Review*, 58 (June 1969), 623-635.

Tanner, Tony. "Fictionalized Recall — or 'The Settling of Scores! The Pursuit of Dreams!' " *City of Words: American Fiction 1950-1970*. New York: Harper and Row, 1971.

Trachtenberg, Stanley. "The Hero in Stasis." *Critique*, 7 (Winter 1964-65), 5-17.

Weinberg, Helen. *The New Novel in America: The Kafkan Mode in Contemporary Fiction*. Ithaca: Cornell University Press, 1970.

White, Robert L. "The English Instructor as Hero: Two Novels by Roth and Malamud." *Forum*, 4 (Winter 1963), 16-22.

Wisse, Ruth. *The Schlemiel as Modern Hero*. Chicago: University of Chicago Press, 1971.

Wolff, Geoffrey. "Beyond Portnoy." *Newsweek*, 3 August 1970, p. 66.

Goodbye Columbus

① Anti Semetism in his works

    1. Take critics who
      say he is anti semetic
      and <u>isn't</u> anti
      semetic

    2. Show mad. in book
      showing both side the